CONTENTS

W9-BGX-697

FOREWORD

When the first edition of *20,000 Words* was published in 1934, it was necessary to explain its purpose at some length. Since that time, thousands of secretaries, typists, word processing operators, and writers have come to rely upon *20,000 Words*—now entitled *20,000+ Words*—as one of their most valued desk reference books.

The book's originator, Dr. Louis A. Leslie, carried *20,000 Words* through seven editions to keep pace with the changing language of society and of the office. The eighth edition continues the process of keeping the book current with the times. In this edition, for example, hundreds of new expressions appear for the first time. A few examples are: *printout, programmer, shared logic system, stand–alone, network, high technology, cursor, byte,* and *salesperson.*

In general, the word list of *20,000+ Words* is in agreement with *Webster's Ninth New Collegiate Dictionary.*

Spelling and Word Division

The word list of *20,000+ Words* serves as a dictionary without definitions. Since most references to a standard dictionary are for the purpose of verifying a spelling or determining a proper point for word division, the absence of definitions from *20,000+ Words* allows for many more words per page and thus increases the speed with which a given word may be found. Further increasing the usefulness of the word list of *20,000+ Words* is the elimination of thousands of English words which are used so infrequently that the typical writer and typist never need to refer to them. Also omitted from the word list are the very frequent monosyllabic words such as *the* and *of* which never pose a problem for most people.

Discerning Among Similar Words

With similar words such as *affect* and *effect* and with homonyms such as *site, cite,* and *sight* a very brief definition follows the word. Also each of these words is followed by the notation *cf.,* meaning "compare with." For a given word, this *cf.* notation lists the similar words of which the user should be aware.

One Word, Two Words, or Hyphenated?

A major problem for the writer and the keyboarder is to determine whether a compound is written as one word, as two words, or with a hyphen. The English language is filled with so many inconsistencies that analogy can be totally useless. A few examples are illustrative of the point: People may secure their *night latches* and put on their *night–robes* and then have *nightmares* before morning dawns. At a *halftime* show a band may march in *half step* past the flag at *half–mast*. Sailors work with *square–rigged* craft, while mathematicians work with *square roots*.

Many expressions go through an evolutionary process of first being two separate words, then hyphenated, and finally solid. People used to hyphenate *picnic* and *percent*. *Output* and *downtime* were originally expressed as separate words. The coverage of two-word and hyphenated expressions has been greatly expanded in the eighth edition in order to help the writer and the keyboarder spell and divide them correctly.

Reference Section

The basic purpose of the Reference Section of *20,000+ Words* is to provide a quick reference for the writer or keyboarder who desires to *see* how to solve a problem of punctuation, number expression, and the like. The quickest way to solve such a problem is by analogy, and thus the Reference Section includes a number of clear examples. Rule statements are kept to a minimum in order to make the reference task as easy as possible. People desiring comprehensive rule statements of matters of

English style should consult *The Gregg Reference Manual*, Sixth Edition, by William A. Sabin.

The Reference Section includes revised and expanded coverage of Numbers, Most-Used Punctuation, and Two-Letter State Abbreviations. New additions to the Reference Section in the eighth edition are Spelling Tips which provide generalizations about spelling patterns, Common Acronyms, and Troublesome U.S. and Foreign Place Names.

Electronic Office Glossary

New to the eighth edition is a glossary of terms encountered frequently in the modern office. Word processing and computer terms are included, making the glossary a handy reference for the writer or typist.

THE WORD LIST

The words included in the eighth edition of *20,000+ Words* contain a dot or dots to indicate the point or points at which a word may be divided. Good typing style requires that at least three characters (one of which is the hyphen) remain at the end of the line and that at least three characters (one of which may be a mark of punctuation) be carried to the next line. The only syllable breaks indicated in *20,000+ Words* are the ones that allow the typist to observe this basic word division rule. The user should keep in mind, then, that two-letter syllables which may be indicated at the ends of certain words may properly be carried to the next line only when they are followed by a mark of punctuation.

Beyond the basic rule of "leave at least three characters, carry at least three characters," there are other considerations affecting the division of words. Excessive word division is distracting to the reader and should be avoided where possible. In general, it is best to avoid dividing words at the ends of more than two consecutive lines, at the end of a page, or at the end of a paragraph.

If, however, a word division must be made, certain points of division are preferable to others. For example, hyphenated expressions such as *self-employed* are best divided at the hyphen. Solid compound words such as *timetable* are best divided between their root words (time•table). Other considerations affecting the preferability of certain word divisions include dividing after prefixes and before suffixes (super•market, not su•per-market) and dividing after single-vowel syllables and not before them (consoli•date, not consol•idate).

How Word Division Is Shown

Word division points are indicated by means of centered dots.

per·ma·nent   **de·duc·tion**

Hyphenated words appear in the Word List with a hyphen, just as they should be typed whether in the middle or at the end of a line.

cost–plus   **let·ter–per·fect**   **heavy–du·ty**

Certain expressions that are two separate words appear in the Word List because they occur together often enough to cause many people to question whether they are solid or hyphenated. No hyphen is needed when these expressions are divided between the root words.

half hour   **air force**   **flight deck**

Certain expressions may be punctuated or spelled differently depending upon their part of speech. Whenever this occurs, the variations are followed by abbreviations such as n. (noun), v. (verb), and adj. (adjective).

re·cord v.   **rec·ord** n.

Words that may be easily confused are cross-referenced. A parenthetical notation follows the word and contains the letters *cf.*, "compare with."

elic·it (draw out; cf. *illicit*)

aba•cus
abaft
ab•a•lo•ne
aban•don
aban•don•ment
abase
abash
abate
abate•ment
ab•at•toir
ab•bé
ab•bess
ab•bey
ab•bot
ab•bre•vi•ate
ab•bre•vi•at•ing
ab•bre•vi•a•tion
ab•di•cate
ab•di•ca•tion
ab•do•men
ab•dom•i•nal
ab•duct
ab•duc•tion
ab•duc•tor
ab•er•rance
ab•er•rant
ab•er•ra•tion
abet
abet•ting
abet•tor

abey•ance
ab•hor
ab•horred
ab•hor•rence
ab•hor•rent
ab•hor•ring
abide
abil•i•ties
abil•i•ty
ab•ject
ab•ject•ly
ab•jure
ab•la•tive
ablaze
able
able–bod•ied
ab•lu•tion
ably
ab•ne•ga•tion
ab•nor•mal
ab•nor•mal•i•ties
ab•nor•mal•i•ty
ab•nor•mal•ly
aboard
abode
abol•ish
ab•o•li•tion
ab•o•li•tion•ism
ab•o•li•tion•ist
A–bomb

abom•i•na•ble
abom•i•nate
abom•i•na•tion
ab•orig•i•nal
ab•orig•i•ne
abort
abor•tion•ist
abor•tive
abound
about
about–face
above
above•board
above•ground
abrade
abra•sion
abra•sive
ab•re•act
abreast
abridge
abridg•ing
abridg•ment
abroad
ab•ro•gate
ab•ro•ga•tion
abrupt
ab•scess
ab•scis•sa
ab•scond
ab•scond•er

ab•sence
ab•sent
ab•sen•tee
ab•sen•tee•ism
ab•sent•mind•ed
ab•sinthe
ab•so•lute
ab•so•lute•ly
ab•so•lu•tion
ab•so•lut•ism
ab•solve
ab•sorb
ab•sor•ben•cy
ab•sor•bent
ab•sorb•ing
ab•sorp•tion
ab•stain
ab•stain•er
ab•ste•mi•ous
ab•sten•tion
ab•sti•nence
ab•sti•nent
ab•stract
ab•strac•tion
ab•stract•ly
ab•stract•ness
ab•struse
ab•surd
ab•sur•di•ty
abun•dance
abun•dant
abuse
abus•ing
abu•sive

abu•sive•ly
abu•sive•ness
abut
abut•ment
abut•ted
abut•ter
abut•ting
abys•mal
abyss
ac•a•de•mia
ac•a•dem•ic
ac•a•de•mi•cian
acad•e•my
ac•cede (to agree; cf. *exceed*)
ac•ce•le•ran•do
ac•cel•er•ate
ac•cel•er•a•tion
ac•cel•er•a•tor
ac•cent
ac•cen•tu•ate
ac•cept (to take; cf. *except*)
ac•cept•abil•i•ty
ac•cept•able
ac•cept•ably
ac•cep•tance
ac•cep•ta•tion
ac•cept•ed
ac•cess (admittance; cf. *excess*)
ac•ces•si•bil•i•ty
ac•ces•si•ble
ac•ces•sion

ac•ces•so•ries
ac•ces•so•ry
ac•ci•dence
ac•ci•dent
ac•ci•den•tal
ac•ci•den•tal•ly
ac•claim
ac•cla•ma•tion
ac•cli•mate
ac•cli•ma•tize
ac•cliv•i•ty
ac•co•lade
ac•com•mo•date
ac•com•mo•dat•ing
ac•com•mo•da•tion
ac•com•pa•nied
ac•com•pa•nies
ac•com•pa•ni•ment
ac•com•pa•nist
ac•com•pa•ny
ac•com•plice
ac•com•plish
ac•com•plished
ac•com•plish•ment
ac•cord
ac•cor•dance
ac•cord•ing•ly
ac•cor•di•on
ac•cost
ac•count
ac•count•abil•i•ty
ac•count•able
ac•coun•tan•cy
ac•coun•tant

ac•count•ing
ac•cou•ter•ment
ac•cred•it
ac•cred•i•ta•tion
ac•cre•tion
ac•cru•al
ac•crue
ac•cru•ing
ac•cu•mu•late
ac•cu•mu•lat•ing
ac•cu•mu•la•tion
ac•cu•mu•la•tive
ac•cu•mu•la•tor
ac•cu•ra•cy
ac•cu•rate•ly
ac•cursed
ac•cu•sa•tion
ac•cu•sa•tive
ac•cu•sa•to•ry
ac•cuse
ac•cus•ing
ac•cus•tom
ac•cus•tomed
acer•bi•ty
ac•e•tate
ace•tic
ac•e•tone
acet•y•lene
ache
achiev•able
achieve
achieve•ment
achiev•ing
ach•ro•mat•ic

ac•id
ac•id–fast
ac•id•head
acid•i•fi•ca•tion
acid•i•fied
acid•i•fy
acid•i•ty
ac•i•do•sis
acid•u•late
acid•u•lous
ac•knowl•edge
ac•knowl•edg•ing
ac•knowl•edg•ment
ac•me (highest point)
ac•ne (skin disorder)
ac•o•lyte
ac•o•nite
acorn
acous•tic
acous•ti•cal
acous•tic cou•pler
ac•ous•ti•cian
acous•tics
ac•quaint
ac•quain•tance
ac•qui•esce
ac•qui•es•cence
ac•qui•es•cent
ac•quire
ac•quire•ment
ac•quir•ing
ac•qui•si•tion
ac•quis•i•tive
ac•quit

ac•quit•tal
ac•quit•ted
ac•quit•ting
acre
acre•age
acre–foot
ac•rid
acrid•i•ty
ac•ri•mo•ni•ous
ac•ri•mo•ny
ac•ro•bat
ac•ro•bat•ic
ac•ro•nym
acrop•o•lis
across
across–the–board
acros•tic
acryl•ic
act•ing
ac•tin•ic
ac•tion
ac•tion•able
ac•ti•vate
ac•tive
ac•tive•ly
ac•tiv•ism
ac•tiv•ist
ac•tiv•i•ties
ac•tiv•i•ty
ac•tor
ac•tu•al
ac•tu•al•i•ty
ac•tu•al•ly
ac•tu•ar•i•al

ac•tu•ar•ies

ac•tu•ary

ac•tu•ate

ac•tu•at•ing

ac•tu•a•tor

acu•ity

acu•men

acu•punc•ture

acute

acute•ness

ad (advertisement; cf. *add*)

ad•age

ada•gio

ad•a•mant

adapt (adjust; cf. *adept, adopt*)

adapt•abil•i•ty

adapt•able

ad•ap•ta•tion

adapt•er

add (plus; cf. *ad*)

ad•den•da pl.

ad•den•dum sing.

ad•der

ad•dict

ad•dict•ed

ad•dic•tion

ad•dic•tive

ad•di•tion (increase; cf. *edition*)

ad•di•tion•al

ad•di•tion•al•ly

ad•di•tive

ad•dle

ad•dress

ad•dress•ee

ad•dress•ees

ad•dress•ing

Ad•dress•o•graph

ad•duce

ad•duc•ing

ad•e•noid

ad•e•noi•dal

ad•ept (skillful; cf. *adapt, adopt*)

ad•e•qua•cy

ad•e•quate

ad•e•quate•ly

ad•here

ad•her•ence

ad•her•ent

ad•her•ing

ad•he•sion

ad•he•sive

ad•he•sive•ly

ad hoc

adieu

ad•i•pose

ad•i•pos•i•ty

ad•ja•cent

ad•jec•tive

ad•join (to be next to)

ad•journ (suspend)

ad•journ•ment

ad•judge

ad•judg•ing

ad•ju•di•cate

ad•ju•di•cat•ed

ad•ju•di•cat•ing

ad•ju•di•ca•tion

ad•ju•di•ca•tor

ad•junct

ad•ju•ra•tion

ad•jure

ad•just

ad•just•able

ad•just•er

ad•just•ment

ad•ju•tant

ad lib adv.

ad–lib adj., v.

ad•min•is•ter

ad•min•is•tra•tion

ad•min•is•tra•tive

ad•min•is•tra•tive sec•re•tary

ad•min•is•tra•tor

ad•min•is•tra•trix

ad•mi•ra•ble

ad•mi•ral

ad•mi•ral•ty

ad•mi•ra•tion

ad•mire

ad•mir•ing

ad•mis•si•bil•i•ty

ad•mis•si•ble

ad•mis•sion

ad•mit

ad•mit•tance

ad•mit•ted

ad•mit•ted•ly

ad•mit•ting
ad•mix•ture
ad•mon•ish
ad•mo•ni•tion
ad•mon•i•to•ry
ad nau•se•am
ado•be
ad•o•les•cence
ad•o•les•cent
ad•o•les•cents
adopt (accept; cf.
   adapt, adept)
adop•tion
adop•tive
ador•able
ad•o•ra•tion
ador•ing
adorn
adorn•ment
ad•re•nal
adren•a•line
adrift
adroit
ad•sorp•tion
ad•u•late
ad•u•la•tion
adult
adul•ter•ate
adul•tery
ad•um•bra•tion
ad va•lo•rem
ad•vance
ad•vanced
ad•vance•ment

ad•vanc•ing
ad•van•tage
ad•van•ta•geous
ad•vent
ad•ven•ti•tious
ad•ven•ture
ad•ven•tur•er
ad•ven•ture•some
ad•ven•tur•ous
ad•verb
ad•ver•bi•al
ad•ver•sar•ies
ad•ver•sary
ad•verse (unfavorable;
   cf. *averse*)
ad•ver•si•ty
ad•vert
ad•ver•tise
ad•ver•tise•ment
ad•ver•tis•er
ad•vice n. (counsel; cf.
   advise)
ad•vis•abil•i•ty
ad•vis•able
ad•vise v. (give
   counsel; cf. *advice*)
ad•vised
ad•vise•ment
ad•vis•er *or*
   ad•vi•sor
ad•vis•ing
ad•vi•so•ry
ad•vo•ca•cy
ad•vo•cate

ae•gis
ae•on
aer•ate
aer•a•tion
ae•ri•al adj.
aer•i•al n.
aero•dy•nam•ics
aero•med•i•cine
aero•nau•tic
aero•nau•ti•cal
aero•sol
aero•space
aes•thet•ic
aes•thet•i•cal•ly
aes•thet•i•cism
aes•thet•ics
af•fa•bil•i•ty
af•fa•ble
af•fair
af•fect (influence; cf.
   effect)
af•fec•ta•tion
af•fect•ed
af•fec•tion
af•fec•tion•ate
af•fi•ance
af•fi•ant
af•fi•da•vit
af•fil•i•ate
af•fin•i•ties
af•fin•i•ty
af•firm
af•fir•ma•tion
af•fir•ma•tive

af•firm•a•to•ry
af•fix
af•flict
af•flic•tion
af•flu•ence
af•flu•ent (cf. *effluent*)
af•ford
af•fray
af•fright
af•front
af•ghan
afield
afire
afloat
afoot
afore•men•tioned
afore•said
afore•thought
afore•time
afraid
afresh
Af•ri•can
Af•ro–Amer•i•can
af•ter
af•ter•burn•er
af•ter•care
af•ter•ef•fect
af•ter•glow
af•ter–hours
af•ter•life
af•ter•math
af•ter•noon
af•ter•taste
af•ter–tax

af•ter•thought
af•ter•ward
again
against
ag•ate
ag•ate ware
aga•ve
age–group
agen•cies
agen•cy
agen•da
ag•glom•er•ate
ag•glom•er•a•tion
ag•glu•ti•nate
ag•glu•ti•na•tive
ag•gran•dize
ag•gran•dize•ment
ag•gra•vate
ag•gra•vat•ing adj.
ag•gra•vat•ing v.
ag•gra•va•tion
ag•gre•gate
ag•gre•gat•ing
ag•gre•ga•tion
ag•gres•sion
ag•gres•sive
ag•gres•sor
ag•grieve
ag•grieved
aghast
ag•ile
ag•ile•ly
agil•i•ty
ag•i•tate

ag•i•tat•ing
ag•i•ta•tion
ag•i•ta•tor
aglow
ag•nos•tic
ag•o•nize
ag•o•niz•ing
ag•o•ny
ag•o•ra•pho•bia
agrar•i•an
agree
agree•abil•i•ty
agree•able
agreed
agree•ing
agree•ment
ag•ri•busi•ness
ag•ri•cul•tur•al
ag•ri•cul•ture
agron•o•my
aground
ague
ahead
ahoy
aid (help; cf. *aide*)
aide (assistant; cf. *aid*)
ail (be ill; cf. *ale*)
ai•le•ron
ail•ment
air (atmosphere; cf.
    heir)
air bag
air base
air•borne

air brake
air•brush
air•bus
air coach
air com•mand
air–con•di•tion v.
air–con•di•tioned
   adj., v.
air con•di•tion•er n.
air–cool v.
air–cooled adj.
air cool•ing n.
air cor•ri•dor
air cov•er
air•craft
air•drome
air–drop v.
air–drop n.
air–dry adj.
Aire•dale
Air Ex•press
air•field
air•flow
air•foil
air force
air•frame
air•freight
air•glow
air gun
air hole
air•i•ly
air•i•ness
air lane
air•lift

air•line
air•lin•er
air lock
air•mail
air•man
air mass
air mile
air•plane
air pock•et
air•port
air•proof
air pump
air raid
air•screw
air•ship
air•sick
air•space
air•speed
air•stream
air•strip
air•tight
air–to–air
air•wave
air•way
air•wor•thi•ness
air•wor•thy
airy
aisle (passageway; cf.
   isle)
aisle•way
akim•bo
Al•a•bama
al•a•bas•ter
a la carte

alac•ri•ty
a la mode
alarm
alarm•ist
Alas•ka
al•ba•tross
al•be•it
Al•ber•ta
al•bi•no
al•bi•nos
al•bum
al•bu•men
Al•bu•quer•que
al•che•mist
al•che•my
al•co•hol
al•co•hol•ic
al•co•hol•ism
al•cove
al•der•man
ale (beer; cf. *ail*)
ale•wife
al•fal•fa
al•fres•co
al•gae
al•ge•bra
al•ge•bra•ic
al•ge•bra•ical
al•go•rithm
alias
al•i•bi
al•i•bied
al•i•bi•ing
alien

alien•ate
alien•at•ing
alien•ation
alien•ist
align
align•ment
alike
al•i•men•ta•ry
al•i•men•ta•tion
al•i•mo•ny
al•i•quot
al•ka•li
al•ka•line
al•ka•loid
al•kyl
all (wholly; cf. *awl*)
all–Amer•i•can
all–around
al•lay (soothe; cf. *alley,*
    ally)
al•le•ga•tion
al•lege
al•leg•ed•ly
Al•le•ghe•nies
Al•le•ghe•ny
al•le•giance
al•leg•ing
al•le•gor•i•cal
al•le•go•ry
al•le•gret•to
al•le•gro
al•ler•gic
al•ler•gies
al•ler•gy

al•le•vi•ate
al•le•vi•a•tion
al•ley (passage; cf.
    allay, ally)
al•leys
al•li•ance
al•lied
al•lies
al•li•ga•tor
all–im•por•tant
al•lit•er•a•tion
al•lit•er•a•tive
al•lo•ca•ble
al•lo•cate
al•lo•cat•ing
al•lo•ca•tion
al•lo•cu•tion
al•lo•path•ic
al•lop•a•thy
al•lot
al•lot•ment
al•lot•ted
al•lot•ting
al•low
al•low•able
al•low•ance
al•lowed (permitted;
    cf. *aloud*)
al•low•ed•ly
all right
al•lude (refer to; cf.
    elude)
al•lure
al•lu•sion

al•lu•vi•al
al•ly (associate; cf.
    allay, alley)
al•mighty
al•mond
al•most
alms (charity; cf. *arms*)
al•ni•co
aloft
alone
along
aloud (audibly; cf.
    allowed)
al•paca
al•pha•bet
al•pha•bet•ic
al•pha•bet•i•cal
al•pha•bet•ize
al•pha•nu•mer•ic
al•ready
al•tar (for worship; cf.
    alter)
al•tar•piece
al•tar rail
al•tar stone
al•ter (change; cf.
    altar)
al•ter•ation
al•ter•ca•tion
al•ter ego
al•ter•nate
al•ter•nat•ing
al•ter•na•tion
al•ter•na•tive

al·ter·na·tor
al·though
al·tim·e·ter
al·ti·pla·no
al·ti·tude
al·to
al·to·geth·er
al·tru·ism
al·tru·ist
al·tru·is·tic
al·um
alu·mi·nous
alu·mi·num
alum·na sing. fem.
alum·nae pl. fem.
alum·ni pl. mas.
alum·nus sing. mas.
Alun·dum
al·ways
amal·gam
amal·gam·ate
amal·gam·ation
aman·u·en·sis
am·a·teur
amaze
amaze·ment
amaz·ing·ly
am·bas·sa·dor
am·ber·gris
am·bi·dex·trous
am·bi·ent
am·bi·gu·ity
am·big·u·ous
am·bi·tion

am·bi·tious
am·biv·a·lence
am·bro·sia
am·bu·lance
am·bu·la·to·ry
am·bus·cade
am·bush
ame·lio·rate
ame·lio·ra·tion
ame·lio·ra·tive
ame·na·ble
amend (to change; cf. *emend*)
amend·ment
ame·ni·ties
ame·ni·ty
Amer·i·can
Amer·i·can·ism
Amer·i·can·iza·tion
Am·er·ind
am·e·thyst
ami·a·bil·i·ty
ami·a·ble
am·i·ca·bil·i·ty
am·i·ca·ble
amid·ships
amidst
am·i·ty
am·me·ter
am·mo·nia
am·mu·ni·tion
am·ne·sia
am·nes·ty
am·nio·cen·te·sis

amoe·ba
among
amor·al
am·o·rous
amor·phous
am·or·ti·za·tion
am·or·tize
am·or·tiz·ing
amount
am·per·age
am·pere
am·per·sand
am·phib·i·an
am·phib·i·ous
am·phi·the·ater
am·ple
am·pli·fi·ca·tion
am·pli·fied
am·pli·fi·er
am·pli·fy
am·pli·fy·ing
am·pli·tude
am·ply
am·pu·tate
am·pu·ta·tion
am·pu·tee
am·u·let
amuse
amuse·ment
amus·ing
anach·ro·nism
anach·ro·nis·tic
an·a·con·da
an·aer·o·bic

an•a•gram
an•al•ge•sia
an•a•log
an•a•log•i•cal
anal•o•gies
anal•o•gous
anal•o•gy
anal•y•sand
anal•y•ses pl.
anal•y•sis sing.
an•a•lyst (one who
   analyzes; cf. *annalist*)
an•a•lyt•i•cal
an•a•lyze
an•a•lyz•ing
an•ar•chic
an•ar•chism
an•ar•chist
an•ar•chis•tic
an•ar•chy
an•astig•mat•ic
anas•to•mo•sis
anas•to•mot•ic
anath•e•ma
an•a•tom•i•cal
anat•o•mist
anat•o•mize
anat•o•my
an•ces•tor
an•ces•tral
an•ces•try
an•chor
an•chor•age
an•chor•man

an•chor•wom•an
an•cho•vies
an•cho•vy
an•cient
an•cil•lary
and•iron
and/or
an•ec•dote
ane•mia
ane•mic
an•e•mom•e•ter
anem•o•ne
an•er•oid
an•es•the•sia
an•es•the•si•ol•o•gist
an•es•thet•ic
anes•the•tist
anes•the•tize
an•eu•rysm
an•gel (a spiritual
   being; cf. *angle*)
an•gel•fish
an•gel food cake
an•gel•ic
An•ge•lus
an•ger
an•gi•na
an•gle (in geometry;
   cf. *angel*)
an•gle iron
an•gler
an•gle•worm
An•gli•can
an•gli•cism

an•gli•cize
an•gling
An•glo•phile
An•glo•phobe
An•glo–Sax•on
an•go•ra
an•gri•ly
an•gry
an•guish
an•gu•lar
an•gu•lar•i•ty
an•i•line
an•i•mad•ver•sion
an•i•mal
an•i•mate
an•i•mat•ed•ly
an•i•ma•tion
an•i•mos•i•ty
an•i•mus
an•ise
ani•seed
an•is•ette
an•kle
an•kle•bone
an•klet
an•nal•ist (writer of
   annals; cf. *analyst*)
an•nals
an•neal
an•nex
an•nex•ation
an•ni•hi•late
an•ni•hi•la•tion
an•ni•hi•la•tor

an•ni•ver•sa•ries
an•ni•ver•sa•ry
an•no•tate
an•no•ta•tion
an•nounce
an•nounce•ment
an•nounc•er
an•nounc•ing
an•noy
an•noy•ance
an•noyed
an•noy•ing
an•nu•al
an•nu•al•ize
an•nu•al•ly
an•nu•itant
an•nu•ity
an•nul
an•nu•lar
an•nulled
an•nul•ling
an•nul•ment
an•nun•ci•a•tion
an•nun•ci•a•tor
an•ode
an•od•ize
an•o•dyne
anoint
anom•a•lous
anom•a•ly
an•o•nym•i•ty
anon•y•mous
anoph•e•les
an•oth•er

an•ox•ia
an•swer
an•swer•able
ant (insect; cf. *aunt*)
ant•ac•id
an•tag•o•nism
an•tag•o•nist
an•tag•o•nis•tic
an•tag•o•nize
ant•arc•tic
ant•eat•er
an•te•bel•lum
an•te•ced•ent
an•te•cham•ber
an•te•date
an•te•di•lu•vi•an
an•te•lope
an•te me•ri•di•em
an•te•na•tal
an•ten•na
an•te•pe•nult
an•te•ri•or
an•te•room
an•them
an•ther
ant•hill
an•thol•o•gy
an•thra•cite
an•thrax
an•thro•poid
an•thro•pol•o•gy
an•thro•po•mor•phic
an•ti•air•craft
an•ti•bi•ot•ic

an•ti•body
an•tic
an•tic•i•pate
an•tic•i•pat•ing
an•tic•i•pa•tion
an•tic•i•pa•tive
an•tic•i•pa•to•ry
an•ti•cli•mac•tic
an•ti•cli•max
an•ti•dote
an•ti•dump•ing
an•ti•freeze
an•ti•gen
an•ti•knock
an•ti•ma•cas•sar
an•ti•ma•lar•i•al
an•ti•mo•ny
an•ti•pa•thet•ic
an•tip•a•thy
an•ti•per•son•nel
an•tiph•o•nal
an•tip•o•des
an•ti•pov•er•ty
an•ti•quar•i•an
an•ti•quary
an•ti•quat•ed
an•tique
an•tiq•ui•ty
an•ti–Se•mit•ic
an•ti•sep•sis
an•ti•sep•tic
an•ti•so•cial
an•tith•e•sis
an•ti•tox•in

an·ti·trust
ant·ler
ant·onym
an·trum
an·vil
anx·i·ety
anx·ious
any
any·body
any·how
any·more
any·one
any·place
any·thing
any·time
any·way
any·ways
any·where
ao·rist
aor·ta
aor·tic
apace
apart
apart·heid
apart·ment
ap·a·thet·ic
ap·a·thy
ap·er·ture
apex
apha·sia
aph·o·rism
Aph·ro·di·te
api·ary (for bees; cf.
   aviary)

api·cal
api·cul·ture
apiece
apoc·a·lypse
apoc·a·lyp·tic
apoc·ry·pha
apoc·ry·phal
apo·gee
apo·lit·i·cal
Apol·lo
apol·o·get·ic
apol·o·get·i·cal·ly
apol·o·get·ics
apol·o·gies
apol·o·gize
apol·o·giz·ing
ap·o·logue
apol·o·gy
ap·o·plec·tic
ap·o·plexy
apos·ta·sy
apos·tate
a pos·te·ri·o·ri
apos·tle
apos·to·late
ap·os·tol·ic
apos·tro·phe
apos·tro·phize
apoth·e·car·ies
apoth·e·cary
apo·the·o·sis
Ap·pa·la·chian
ap·pall
ap·palled

ap·pall·ing
ap·pa·ra·tus
ap·par·el
ap·par·eled
ap·par·ent
ap·pa·ri·tion
ap·peal
ap·peal·ing·ly
ap·pear
ap·pear·ance
ap·pease
ap·pease·ment
ap·pel·lant
ap·pel·late
ap·pel·la·tion
ap·pel·lee
ap·pend
ap·pend·age
ap·pen·dec·to·my
ap·pen·di·ci·tis
ap·pen·dix
ap·per·ceive
ap·per·cep·tion
ap·per·tain
ap·pe·tite
ap·pe·tiz·er
ap·pe·tiz·ing
ap·plaud
ap·plause
ap·ple
ap·ple·jack
ap·pli·ance
ap·pli·ca·bil·i·ty
ap·pli·ca·ble

ap•pli•cant
ap•pli•ca•tion
ap•pli•ca•tor
ap•plied
ap•pli•qué
ap•ply
ap•ply•ing
ap•point
ap•poin•tee
ap•point•ive
ap•point•ment
ap•por•tion
ap•por•tion•ment
ap•po•site
ap•po•si•tion
ap•prais•al
ap•praise (value; cf. *apprise*)
ap•prais•er
ap•prais•ing
ap•pre•cia•ble
ap•pre•ci•ate
ap•pre•ci•a•tion
ap•pre•cia•tive
ap•pre•hend
ap•pre•hen•si•ble
ap•pre•hen•sion
ap•pre•hen•sive
ap•pren•tice
ap•pren•ticed
ap•pren•tice•ship
ap•prise (inform; cf. *appraise*)
ap•proach

ap•pro•ba•tion
ap•pro•ba•to•ry
ap•pro•pri•ate
ap•pro•pri•ate•ness
ap•pro•pri•a•tion
ap•prov•al
ap•prov•als
ap•prove
ap•prov•ing
ap•prox•i•mate
ap•prox•i•ma•tion
ap•pur•te•nance
ap•pur•te•nant
apri•cot
April
a pri•o•ri
apron
ap•ro•pos
ap•ti•tude
apt•ly
apt•ness
aqua•cade
Aqua•lung
aqua•ma•rine
aqua•plane
aqua•relle
aquar•i•um
aquat•ic
aqua•tint
aq•ue•duct
aque•ous
aq•ui•line
ar•a•besque
Ara•bi•an

Ar•a•bic
ar•a•ble
arach•noid
ar•bi•ter
ar•bi•tra•ble
ar•bi•trage
ar•bit•ra•ment
ar•bi•trari•ly
ar•bi•trary
ar•bi•trate
ar•bi•tra•tion
ar•bi•tra•tive
ar•bi•tra•tor
ar•bor
ar•bo•re•al
ar•bo•re•tum
ar•bor•vi•tae
ar•bu•tus
arc (curved line; cf. *ark*)
ar•cade
ar•chae•o•log•i•cal
ar•chae•ol•o•gist
ar•chae•ol•o•gy
ar•cha•ic
arch•an•gel
arch•bish•op
arch•dea•con
arch•di•o•cese
arch•du•cal
arch•duch•ess
arch•duchy
arch•duke
arch•en•e•my

ar•cher
ar•chery
ar•che•type
arch•fiend
ar•chi•epis•co•pal
ar•chi•pel•a•go
ar•chi•tect
ar•chi•tec•tur•al
ar•chi•tec•ture
ar•chi•trave
ar•chiv•al
ar•chive dis•kette
ar•chives
arch•ness
arch•way
arc•ing
arc•tic
ar•dent
ar•dor
ar•du•ous
ar•ea (space; cf. *aria*)
ar•eas
area•way
are•na
are•nas
ar•gon
ar•go•naut
ar•go•sy
ar•got
ar•gu•able
ar•gue
ar•gued
ar•gues
ar•gu•ing

ar•gu•ment
ar•gu•men•ta•tion
ar•gu•men•ta•tive
ar•gyle
Ar•gy•rol
aria (melody; cf. *area*)
ar•id
arid•i•ty
ari•o•so
ar•is•toc•ra•cy
aris•to•crat
aris•to•crat•ic
Ar•is•to•te•lian
arith•me•tic
ar•ith•met•i•cal
arith•me•ti•cian
Ar•i•zo•na
ark (refuge; cf. *arc*)
Ar•kan•sas
ar•ma•da
ar•ma•dil•lo
ar•ma•ment
ar•ma•ture
arm•chair
arm•ful
arm•hole
ar•mies
ar•mi•stice
arm•let
ar•mor
ar•mor•er
ar•mo•ri•al
ar•mory
arm•pit

arm•rest
arms (of body; cf.
    alms)
ar•my
ar•my ant
ar•my•worm
ar•ni•ca
aro•ma
ar•o•mat•ic
around
around–the–clock
ar•peg•gio
ar•raign
ar•raign•ment
ar•range
ar•range•ment
ar•rang•ing
ar•rant
ar•ras
ar•ray
ar•rayed
ar•ray•ing
ar•rear
ar•rear•age
ar•rears
ar•rest
ar•riv•al
ar•rive
ar•riv•ing
ar•ro•gance
ar•ro•gant
ar•ro•gate
ar•row
ar•row•head

ar•row•root
ar•royo
ar•se•nal
ar•se•nate
ar•se•nic
ar•son
ar•te•ri•al
ar•ter•ies
ar•te•rio•scle•ro•sis
ar•tery
ar•te•sian
art•ful
art•ful•ly
ar•thri•tis
ar•ti•choke
ar•ti•cle
ar•ti•cled
ar•tic•u•late
ar•tic•u•la•tion
ar•ti•fact
ar•ti•fice
ar•ti•fi•cer
ar•ti•fi•cial
ar•ti•fi•ci•al•i•ty
ar•til•lery
ar•ti•san
art•ist
ar•tiste
ar•tis•tic
art•ist•ry
art•less
art•work
Ary•an
as•bes•tos

as•cend
as•cen•dan•cy
as•cen•dant
as•cend•ing
as•cen•sion
as•cent (motion
  upward; cf. *assent*)
as•cer•tain
as•cer•tain•able
as•cer•tain•ment
as•cet•ic
as•cet•i•cism
as•cribe
as•crib•ing
as•crip•tion
asep•sis
asep•tic
asep•ti•cal•ly
ashamed
ash can n.
ash•can adj.
ash•en
ashore
ash•tray
ashy
Asian
Asi•at•ic
aside
as•i•nine
as•i•nin•i•ty
askance
askew
asleep
as•par•a•gus

as•pect
as•pen
as•per•i•ty
as•perse
as•per•sion
as•phalt
as•phyx•ia
as•phyx•i•ate
as•phyx•i•at•ing
as•phyx•i•a•tion
as•pic
as•pi•rant
as•pi•rate
as•pi•ra•tion
as•pi•ra•tor
as•pire
as•pi•rin
as•pir•ing
as•sail
as•sail•ant
as•sas•sin
as•sas•si•nate
as•sas•si•na•tion
as•sault
as•say (analyze; cf.
  essay)
as•sayed
as•say•ing
as•sem•blage
as•sem•ble
as•sem•blies
as•sem•bling
as•sem•bly
as•sem•bly•man

as•sem•bly•wom•an
as•sent (consent;
   cf. *ascent*)
as•sert
as•ser•tion
as•ser•tive
as•sess
as•sess•able
as•sess•ment
as•ses•sor
as•set
as•sev•er•ate
as•sev•er•a•tion
as•si•du•ity
as•sid•u•ous
as•sign
as•sign•abil•i•ty
as•sign•able
as•sig•nat
as•sig•na•tion
as•sign•ee
as•sign•er
as•sign•ment
as•sim•i•la•ble
as•sim•i•late
as•sim•i•lat•ing
as•sim•i•la•tion
as•sim•i•la•tive
as•sim•i•la•to•ry
as•sist
as•sis•tance (help;
   cf. *assistants*)
as•sis•tant

as•sis•tants (helpers;
   cf. *assistance*)
as•sis•tant•ship
as•size
as•so•ci•ate n.
as•so•ci•ate v.
as•so•ci•at•ing
as•so•ci•a•tion
as•so•cia•tive
as•so•nance
as•so•nant
as•sort
as•sort•ment
as•suage
as•suag•ing
as•sume
as•sum•ing
as•sump•tion
as•sur•ance
as•sure
as•sured
as•sur•ing
as•ter
as•ter•isk
as•ter•oid
as•the•nia
asth•ma
as•tig•mat•ic
astig•ma•tism
as•ton•ish
as•ton•ish•ment
as•tound
as•tra•khan

as•tral
astride
as•trin•gen•cy
as•trin•gent
as•tro•dome
as•tro•labe
as•trol•o•ger
as•trol•o•gy
as•tro•naut
as•tro•nau•ti•cal
as•tro•nau•tics
as•tron•o•mer
as•tro•nom•ic
as•tro•nom•i•cal
as•tron•o•my
as•tute
asun•der
asy•lum
asym•met•ric
asyn•chro•nous
at•a•rac•tic
at•a•vism
ate•lier
athe•ism
athe•ist
athe•is•tic
ath•e•nae•um
ath•lete
ath•let•ic
ath•let•ics
athwart
At•lan•tic
at•las

at•mo•sphere
at•mo•spher•ic
at•om
atom•ic
at•om•ize
at•om•iz•er
aton•al
atone•ment
aton•ing
atri•um
atro•cious
atroc•i•ty
at•ro•phied
at•ro•phy
at•tach
at•ta•ché
at•ta•ché case
at•tached
at•tach•ment
at•tack
at•tain
at•tain•able
at•tain•der
at•tain•ment
at•taint
at•tar
at•tempt
at•tend
at•ten•dance
at•ten•dant
at•ten•dants
at•ten•tion
at•ten•tive

at•ten•u•ate
at•ten•u•a•tion
at•test
at•tes•ta•tion
at•tic
at•tire
at•ti•tude
at•ti•tu•di•nal
at•tor•ney
at•tor•ney–at–law
at•tor•neys
at•tract
at•trac•tion
at•trac•tive
at•trib•ut•able
at•tri•bute n.
at•trib•ute v.
at•tri•bu•tion
at•trib•u•tive
at•tri•tion
at•tune
atyp•i•cal
au•burn
au cou•rant
auc•tion
auc•tion•eer
au•da•cious
au•dac•i•ty
au•di•bil•i•ty
au•di•ble
au•di•bly
au•di•ence
au•dio

au•di•ol•o•gy
au•dio•phile
au•dio•vi•su•al
au•dit
au•di•tion
au•di•tor
au•di•to•ri•um
au•di•to•ry
au fait
au fond
auf Wie•der•seh•en
au•ger (tool; cf.
    augur)
aught (slightest thing;
    cf. *ought*)
aug•ment
aug•men•ta•tion
au gra•tin
au•gur (predict; cf.
    auger)
au•gu•ry
au•gust (majestic)
Au•gust (month)
au jus
auk
au lait
au na•tu•rel
aunt (relative; cf. *ant*)
au•ra
au•ral (heard; cf.
    oral)
au•re•ate
au•re•ole

Au•reo•my•cin
au•ri•cle
au•ric•u•lar
au•rif•er•ous
au•ro•ra bo•re•al•is
aus•cul•tate
aus•cul•ta•tion
aus•pice
aus•pic•es
aus•pi•cious
aus•tere
aus•ter•i•ty
Aus•tra•lian
au•then•tic
au•then•ti•cate
au•then•tic•i•ty
au•thor
au•thor•i•tar•i•an
au•thor•i•ta•tive
au•thor•i•ty
au•tho•ri•za•tion
au•tho•rize
au•tho•riz•ing
au•thor•ship
au•tis•tic
au•to•bahn
au•to•bio•graph•i•cal
au•to•bi•og•ra•phy
au•toch•tho•nous
au•toc•ra•cy
au•to•crat
au•to•crat•ic
au•to–da–fé
au•to•gi•ro

au•to•graph
au•to•graph•ic
au•to•hyp•no•sis
au•to•in•fec•tion
au•to•in•tox•i•ca•
    tion
Au•to•mat
au•to•mate
au•to•mat•ic
au•to•ma•tion
au•tom•a•tism
au•tom•a•ti•za•tion
au•tom•a•tize
au•tom•a•ton
au•to•mo•bile
au•to•mo•tive
au•ton•o•mous
au•ton•o•my
au•top•sy
au•to•sug•ges•tion
au•tumn
au•tum•nal
aux•il•ia•ry
avail
avail•abil•i•ty
avail•able
av•a•lanche
avant–garde
av•a•rice
av•a•ri•cious
avenge
av•e•nue
aver
av•er•age

averred
aver•ring
averse (disinclined;
    cf. *adverse*)
aver•sion
avert
avi•ary (for birds; cf.
    apiary)
avi•a•tion
avi•a•tor
avi•cul•ture
av•id
avid•ity
avi•on•ics
av•o•ca•do
av•o•ca•dos
av•o•ca•tion (hobby;
    cf. *vocation*)
avoid
avoid•able
avoid•ance
av•oir•du•pois
avow
avow•al
avowed
avun•cu•lar
await
awake
awak•en
award
aware
aware•ness
awash
away (absent)

aweigh (of anchor)
awe•some
aw•ful
awhile
awk•ward
awl (tool; cf. *all*)
aw•ning

awoke
awry
ax
ax•i•al
ax•i•om
ax•i•om•at•ic
ax•is

ax•le
ax•le•tree
aza•lea
az•i•muth
Az•tec
azure

B

bab•bitt met•al
bab•ble (chatter; cf.
  bauble, bubble)
bab•bling
ba•bies
ba•boon
ba•bush•ka
ba•by
ba•by•ing
ba•by–sit
ba•by–sit•ter
bac•ca•lau•re•ate
bac•ca•rat
bac•cha•nal
bac•cha•na•lian
bac•chant
bach•e•lor
bach•e•lor's
  de•gree
ba•cil•li pl.
ba•cil•lus sing.

back•ache
back•bite
back•board
back•bone
back•break•ing
back•cross
back door n.
back•door adj.
back•drop
back•er
back•field
back•fire
back•gam•mon
back•ground
back•hand
back•hand•ed
back•hoe
back•lash
back•log
back off
back•pack

back•rest
back room n.
back•room adj.
back•scat•ter
back•seat adj., n.
back•set
back•slide
back•spac•er
back•stage
back•stairs
back•stitch
back•stop
back•stretch
back•stroke
back talk
back–to–back
back•track v.
back up v.
back•up adj., n.
back•ward
back•ward•ly

back·ward·ness
back·wash
back·wa·ter
back·woods
back·woods·man
back·yard
ba·con
bac·te·ria pl.
bac·te·ri·al
bac·te·ri·cid·al
bac·te·ri·cide
bac·te·ri·o·log·i·cal
bac·te·ri·ol·o·gist
bac·te·ri·ol·o·gy
bac·te·ri·um sing.
bad (not good)
bade (commanded)
bad·ger
ba·di·nage
bad·lands
bad·min·ton
baf·fle
baf·fle·ment
baf·fling
bag·a·telle
bag·gage
bag·gage·mas·ter
bagged
bag·gi·ly
bag·ging
bag·gy
bag·pipe
ba·guette

bailed (set free; cf. *baled*)
bail·ee
bai·liff
bai·li·wick
bail·ment
bail·or
bait (a lure; cf. *bate*)
Ba·ke·lite
bak·er's doz·en
bak·ing
bal·a·lai·ka
bal·ance
bal·anc·ing
bal·co·nies
bal·co·ny
bald (hairless; cf. *balled, bawled*)
bal·der·dash
baled (packaged; cf. *bailed*)
bale·ful
bal·ing
balk
bal·kan·iza·tion
bal·kan·ize
balk·line
balky
bal·lad
bal·lad·ry
bal·last
ball bear·ing
balled (in a ball; cf. *bald, bawled*)

bal·le·ri·na
bal·let
bal·lis·tic
bal·lis·tics
bal·loon
bal·loon·ist
bal·lot
ball·park
ball·point pen
ball·room
bal·ly·hoo
balm
balm·i·ness
bal·mor·al
balmy
bal·sa
bal·sam
Bal·tic
bal·us·trade
bam·boo
bam·boo·zle
ba·nal
ba·nal·i·ty
ba·nana
band (narrow strip; cf. *banned*)
ban·dage
ban·dag·ing
ban·dan·na
band·box
ban·deau
ban·de·role
ban·dit
band·mas·ter

ban•do•lier

bands (groups; cf.
   banns, bans)

band saw

band shell

band•stand

band•wag•on

ban•dy

ban•dy–legged

bane•ful

ban•gle

ban•ish

ban•ish•ment

ban•is•ter

ban•jo

bank•book

bank•card

bank dis•count

bank draft

bank•er

bank mon•ey

bank note

bank pa•per

bank rate

bank•roll

bank•rupt

bank•rupt•cy

banned (forbidden; cf.
   band)

ban•ner

ban•ner•et

ban•nock

banns (of marriage; cf.
   bands, bans)

ban•quet

ban•quette

bans (forbids; cf.
   bands, banns)

ban•shee

ban•tam

ban•ter•ing•ly

ban•yan

ban•zai

bao•bab

bap•tism

bap•tist

bap•tis•tery

bap•tize

bar•bar•i•an

bar•bar•ic

bar•ba•rism

bar•bar•i•ty

bar•ba•rize

bar•ba•rous

bar•be•cue

bar•bell

bar•ber

bar•ber•shop

bar•bette

bar•bi•tu•rate

bar•ca•role

bar chart

bard (poet; cf. *barred*)

bard•ol•a•ter

bare (uncover; cf. *bear*)

bare•back

bare•faced

bare•foot

bare–hand•ed

bare•head•ed

bare•ly

bar•gain

barge•board

barg•ee

barge•man

bari•tone

bar•i•um

bar•keep•er

bar•ken•tine

bark•er

bar•ley

bar•ley•corn

bar•maid

bar•na•cle

barn•storm•er

barn•yard

baro•graph

ba•rom•e•ter

baro•met•ric

bar•on (nobleman; cf.
   barren)

bar•on•age

bar•on•ess

bar•on•et

bar•on•et•cy

ba•ro•ni•al

bar•ony

ba•roque

ba•rouche

bar•rack

bar•ra•cu•da

bar•rage

barred (shut out; cf. *bard*)

bar•rel

bar•ren (sterile; cf. *baron*)

bar•rette

bar•ri•cade

bar•ri•er

bar•ring

bar•ris•ter

bar•room

bar•row

bar•tend•er

bar•ter

bas•al

ba•salt

bas•cule

base (foundation; cf. *bass*)

base•ball

base•board

base•born

base burn•er

base•less

base•line

base•ment

base•ness

base pay

ba•ses (pl. of *basis*)

bas•es (pl. of *base*)

bash•ful

ba•sic

ba•si•cal•ly

ba•sil

ba•sil•i•ca

bas•i•lisk

ba•sin

bas•i•net (helmet; cf. *bassinet*)

ba•sis (foundation; cf. *bases*)

bas•ket

bas•ket•ball

bas•ket•work

bas—re•lief

bass (deep voice; cf. *base*)

bas•si•net (cradle; cf. *basinet*)

bas•soon

bass•wood

bas•tion

batch

bate (moderate; cf. *bait*)

ba•teau

bat•fish

bath

bathe

ba•thet•ic

bath•house

Bath•i•nette

bath•ing

bath mat

ba•thom•e•ter

ba•thos

bath•robe

bath•room

bath•tub

bathy•scaphe

bathy•sphere

ba•tiste

ba•ton

Bat•on Rouge La.

bat•tal•ion

bat•ten

bat•ter

bat•ter•ies

bat•tery

bat•tle

bat•tle—ax

bat•tle cruis•er

bat•tle cry

bat•tle•field

bat•tle flag

bat•tle•ground

bat•tle group

bat•tle•ment

bat•tle—scarred

bat•tle•ship

bau•ble (trifle; cf. *babble, bubble*)

baux•ite

Ba•var•i•an

bawled (shouted; cf. *bald, balled*)

bay•ber•ry

bay•o•net

Bay•onne N.J.

bay•ou

bay rum

ba•zaar (market; cf. *bizarre*)

ba•zoo•ka

beach (shore; cf. *beech*)

beach•comb•er

beach•head

bea•con

bea•dle

bead•work

beady

bea•gle

bean•ie

bear (animal; cf. *bare*)

bear•able

beard•ed

bear•er

bear•skin

beat (flog; cf. *beet*)

be•atif•ic

be•at•i•fi•ca•tion

be•at•i•fy

be•at•i•tude

beat•nik

beau (suitor; cf. *bow*)

beau•te•ous

beau•ti•cian

beau•ties

beau•ti•fied

beau•ti•ful

beau•ti•fy

beau•ti•fy•ing

beau•ty

bea•ver

be•calm

be•cause

beck•on

be•cloud

be•come

be•com•ing•ly

be•daub

be•daz•zle

bed board

bed•bug

bed•clothes

bed•ding

be•deck

be•dev•il

bed•fast

bed•fel•low

be•dight

be•di•zen

bed•lam

bed•ou•in

bed•post

be•drag•gled

bed•rid•den

bed•rock

bed•room

bed•side

bed•sore

bed•spread

bed•stead

bed•time

beech (tree; cf. *beach*)

beech•nut

beef•eat•er

beef•steak

bee•hive

bee•keep•er

bee•line

beer (liquor; cf. *bier*)

bees•wax

beet (vegetable; cf. *beat*)

bee•tle

bee•tle–browed

be•fall

be•fit

be•fit•ting

be•fog

be•fool

be•fore

be•fore•hand

be•fore•time

be•friend

be•fud•dle

beg•gar

beg•gar•li•ness

beg•gar•ly

beg•gar•weed

beg•gary

be•gin

be•gin•ning

be•grime

be•grudge

be•guile

be•gum

be•gun
be•half
be•have
be•hav•ing
be•hav•ior
be•hav•ior•al
be•hav•ior•ism
be•head
be•held
be•he•moth
be•hest
be•hind
be•hind•hand
be•hind–the–
 scenes
be•hold
be•hoove
be•hooves
beige
be•la•bor
be•lat•ed•ly
be•lay
bel can•to
be•lea•guer
bel•fry
Bel•gian
Be•lial
be•lie
be•lief
be•liev•able
be•lieve
be•liev•ing
be•lit•tle
be•lit•tling

bell (that rings; cf.
 belle)
bel•la•don•na
bell•boy
belle (girl; cf. *bell*)
belles let•tres
bell•flow•er
bell•hop
bel•li•cose
bel•lig•er•ence
bel•lig•er•ent
bell jar
bell met•al
bel•lows
bell•pull
bell rope
bell tow•er
bell•weth•er
bel•ly
bel•ly•ache
bel•ly•band
be•long
be•loved
be•low
belt•ing
bel•ve•dere
be•moan
bench mark
bench show
bench war•rant
ben•day
be•neath
ben•e•dict
bene•dic•tion

bene•dic•to•ry
bene•fac•tion
bene•fac•tor
ben•e•fice
be•nef•i•cence
be•nef•i•cent
be•nef•i•cent•ly
ben•e•fi•cial
ben•e•fi•cia•ries
ben•e•fi•cia•ry
ben•e•fit
ben•e•fit•ed
ben•e•fit•ing
be•nev•o•lence
be•nev•o•lent
be•night•ed
be•nign
be•nig•nant•ly
be•nig•ni•ty
be•nign•ly
ben•i•son
ben•zene
be•queath
be•quest
ber•ceuse
be•reave
be•reave•ment
beri•beri
Berke•ley Calif.
Berk•ley Mich.
ber•lin
ber•ries
ber•ry (fruit; cf. *bury*)
ber•serk

berth (bed; cf. *birth*)
ber•yl
be•ryl•li•um
be•seech
be•set•ting
be•side
be•sides
be•siege
be•smear
be•smirch
be•speak
Bes•se•mer
bes•tial
bes•ti•al•i•ty
best man
be•stow
best–sell•er
best–sell•ing
bet
be•tide
be•times
be•to•ken•ing
be•tray
be•tray•al
be•troth
be•troth•al
bet•ter (good; cf. *bettor*)
bet•ter•ment
bet•ting
bet•tor (one who wagers; cf. *better*)
be•tween
be•tween•times

be•tween•whiles
be•twixt
bev•el
bev•eled
bev•el•ing
bev•er•age
bev•ies
bevy
be•wail
be•ware
be•wil•der
be•wil•dered
be•wil•der•ment
be•witch
be•wray
be•yond
be•zant
be•zel
bi•an•nu•al (twice yearly; cf. *biennial*)
bi•as
bi•ased
bi•be•lot
bi•ble
bib•li•cal
bib•li•og•ra•pher
bib•li•og•ra•phy
bib•lio•phile
bib•u•lous
bi•cam•er•al
bi•car•bon•ate
bi•cen•te•na•ry
bi•cen•ten•ni•al
bi•ceps

bi•chlo•ride
bi•chro•mate
bi•cus•pid
bi•cy•cle
bi•cy•clist
Bid•de•ford Maine
Bid•e•ford England
bi•en•ni•al (once in two years; cf. *biannual*)
bi•en•ni•um
bier (for funeral; cf. *beer*)
bi•fur•cate
big•a•mist
big•a•mous
big•a•my
Big Ben
bi•gem•i•nal
big•eyed
big game
big•ger
big•gest
big•head•ed
big•heart•ed
big•horn
bight
big•mouthed
big•ot•ed
big•ot•ry
big shot
big time
big top
big•wig

bi•jou

bi•ki•ni

bi•lat•er•al

bi–lev•el

bilge

bilge wa•ter

bi•lin•gual

bil•ious

bill•board

billed (charged; cf. *build*)

bil•let

bil•let–doux

bill•fish

bill•fold

bill•head

bill•hook

bil•liards

bil•lings•gate

bil•lion

bil•lion•aire

bil•lionth

bill of fare

bill of lad•ing

bill of sale

bil•low

bil•lowy

bill•post•er

bil•ly goat

bi•me•tal•lic

bi•met•al•lism

bi•met•al•list

bi•month•ly

bi•na•ry

bind•er

bind•ery

bind•ing

bind•weed

bin•na•cle

bin•oc•u•lar

bi•no•mi•al

bio•chem•is•try

bio•de•grad•able

bio•feed•back

bi•og•ra•pher

bio•graph•ic

bio•graph•i•cal

bi•og•ra•phy

bi•o•log•i•cal

bi•ol•o•gy

bi•op•sy

bio•sci•ence

bi•par•ti•san

bi•par•tite

bi•ped

bi•plane

bi•po•lar

bird•bath

bird•brain

bird•call

bird dog n.

bird–dog v.

bird•house

bird•lime

bird•man

bird•seed

bird's–eye

bi•ret•ta

birth (beginning; cf. *berth*)

birth•day

birth•mark

birth•place

birth•rate

birth•right

birth•stone

bis•cuit

bi•sect

bish•op

bish•op•ric

Bis•marck N. Dak.

bis•muth

bi•son

bisque

bit

bit•ing

bit•stock

bit•ter

bit•tern

bit•ter•ness

bit•ter•root

bit•ter•sweet

bit•ter•weed

bi•tu•men

bi•tu•mi•nous

bi•va•lent

bi•valve

biv•ouac

biv•ouacked

bi•zarre (odd; cf. *bazaar*)

bi•zon•al

black–and–blue
black•ball
black•ber•ry
black•bird
black•board
black•cap
black•ened
black–eyed Su•san
black•head
black•jack
black lead
black light
black•list
black•mail
black•ness
black out v.
black•out n.
black•poll
black sheep
black•smith
black•snake
black•thorn
black•top
blad•der
blam•able
blame•ful
blame•less
blame•wor•thy
blam•ing
blanc•mange
blan•dish
blank
  en•dorse•ment
blan•ket

blar•ney
bla•sé
blas•pheme
blas•phem•ing
blas•phe•mous
blas•phe•my
blast off v.
blast–off n.
bla•tan•cy
bla•tant
blath•er•skite
blaze
blaz•ing
bla•zon
bla•zon•ry
bleach•er
blem•ish
blend•ed
bless•ed•ness
blew (air; cf. *blue*)
blind•er
blind•fish
blind•fold
blind•ing
blind•ly
blind word
  pro•ces•sor
blink•er
bliss•ful
blis•ter
blithe
blithe•some
blitz•krieg
bliz•zard

bloat•er
bloc (political)
block (of wood)
block•ade
block•bust•er
block•head
block•house
blond
blood
blood bank
blood count
blood•cur•dling
blood•ed
blood•hound
blood•i•est
blood•i•ly
blood•i•ness
blood•less
blood•let•ting
blood•mo•bile
blood mon•ey
blood pres•sure
blood•root
blood•shed
blood•shot
blood•stain
blood•stone
blood•suck•er
blood•thirst•i•ness
blood•thirsty
blood ves•sel
blood•wort
bloody
blos•som

blot·ter
blot·ting
blouse
blow–dry
blow·er
blow·fish
blow·fly
blow·gun
blow out v.
blow·out n.
blow·pipe
blow·torch
blow·tube
blub·ber
blub·bery
blu·cher
blud·geon
blue (color; cf. *blew*)
blue·bell
blue·ber·ry
blue·bird
blue·bon·net
blue book
blue·bot·tle
blue·coat
blue–col·lar
blue–eyed
blue·fish
blue·grass
blue·jack
blue jay
blue law
blue moon
blue–pen·cil

blue·print
blue·stock·ing
blu·et
bluff
blu·ing
blu·ish
blun·der
blun·der·buss
blunt·ly
blunt·ness
blur
blurred
blur·ring
blurt
blus·ter
blus·ter·ous
boa
boar (animal; cf. *bore*)
board (wood; cf. *bored*)
board·er (one who
    pays for meals; cf.
    border)
board foot
board·ing·house
board·ing school
board·room
board rule
board·walk
boast·ful
boast·ing·ly
boat hook
boat·house
boat·load
boat·man

boat·swain
boat train
bob·bin
bob·bi·net
bob·cat
bob·o·link
bob·sled
bob·tail
bob·white
bo·cac·cio
bod·ice
bodi·less
bodi·ly
bod·kin
body·guard
Boer
bo·gey
bo·gey·man
bog·gle
bo·gus
Bo·he·mi·an
boil·er
boil·er·plate
bois·ter·ous
bold·er (braver; cf.
    boulder)
bold·face n.
bold–faced
bold·ly
bold·ness
bole (trunk of tree; cf.
    boll, bowl)
bo·le·ro
bo·li·var

boll (of cotton; cf. *bole*, *bowl*)
boll wee•vil
boll•worm
bol•ster
bolt•er
bolt•rope
bo•lus
bomb
bom•bard
bom•bar•dier
bom•bard•ment
bom•bast
bom•bas•tic
bom•ba•zine
bomb•proof
bomb•shell
bomb•sight
bo•na fide
bo•nan•za
bon•bon
bon•bon•nière
bond•age
bond•hold•er
bond•maid
bond ser•vant
bonds•man
bone•meal
bon•fire
bo•ni•to
bon mot
bon•net
bon•ny
bo•nus

bon vi•vant
bon voy•age
bonze
boo•dle
book
book•bind•er
book•case
book club
book•deal•er
book•end
book•fair
book•ie
book•ish
book•keep•er
book•keep•ing
book•let
book list
book•lore
book•mak•er
book•mak•ing
book•man
book•mark
book•mo•bile
book•plate
book•rack
book•rest
book re•view
book•sell•er
book•shelf
book•store
book val•ue
book•work
book•worm
boo•mer•ang

boon•dog•gle
boor•ish•ness
boost•er
boot•black
boot•ed
boo•tee
booth
boot•jack
boot•leg
boot•less
boo•ty
booze
boozy
bo•rac•ic
bo•rate
bo•rax
Bor•deaux
bor•der (edge; cf. *boarder*)
bor•der•line
bore (weary; cf. *boar*)
bo•re•al
Bo•re•as
bored (uninterested; cf. *board*)
bore•dom
bor•ing
born–again
bo•ron
bor•ough (division of city; cf. *burro*, *burrow*)
bor•row
bosky

Bos·ni·an
bo·som
boss·i·ness
bossy
bo·tan·i·cal
bot·a·nist
bot·a·nize
bot·a·ny
botch
both
both·er
both·er·some
bot·tle
bot·tle·neck
bot·tler
bot·tling
bot·tom
bot·tom·less
bot·tom·ry
bot·u·lism
bou·doir
bouf·fant
bough (of tree; cf. bow)
bought
bouil·la·baisse
bouil·lon (soup; cf. bullion)
boul·der (rock; cf. bolder)
bou·le·vard
bounce
bounc·er
bounc·ing

bound
bound·aries
bound·ary
bound·en
bound·er
bound·less
boun·te·ous
boun·ti·ful
boun·ty
bou·quet
bour·bon
bour·geois
bour·geoi·sie
bourse
bou·tique
bou·ton·niere
bo·vine
bow (knot; cf. beau)
bow (salutation; cf. bough)
bowd·ler·ize
bow·el
bow·er
bow·ery
bow·fin
bow·knot
bowl (dish; cf. bole, boll)
bowl·er
bow·line
bowl·ing
bow·man
bow·shot
bow·sprit

bow·string
bow tie
bow·yer
box calf
box·car
box coat
box·er
box·ing
box kite
box of·fice
box score
box spring
box·thorn
box·wood
boy (youth; cf. buoy)
boy·cott
boy·hood
boy·ish
boy·sen·ber·ry
brace·let
brac·er
brack·et
brack·et·ing
brack·ish
brad·awl
brag
brag·ga·do·cio
brag·gart
bragged
brag·ging
braille
brain·child
brain cor·al
brain·less

brain•pow•er
brain•sick
brain•storm
brain trust
brain•wash•ing
brain wave
brainy
braise (cook slowly; cf.
    braze)
brake (on a car; cf.
    break)
brake•man
bram•ble
brand
bran•died
bran•dish
brand–new
bran•dy
bras•sard
brass•bound
brass hat
brass•ie
bras•siere
brass•i•ness
bra•va•do
brav•ery
brav•est
bra•vo
bra•vu•ra
brawl
brawn•i•est
brawny
braze (solder; cf.
    braise)

bra•zen
bra•zen–faced
bra•zier
Bra•zil•ian
bra•zil•wood
breach (violation; cf.
    breech)
bread (food; cf. *bred*)
bread•board•ing
bread•fruit
bread•root
bread•stuff
breadth (size; cf.
    breath)
bread•win•ner
break (shatter; cf.
    brake)
break•able
break•age
break down v.
break•down n.
break•er
break–even
break•fast
break•neck
break•out n.
break•through n.
break•wa•ter
breast
breast•bone
breast•stroke
breath (of air; cf.
    breadth)
breathe

breath•er
breath•ing
breath•less
breath•tak•ing
bred (produced; cf.
    bread)
breech (rear; cf.
    breach)
breech•es
breech•load•er
breech–load•ing
breed
breed•ing
breeze
breeze•way
breezy
breth•ren
bre•vet
bre•via•ry
brev•i•ty
brew
brew•ery
brew•ing
brews (ferments; cf.
    bruise)
bribe
brib•ery
brib•ing
bric–a–brac
brick
brick•bat
brick•kiln
brick•lay•er
brick red

brick•work
brick•yard
brid•al (wedding; cf. *bridle*)
bride
bride•groom
brides•maid
bride•well
bridge
bridge•head
bridge•work
bri•dle (harness; cf. *bridal*)
brief
brief•case
brief•less
bri•er
bri•er•root
bri•er•wood
brig
bri•gade
brig•a•dier
brig•and
brig•an•tine
bright
bright•en
bright•ly
bright•ness
bright•work
bril•liance
bril•lian•cy
bril•liant
bril•lian•tine
bril•liant•ly

brim
brim•ful
brimmed
brim•mer
brim•ming
brim•stone
brin•dle
bring
brink
brink•man•ship
briny
bri•quette
brisk
bris•ket
bris•tle
bris•tle•tail
bris•tling
bris•tol (cardboard)
Brit•ain (country; cf. *Briton*)
Bri•tan•nia
Bri•tan•nic
Brit•ish
Brit•ish Co•lum•bia
Brit•ish•er
Brit•on (person; cf. *Britain*)
brit•tle
broach (open; cf. *brooch*)
broad
broad•ax
broad•cast
broad•cloth

broad•en
broad jump
broad•leaf adj.
broad–leaved adj.
broad•loom
broad•ly
broad–mind•ed
broad–mind•ed•ness
broad•side
broad•sword
broad•tail
bro•cade
broc•co•li
bro•chette
bro•chure
brogue
broil
broil•er
broke
bro•ken
bro•ken•heart•ed
bro•ker
bro•ker•age
bro•mate
bro•mide
bro•mine
bron•chi•al
bron•chi•tis
bron•cho- (medical prefix; cf. *bronco*)
bron•cho•scope
bron•co (horse; cf. *broncho*)

bronze
brooch (pin; cf.
  broach)
brood
brood•er
brook
brook•let
Brook•line Mass.
Brook•lyn N.Y.
broom•stick
broth
broth•er
broth•er•hood
broth•er–in–law
broth•er•ly
brougham
brought
brow
brow•beat
brown bread
brown•ish
brown•out
brown•stone
brown sug•ar
browse
bru•in
bruise (crush; cf.
  brews)
bruis•er
bru•net *or*
  bru•nette
brunt
brush
brush–off n.

brush up v.
brush•up n.
brush•wood
brush•work
brusque
bru•tal
bru•tal•i•ty
bru•tal•iza•tion
bru•tal•ize
brute
brut•ish
bub•ble (soap; cf.
  babble, bauble)
bub•bly
bu•bon•ic
buc•ca•neer
Bu•ceph•a•lus
buck•board
buck•et
buck•eye
buck•hound
buck•le
buck•ler
buck•ling
buck•ram
buck•saw
buck•shot
buck•skin
buck•thorn
buck•wheat
bu•col•ic
Bud•dha
Bud•dhism
bud•ding

bud•get
bud•get•ary
buf•fa•lo sing. (pl.:
  buffalo or *buffaloes*)
buff•er
buf•fet
buf•foon
buf•foon•ery
bug•bear
bu•gle
bu•gling
build (construct; cf.
  billed)
build•er
build•ing
build•up n.
built–in
built–up
bul•bous
Bul•gar•i•an
bulge
bulg•ing
bulk•head
bulky
bull•dog
bull•doze
bull•doz•er
bul•let
bul•le•tin
bul•let•proof
bull•fight
bull•finch
bull•frog
bull•head

bul•lion (gold or silver; cf. *bouillon*)
bull•ock
bull pen
bull•pout
bull's—eye
bull•ter•ri•er
bull•whip
bul•ly
bul•ly•rag
bul•rush
bul•wark
bum•ble•bee
bum•boat
bump•er
bump•kin
bumpy
bunch
bun•dle
bun•ga•low
bun•gle
bun•gling
bun•ion
bunk
bunk beds
bun•ker
bun•kum *or* bun•combe
bun•ting
buoy (signal; cf. *boy*)
buoy•an•cy
buoy•ant
bur•den
bur•den•some

bur•dock
bu•reau
bu•reau•cra•cy
bu•reau•crat
bu•reau•crat•ic
bu•rette
bur•geon
bur•gher
bur•glar
bur•glar•ies
bur•glar•i•ous
bur•glar•ize
bur•glar•proof
bur•glary
bur•go•mas•ter
bur•gun•dy
buri•al
bur•ied
bur•ies
bur•lap
bur•lesque
bur•ly
Bur•mese
burn
burned
burn•er
bur•nish
bur•noose
burn•outs
burn•sides
burnt
burr
bur•ro (donkey; cf. *borough, burrow*)

bur•ros
bur•row (dig; cf. *borough, burro*)
bur•sar
bur•sa•ry
bur•si•tis
burst
bury (conceal; cf. *berry*)
bury•ing
bus•boy
bush•el
bush•rang•er
bush•whack•er
bus•ied
busi•er
busi•est
busi•ly
busi•ness (enterprise; cf. *busyness*)
busi•ness•like
busi•ness•man
busi•ness•men
busi•ness•wom•an
busi•ness•wom•en
bus•kin
bus•tle
bus•tling
busy
busy•ness (busy state; cf. *business*)
busy•work
but (conjunction; cf. *butt*)

butch•er
butch•ery
butt (end; cf. *but*)
butte
but•ter
but•ter•cup
but•ter•fat
but•ter•fish
but•ter•fly
but•ter•milk
but•ter•nut
but•ter•scotch
but•ter•weed
but•tery
but•tock

but•ton
but•ton•hole
but•ton•hook
but•ton•wood
but•tress
bux•om
buy•er
buy•ing
buzz
buz•zard
buzz•er
buzz saw
buzz•word
by and large
by–elec•tion

by•gone
by•law
by•line
by•pass
by•path
by•play
by–prod•uct
by•road
bys•sus
by•stand•er
byte
by•way
by•word
Byz•an•tine

ca•bal
cab•a•lis•tic
ca•bana
cab•a•ret
cab•bage
cab•driv•er
cab•in
cab•i•net
cab•i•net•mak•er
cab•i•net•work
ca•ble
ca•ble•gram
ca•bling

cab•man
cab•o•chon
ca•boose
cab•ri•o•let
cab•stand
ca•cao
cach•a•lot
cache
ca•chet
cach•in•na•tion
ca•cique
cack•le
ca•coph•o•ny

cac•tus (pl.: *cacti* or
    cactuses or *cactus*)
ca•dav•er
ca•dav•er•ous
ca•dence
ca•den•za
ca•det
cad•mi•um
ca•du•ceus
Cae•sar
cae•su•ra
caf•e•te•ria
caf•feine

cairn•gorm
cais•son
cai•tiff
ca•jole
ca•jol•ery
cake•walk
cal•a•bash
cal•a•boose
ca•lam•i•tous
ca•lam•i•ty
cal•car•e•ous
cal•cif•er•ous
cal•ci•fi•ca•tion
cal•ci•fy
cal•ci•mine
cal•ci•na•tion
cal•cine
cal•ci•um
cal•cu•la•ble
cal•cu•late
cal•cu•lat•ing
cal•cu•la•tion
cal•cu•la•tor
cal•cu•lus (pl.: *calculi*)
cal•dron
cal•en•dar (for dates)
cal•en•der (machine)
calf (pl.: *calves*)
calf•skin
cal•i•ber
cal•i•brate
cal•i•co
Cal•i•for•nia
cal•i•per

ca•liph
cal•is•then•ics
calk
calk•er
call•able
cal•lig•ra•pher
cal•lig•ra•phy
call•ing
cal•los•i•ty
cal•lous (hardened; cf. *callus*)
cal•low
cal•lus (hardened surface; cf. *callous*)
calm
calm•ly
calm•ness
cal•o•mel
ca•lo•ric
ca•lo•rie
ca•lo•ries
ca•lo•rim•e•ter
ca•lum•ni•ate
ca•lum•ni•a•tion
ca•lum•ni•a•tor
cal•um•nies
ca•lum•ni•ous
cal•um•ny
cal•va•ry
Cal•vin•ism
Cal•vin•ist
Cal•vin•is•tic
ca•lyp•so
ca•lyx

ca•ma•ra•de•rie
cam•ber
cam•bi•um
cam•bric
cam•el
ca•mel•lia
ca•mel•o•pard
Cam•em•bert
cam•eo
cam•eos
cam•era
cam•era•man
cam•i•sole
cam•ou•flage
cam•paign
cam•pa•ni•le
camp•er
camp•fire
camp•ground
cam•phor
cam•pus
cam•shaft
cam wheel
Can•a•da
Ca•na•di•an
ca•naille
ca•nal
can•a•li•za•tion
can•a•pé
ca•nard
ca•nar•ies
ca•nary
can•cel
can•celed

can·cel·er
can·cel·ing
can·cel·la·tion
can·cer
can·cer·ous
can·de·la·bra
can·did
can·di·da·cy
can·di·date
can·did·ly
can·did·ness
can·died
can·dies
can·dle
can·dle·ber·ry
can·dle·fish
can·dle·light
can·dle·nut
can·dle·pin
can·dle·pow·er
can·dle·stick
can·dle·wick
can·dle·wood
can·dor
can·dy
cane·brake
ca·nine
can·is·ter
can·ker
can·ker·ous
can·ker·worm
can·na
can·nery
can·ni·bal

can·ni·bal·ism
can·ni·bal·ize
can·ni·ly
can·ni·ness
can·ning
can·non (gun; cf.
    canon, canyon)
can·non·ade
can·non·eer
can·not
can·ny
ca·noe
ca·noe·ing
ca·noes
can·on (rule; cf.
    cannon, canyon)
ca·non·i·cal
can·on·ize
can·o·pies
can·o·py
can·ta·bi·le
can·ta·loupe
can·tan·ker·ous
can·ta·ta
can·ta·trice
can·teen
can·ter
can·ti·cle
can·ti·le·ver
can·to
can·ton
can·ton·al
Can·ton·ese
can·ton·ment

can·tor
can·vas n. (cloth)
can·vass v. (solicit)
can·yon (ravine; cf.
    cannon, canon)
ca·pa·bil·i·ties
ca·pa·bil·i·ty
ca·pa·ble
ca·pa·bly
ca·pa·cious
ca·pac·i·tor
ca·pac·i·ty
cap–a–pie
ca·par·i·son
ca·per
cap·il·lar·i·ty
cap·il·lary
cap·i·tal (city,
    property; cf. *capitol*)
cap·i·tal·ism
cap·i·tal·ist
cap·i·tal·iza·tion
cap·i·tal·ize
cap·i·tol (building; cf.
    capital)
ca·pit·u·late
ca·pit·u·la·tion
ca·price
ca·pri·cious
cap·size
cap·stan
cap·stone
cap·sule
cap·tain

cap•tion
cap•tious
cap•ti•vate
cap•ti•va•tion
cap•tive
cap•tiv•i•ty
cap•tor
cap•ture
cap•tur•ing
car•a•cole
car•a•cul
car•a•mel
car•a•mel•ize
car•at *or* kar•at
  (weight; cf. *caret,*
  carrot)
car•a•van
car•a•van•sa•ry
car•a•vel
car•a•way
car•bide
car•bine
car•bo•hy•drate
car•bol•ic
car•bon
car•bo•na•ceous
car•bon•ate
car•bon•ic
car•bon•if•er•ous
Car•bo•run•dum
car•box•yl
car•boy
car•bun•cle
car•bu•re•tor

car•cass
car•cin•o•gen
car•ci•no•ma
car•da•mom
card•board
card cat•a•log
card•hold•er
car•di•ac
car•di•gan
car•di•nal
car•di•nal•ate
car•dio•gram
car•dio•graph
car•di•ol•o•gist
car•dio•vas•cu•lar
card ta•ble
ca•reen
ca•reer
care•ful
care•ful•ly
care•less
ca•ress
car•et (a symbol; cf.
  carat, carrot)
care•worn
car•fare
car•go *sing.*
car•goes *pl.*
car•hop
Ca•rib•be•an
car•i•bou
car•i•ca•ture
car•ies
car•il•lon

ca•ri•o•ca
car•line
car•load
car•mi•na•tive
car•mine
car•nage
car•nal
car•nal•i•ty
car•na•tion
car•ne•lian
car•ni•val
car•niv•o•rous
car•ol
car•om
ca•rot•id
ca•rous•al
ca•rouse
car•pen•ter
car•pen•try
car•pet
car•pet•bag
car•pet•bag•ger
car•pet•ing
car•port
car•riage
car•ri•er
car•ri•on
car•rot (vegetable; cf.
  carat, caret)
car•rou•sel
car•ry
car•ry•all
car•ry•over *n.*
cart•age

carte blanche
car•tel
car•ti•lage
car•ti•lag•i•nous
car•tog•ra•pher
car•tog•ra•phy
car•ton (box)
car•toon (picture)
car•toon•ist
car•touche
car•tridge
carve
cary•at•id
ca•sa•ba
cas•cade
case hard•en
ca•sein
case knife
case•mate
case•ment
ca•sern
case•work
cash–and–car•ry
cash•book
ca•shew
cash•ier n.
ca•shier v.
cash•mere
ca•si•no
cas•ket
casque
cas•se•role
cas•sette
cas•sia

cas•sock
cas•so•wary
cast (throw; cf. *caste*)
cas•ta•net
cast•away
caste (social class; cf. *cast*)
cas•tel•lat•ed
cas•ti•gate
cas•ti•ga•tion
Cas•til•ian
cast iron n.
cast–iron adj.
cas•tle
cast–off adj.
cast•off n.
cas•tor
ca•su•al
ca•su•al•ty
ca•su•ist
ca•su•ist•ry
cat•a•clysm
cat•a•comb
cat•a•falque
Cat•a•lan
cat•a•lep•sy
cat•a•lep•tic
cat•a•log
ca•tal•pa
ca•tal•y•sis
cat•a•lyst
cat•a•lyt•ic
cat•a•ma•ran
cat•a•mount

cat•a•pult
cat•a•ract
ca•tarrh
ca•tarrh•al
ca•tas•ta•sis
ca•tas•tro•phe
cat•a•stroph•ic
Ca•taw•ba
cat•bird
cat•boat
cat•call
catch–22
catch•all
catch•er
catch•pen•ny
catch•word
cat•e•che•sis
cat•e•chism
cat•e•chist
cat•e•chu•men
cat•e•gor•i•cal
cat•e•go•rize
cat•e•go•ry
cat•e•nary
cat•er–cor•nered
ca•ter•er
cat•er•pil•lar
cat•er•waul
cat•fish
cat•gut
ca•thar•sis
ca•thar•tic
ca•the•dral
cath•e•ter

cath•ode
cath•ode–ray tube
cath•o•lic
Ca•thol•i•cism
cath•o•lic•i•ty
ca•thol•i•cize
cat•like
cat•nip
cat–o'–nine–tails
cat's–eye
cat's–paw
cat•sup
cat•tail
cat•tle
cat•walk
Cau•ca•sian
cau•cus
cau•dal
cau•li•flow•er
caulk
caus•al
cau•sal•i•ty
cau•sa•tion
caus•ative
cau•se•rie
cause•way
caus•ing
caus•tic
cau•ter•i•za•tion
cau•ter•ize
cau•tery
cau•tion
cau•tion•ary
cau•tious

cav•al•cade
cav•a•lier
cav•a•lier•ly
cav•al•ry
cav•a•ti•na
ca•ve•at emp•tor
cav•ern
cav•ern•ous
cav•i•ar
cav•il
cav•iled
cav•i•ties
cav•i•ty
ca•vort
cease
ceased
cease•less
ce•dar
cede (yield; cf. *seed*)
ce•dil•la
ceil
ceil•ing
cel•e•brant
cel•e•brate
cel•e•brat•ed
cel•e•bra•tion
cel•e•bra•tor
ce•leb•ri•ty
ce•ler•i•ty
cel•ery
ce•les•ta
ce•les•tial
cel•i•ba•cy
cel•i•bate

cel•lar (underground
   storeroom; cf. *seller*)
cel•lar•age
cel•lar•er
cel•lar•ette
cel•list
cel•lo
cel•lo•phane
cel•lu•lar
cel•lu•loid
cel•lu•lose
Cel•sius
ce•ment
ce•men•ta•tion
cem•e•ter•ies
cem•e•tery
cen•o•bite
ceno•taph
cen•ser (for incense)
cen•sor (examiner)
cen•so•ri•al
cen•so•ri•ous
cen•sor•ship
cen•sur•able
cen•sure
cen•sur•ing
cen•sus (count; cf.
   senses)
cent (penny; cf. *scent,
   sent*)
cen•taur
cen•ta•vo
cen•te•na•ry
cen•ten•ni•al

cen·ter·board
cen·ter·piece
cen·ti·grade
cen·ti·gram
cen·ti·li·ter
cen·time
cen·ti·me·ter
cen·ti·pede
cen·tral
cen·tral·iza·tion
cen·tral·ize
cen·tral pro·cess·ing unit
cen·trif·u·gal
cen·tri·fuge
cen·trip·e·tal
cen·trist
cen·tu·ri·on
cen·tu·ry
ce·phal·ic
ce·ram·ic
Cer·ber·us
ce·re·al (grain; cf. serial)
cer·e·bel·lum
ce·re·bral
ce·re·bro·spi·nal
cer·e·mo·ni·al
cer·e·mo·nies
cer·e·mo·ni·ous
cer·e·mo·ny
Ce·res
ce·rise
ce·ri·um

cer·tain
cer·tain·ly
cer·tain·ties
cer·tain·ty
cer·ti·fi·able
cer·tif·i·cate
cer·ti·fi·ca·tion
cer·ti·fies
cer·ti·fy
cer·tio·ra·ri
cer·ti·tude
ce·ru·le·an
cer·vi·cal
cer·vix
ce·si·um
ces·sa·tion
ces·sion (yielding; cf. session)
cess·pit
cess·pool
chafe (irritate)
chaff (banter)
chaf·finch
cha·grin
cha·grined
chain gang
chain mail
chain saw
chain–smoke
chain stitch
chair·man
chair·per·son
chair·wom·an
chaise longue

chal·ce·do·ny
cha·let
chal·ice
chalky
chal·lenge
chal·lis
cham·ber
cham·ber·lain
cham·ber·maid
cha·me·leon
cham·fer
cham·ois
cham·pagne (wine)
cham·paign (plain)
cham·per·ty
cham·pi·on
cham·pi·on·ship
chance·ful
chan·cel
chan·cel·lery
chan·cel·lor
chan·cery
chan·de·lier
chan·dler
chan·dlery
change·abil·i·ty
change·able
change·less
change·ling
change·over
chang·ing
chan·nel
chan·neled
chan·nel·ing

chan·son
chan·te·relle
chan·teuse
chan·ti·cleer
cha·os
cha·ot·ic
chap·ar·ral
chap·book
cha·peau (pl.:
  chapeaus)
cha·pel
chap·er·on
chap·fall·en
chap·lain
chap·let
chap·ter
char·ac·ter
char·ac·ter·is·tic
char·ac·ter·iza·tion
char·ac·ter·ize
char·ac·ter print·er
cha·rade
char·coal
charge·abil·i·ty
charge·able
charge ac·count
charge card
char·gé d'af·faires
charge plate
charg·ing
char·i·ot
char·i·o·teer
cha·ris·ma
char·i·ta·ble

char·i·ta·bly
char·i·ties
char·i·ty
char·la·tan
Charles·ton S.C.,
  W. Va.
Charles·town Mass.
char·ley horse
char·nel
char·ter
char·treuse
char·wom·an
Cha·ryb·dis
chased (pursued; cf.
  chaste)
chasm
chasse·pot
chas·sis
chaste (virtuous; cf.
  chased)
chas·ten
chas·tise
chas·tise·ment
chas·ti·ty
cha·su·ble
châ·teau (pl.:
  châteaus)
chat·e·laine
chat·tel
chat·ter
chat·ter·box
chat·ter·er
chat·ting
chauf·feur

chau·tau·qua
chau·vin·ism
cheap·en
cheap·ened
cheap·skate
check·book
check·er·ber·ry
check·er·board
check·ered
check in v.
check–in n.
check·list
check mark
check·mate
check off v.
check·off n.
check out v.
check·out n.
check·point
check·rein
check·room
check up v.
check·up n.
check·writ·er
cheek·bone
cheek·i·ly
cheek·i·ness
cheeky
cheer·ful
cheer·ful·ness
cheer·i·ly
cheer·less
cheery
cheese·burg·er

cheese•cake
cheese•cloth
cheese•par•ing
chef
chef d'oeu•vre
chem•i•cal
che•mise
chem•ist
chem•is•try
che•mo•ther•a•py
che•nille
cher•ish
Cher•o•kee
che•root
cher•ries
cher•ry
cher•ub (pl.: *cherubim*
    or *cherubs*)
chess•board
chess•man
ches•ter•field
chest•nut
che•va•lier
chev•i•ot
chev•ron
Chi•an•ti
chiar•oscu•ro
chi•ca•nery
chick•a•dee
chick•a•ree
chick•en
chick•en•heart•ed
chick•en pox
chick–pea

chick•weed
chi•cle
chic•o•ry
chief•ly
chief•tain
chif•fon
chif•fo•nier
chi•gnon
chil•blain
child•bed
child•birth
child•hood
child•ish
child•less
child•like
child•proof
chil•dren
chill
chill•i•ness
chill•ing•ly
chilly
chi•me•ra
chi•me•ri•cal
chim•ney
chim•neys
chim•pan•zee
chi•na•ber•ry
Chi•na•town
chi•na•ware
chin•chil•la
Chi•nese
Chi•nook
chintz
chip•munk

chip•ping
chi•rog•ra•phy
chi•rop•o•dist
chi•ro•prac•tor
chis•el
chis•eled
chis•el•er
chis•el•ing
chit•chat
chi•val•ric
chiv•al•rous
chiv•al•ry
chlo•ral
chlo•rate
chlor•dane
chlo•ric
chlo•ride
chlo•ri•nate
chlo•rine
chlo•rite
chlo•ro•form
chlo•ro•phyll
chlo•rous
chock–full
choc•o•late
Choc•taw
choir (singers; cf.
    quire)
choke•ber•ry
choke•cher•ry
choke•damp
chok•er
cho•ler
chol•era

cho•ler•ic
cho•les•ter•ol
choose (select; cf. *chose*)
choos•ing
chop•house
chop•per
chop•ping
chop•stick
chop su•ey
cho•ral (of a chorus; cf. *chorale, coral, corral*)
cho•rale (sacred song; cf. *choral, coral, corral*)
chord (music; cf. *cord*)
chore
cho•rea
cho•re•og•ra•phy
cho•ris•ter
chor•tle
cho•rus
chose (selected; cf. *choose*)
cho•sen
chow•der
chrism
chris•ten
Chris•ten•dom
Chris•tian
Chris•tian•i•ty
Chris•tian•ize
Christ•like
Christ•ly

Christ•mas
Christ•mas•tide
chro•mate
chro•mat•ic
chro•ma•tog•ra•phy
chrome
chro•mite
chro•mi•um
chro•mo•some
chron•ic
chron•i•cle
chro•no•graph
chro•no•log•i•cal
chro•nol•o•gy
chro•nom•e•ter
chro•no•met•ric
chrys•a•lis
chry•san•the•mum
chryso•ber•yl
chrys•o•lite
chrys•o•prase
chuck•le
chuck•le•head
chuk•ker
chum
chum•mi•ness
chum•my
chump
chunk
church•go•er
church•man
church•war•den
church•wom•an
church•yard

churl
churl•ish
churn
chute (slide; cf. *shoot*)
chut•ney
chyle
chyme
ci•bo•ri•um
ci•ca•da
ci•ca•la
ci•ca•trix
ci•der
ci–de•vant
ci•gar
cig•a•rette
Cim•me•ri•an
cin•cho•na
Cin•cin•nati Ohio
cinc•ture
cin•der
Cin•der•el•la
cin•e•ma
cin•e•mat•o•graph
cin•na•bar
cin•na•mon
cin•que•cen•to
cin•que•foil
ci•pher
Cir•cas•sian
Cir•ce
cir•cle
cir•clet
cir•cling
cir•cuit

cir•cu•itous
cir•cuit•ry
cir•cu•lar
cir•cu•lar•iza•tion
cir•cu•lar•ize
cir•cu•late
cir•cu•la•tion
cir•cu•la•tive
cir•cu•la•tor
cir•cu•la•to•ry
cir•cum•am•bi•ent
cir•cum•cise
cir•cum•ci•sion
cir•cum•fer•ence
cir•cum•fer•en•tial
cir•cum•flex
cir•cum•lo•cu•tion
cir•cum•nav•i•gate
cir•cum•scribe
cir•cum•scrip•tion
cir•cum•spect
cir•cum•spec•tion
cir•cum•stance
cir•cum•stan•tial
cir•cum•stan•ti•al•
  i•ty
cir•cum•stan•tial•ly
cir•cum•stan•ti•ate
cir•cum•vent
cir•cum•ven•tion
cir•cus
cir•rho•sis
cir•ro•cu•mu•lus
cir•ro•stra•tus

cis•tern
cit•a•del
ci•ta•tion
cite (quote; cf. *sight,
  site*)
cit•ing
cit•i•zen
cit•i•zen•ry
cit•i•zen•ship
ci•trate
cit•ric
cit•ron
cit•ro•nel•la
cit•rus
city
civ•et
civ•ic
civ•il
ci•vil•ian
ci•vil•i•ty
civ•i•li•za•tion
civ•i•lize
civ•il•ly
claim•ant
clair•voy•ance
clair•voy•ant
cla•mant
clam•bake
clam•ber (climb; cf.
  clamor)
clam•mi•ness
clam•my
clam•or (outcry; cf.
  clamber)

clam•or•ous
clam•shell
clan•des•tine
clan•gor
clan•gor•ous•ly
clan•nish
clans•man
clap•board
clap•per
clap•ping
clap•trap
claque
clar•et
clar•i•fi•ca•tion
clar•i•fied
clar•i•fy
clar•i•net
clar•i•on
clar•i•ty
clas•sic
clas•si•cal
clas•si•cism
clas•si•cist
clas•si•fi•able
clas•si•fi•ca•tion
clas•si•fied
clas•si•fy
class•mate
class•room
clat•ter
clause (grammatical; cf.
  claws)
claus•tro•pho•bia
clav•i•chord

clav•i•cle
cla•vier
claws (animal's nails; cf. *clause*)
clay•bank
clay•more
clean–cut
clean•er
clean•hand•ed
clean–limbed
clean•li•ness
clean•ly
clean•ness
cleanse
cleans•er
cleans•ing
clear•ance
clear–cut
clear–eyed
clear•head•ed
clear•ing•house
clear–sight•ed
cleav•age
cleav•er
cle•ma•tis
clem•en•cy
clem•ent
clep•sy•dra
clere•sto•ry
cler•gy
cler•gy•man
cler•gy•wom•an
cler•ic
cler•i•cal

cler•i•cal•ism
clev•er
clew *or* clue
cli•ché
cli•ent
cli•en•tele
cliff–hang•er
cli•mac•ter•ic
cli•mac•tic (of a climax; cf. *climatic*)
cli•mate
cli•ma•tic (of climate; cf. *climactic*)
cli•ma•to•log•i•cal
cli•max
cling•stone
clin•ic
clin•i•cal
cli•ni•cian
cli•ni•cians
clin•ker
clip•per
clip•ping
clique
clo•aca
cloak–and–dag•ger
clob•ber
clock–watch•er
clock•wise
clock•work
clod•hop•per
clog•ging
clois•ter
closed–end

close•fist•ed
close–hauled
close–knit
close•ness
clos•et
close–up n.
clo•sure
cloth n.
clothe v.
clothes•pin
cloth•ier
cloth•ing
clo•ture
cloud•burst
cloud•i•ly
cloud•i•ness
cloud•less
clout
clo•ven–foot•ed
clo•ver
clo•ver•leaf
club•bing
club car
club chair
club•foot
club•house
club steak
clum•si•er
clum•si•est
clum•si•ly
clum•si•ness
clum•sy
clus•ter
clutch

clut•ter
coach dog
coach•man
co•ad•ju•tor
co•ag•u•late
co•ag•u•la•tion
co•alesce
co•ales•cence
co•ales•cent
coal gas
co•ali•tion
coal tar
coarse (rough; cf.
    corse, course)
coars•en
coast•al
coast•er
coast guard
coast•line
coast–to–coast
coast•wise
coat•tail
co•au•thor
coax
co•ax•i•al
co•balt
cob•bler
cob•ble•stone
CO•BOL
co•bra
cob•web
co•caine
coc•cyx
co•chair•man

co•chair•per•son
co•chair•wom•an
Co•chin Chi•na
co•chi•neal
cock•ade
cock•a•too
cock•a•trice
cock•boat
cock•cha•fer
cock•crow
cock•le•bur
cock•les
cock•le•shell
cock•ney
cock•pit
cock•roach
cock•sure
cock•tail
co•coa
co•co•nut
co•coon
co•de•fen•dant
co•deine
co•dex
cod•fish
cod•i•cil
cod•i•fi•ca•tion
cod•i•fied
cod•i•fy
co•ed
co•ed•i•tor
co•ed•u•ca•tion
co•ef•fi•cient
coel•acanth

co•erce
co•er•cion
co•er•cive
co•eval
co•ex•is•tence
cof•fee
cof•fee•house
cof•fee•pot
cof•fee shop
cof•fee ta•ble
cof•fer
cof•fer•dam
cof•fin
co•gen•cy
co•gent
cog•i•tate
cog•i•ta•tion
cog•i•ta•tive
co•gnac
cog•nate
cog•ni•zance
cog•ni•zant
cog•no•men
cog•wheel
co•hab•it
co•heir
co•here
co•her•ence
co•her•en•cy
co•her•ent
co•he•sion
co•he•sive
co•hort
co•host

co•host•ess
coif•feur (person)
coif•fure (style)
coign (position; cf. *coin, quoin*)
coin (money; cf. *coign, quoin*)
coin•age
co•in•cide
co•in•ci•dence
co•in•ci•dent
co•in•ci•den•tal
co•in•sur•ance
co•in•sure
co•ition
col•an•der
cold–blood•ed
cold chis•el
cold cream
cold cuts
cold frame
cold front
cold sore
cold sweat
cold war
cold wave
co•le•op•ter•ous
cole•slaw
col•ic
col•ic•root
col•ic•weed
co•li•se•um
co•li•tis
col•lab•o•rate

col•lab•o•ra•tion
col•lab•o•ra•tor
col•lage
col•lapse
col•lapsed
col•laps•ible
col•lar
col•lar•bone
col•late
col•lat•er•al
col•la•tion
col•league
col•lect
col•lect•ed
col•lect•ible
col•lec•tion
col•lec•tive
col•lec•tive•ly
col•lec•tiv•ism
col•lec•tiv•ize
col•lec•tor
col•lege
col•le•gial
col•le•gi•al•i•ty
col•le•gian
col•le•giate
col•le•gi•um
col•lide
col•lie (dog; cf. *coolie, coolly*)
col•lier
col•liery
col•li•sion (crash; cf. *collusion*)

col•lo•ca•tion
col•lo•di•on
col•loid
col•lop
col•lo•qui•al
col•lo•qui•al•ism
col•lo•qui•al•ly
col•lo•quies
col•lo•qui•um
col•lo•quy
col•lu•sion (secret agreement; cf. *collision*)
col•lu•sive
co•logne
co•lon
col•o•nel (officer; cf. *kernel*)
col•o•nel•cy
co•lo•nial
co•lo•nial•ism
col•o•nies
col•o•nist
col•o•ni•za•tion
col•o•nize
col•on•nade
col•o•ny
col•o•phon
col•or
Col•o•ra•do
col•or•ation
col•or•a•tu•ra
col•or–blind
col•ored

col•or•fast
col•or•ful
col•or guard
col•or•less
co•los•sal
col•os•se•um
co•los•sus
col•umn
co•lum•nar
col•um•nist
co•ma (insensibility; cf. *comma*)
co•ma•tose
com•bat
com•bat•ant
com•bat•ed
com•bat•ing
com•bat•ive
com•bi•na•tion
com•bine
com•bo
com•bus•ti•ble
com•bus•tion
come•back n.
co•me•di•an (mas.)
co•me•di•enne (fem.)
com•e•dy
come•li•ness
come•ly
come–on n.
co•mes•ti•ble
com•et
com•fit
com•fort

com•fort•able
com•fort•er
com•ic
com•i•cal
com•ing
co•mi•ty
com•ma (punctuation; cf. *coma*)
com•mand (order; cf. *commend*)
com•man•dant
com•man•deer
com•mand•er
com•mand•ment
com•mand mod•ule
com•man•do
com•man•dos
com•mem•o•rate
com•mem•o•ra•tion
com•mem•o•ra•tive
com•mence
com•mence•ment
com•menc•ing
com•mend (praise; cf. *command*)
com•mend•able
com•men•da•tion
com•men•da•to•ry
com•men•su•ra•bil•i•ty
com•men•su•ra•ble
com•men•su•rate
com•men•su•rate•ly
com•ment

com•men•tary
com•men•ta•tor
com•merce
com•mer•cial
com•mer•cial•ism
com•mer•cial•iza•tion
com•mer•cial•ize
com•min•gle
com•mi•nu•tion
com•mis•er•ate
com•mis•er•a•tion
com•mis•sar
com•mis•sar•i•at
com•mis•sary
com•mis•sion
com•mis•sion•aire
com•mis•sion•er
com•mit
com•mit•ment
com•mit•ted
com•mit•tee
com•mit•tee•man
com•mit•tee•men
com•mit•tee•wom•an
com•mit•ting
com•mode
com•mo•di•ous
com•mod•i•ties
com•mod•i•ty
com•mo•dore
com•mon
com•mon•al•ty

com·mon·er
com·mon·place
com·mon sense n.
com·mon·sense adj.
com·mon·wealth
com·mo·tion
com·mu·nal
com·mune
com·mu·ni·ca·ble
com·mu·ni·cant
com·mu·ni·cate
com·mu·ni·cat·ing
  word pro·ces·sor
com·mu·ni·ca·tion
com·mu·ni·ca·tive
com·mu·ni·ca·tor
com·mu·nion
com·mu·ni·qué
com·mu·nism
com·mu·nist
com·mu·ni·ties
com·mu·ni·ty
com·mu·ta·tion
com·mu·ta·tor
com·mute
com·mu·ter
com·pact
com·pac·tor
com·pa·nies
com·pan·ion
com·pan·ion·able
com·pan·ion·ship
com·pan·ion·way

com·pa·ny
com·pa·ra·ble
com·par·a·tive
com·pare
com·par·i·son
com·part·ment
com·pass
com·pas·sion
com·pas·sion·ate
com·pat·i·bil·i·ty
com·pat·i·ble
com·pa·tri·ot
com·peer
com·pel
com·pelled
com·pel·ling
com·pen·di·ous
com·pen·di·um
com·pen·sate
com·pen·sa·tion
com·pen·sa·tive
com·pen·sa·to·ry
com·pete
com·pe·tence
com·pe·ten·cy
com·pe·tent
com·pe·ti·tion
com·pet·i·tive
com·pet·i·tor
com·pi·la·tion
com·pile
com·pil·er
com·pla·cence

com·pla·cen·cy
com·pla·cent (self-
  satisfied; cf.
  complaisant)
com·plain
com·plain·ant
com·plaint
com·plai·sance
com·plai·sant
  (obliging; cf.
  complacent)
com·ple·ment (full
  quantity; cf.
  compliment)
com·ple·men·tal
com·ple·men·ta·ry
com·plete
com·ple·tion
com·plex
com·plex·ion
com·plex·ioned
com·plex·i·ty
com·pli·an·cy
com·pli·ant
com·pli·cate
com·pli·cat·ed
com·pli·ca·tion
com·plic·i·ty
com·plied
com·pli·ment (flatter;
  cf. *complement*)
com·pli·men·ta·ry
com·ply

com·po·nent
com·port
com·port·ment
com·pose
com·posed
com·pos·er
com·pos·ite
com·pos·ite·ly
com·po·si·tion
com·pos·i·tor
com·post
com·po·sure
com·pound
com·pre·hend
com·pre·hen·si·ble
com·pre·hen·sion
com·pre·hen·sive
com·press
com·pressed
com·press·ible
com·pres·sion
com·pres·sor
com·prise
com·pro·mise
comp·trol·ler
com·pul·sion
com·pul·so·ry
com·punc·tion
com·put·able
com·pu·ta·tion
com·pute
com·put·er
com·put·er·ize

com·put·er out·put
   mi·cro·film
com·rade
con·cat·e·na·tion
con·cave
con·cav·i·ty
con·ceal
con·ceal·ment
con·cede
con·ced·ed·ly
con·ceit
con·ceit·ed
con·ceiv·able
con·ceive
con·cen·trate
con·cen·tra·tion
con·cen·tra·tor
con·cen·tric
con·cept
con·cep·tion
con·cep·tu·al
con·cern
con·cert
con·cer·ti·na
con·cert·mas·ter
con·cer·to
con·ces·sion
con·ces·sion·aire
conch
con·cierge
con·cil·i·ate
con·cil·i·a·tion
con·cil·ia·to·ry

con·cise
con·clave
con·clude
con·clu·sion
con·clu·sive
con·coct
con·coc·tion
con·com·i·tant
con·cord
con·cor·dance
con·cor·dat
con·course
con·crete
con·crete·ly
con·cu·bine
con·cur
con·curred
con·cur·rence
con·cur·rent
con·cur·ring
con·cus·sion
con·demn
con·dem·na·tion
con·dem·na·to·ry
con·demned
con·den·sa·tion
con·dense
con·dens·er
con·de·scend
con·de·scend·ing·ly
con·de·scen·sion
con·dign
con·di·ment

con•di•tion
con•di•tion•al
con•di•tioned
con•dole
con•do•lence
con•do•min•i•um
con•do•na•tion
con•done
con•dor
con•duce
con•du•cive
con•duct
con•duc•tion
con•duc•tor
con•duit
con•el•rad
con•fab•u•late
con•fec•tion
con•fec•tion•er
con•fec•tion•ery
con•fed•er•a•cy
con•fed•er•ate
con•fed•er•a•tion
con•fer
con•fer•ee
con•fer•ence
con•ferred
con•fer•ring
con•fess
con•fessed•ly
con•fes•sion
con•fes•sion•al
con•fes•sor
con•fet•ti

con•fi•dant (friend; cf.
   confident)
con•fide
con•fi•dence
con•fi•dent (sure; cf.
   confidant)
con•fi•den•tial
con•fi•den•ti•al•i•ty
con•fid•ing
con•fig•u•ra•tion
con•fine
con•fine•ment
con•firm
con•fir•ma•tion
con•firmed
con•fis•cate
con•fis•ca•tion
con•fis•ca•to•ry
con•fi•ture
con•fla•gra•tion
con•flict
con•flic•tion
con•flu•ence
con•form
con•form•able
con•for•ma•tion
con•form•ist
con•for•mi•ty
con•found
con•found•ed•ly
con•fra•ter•ni•ty
con•front
con•fron•ta•tion
Con•fu•cian

con•fuse
con•fused•ly
con•fus•ing
con•fu•sion
con•fu•ta•tion
con•fute
con•ga
con•gé
con•geal
con•ge•ner
con•ge•nial
con•ge•nial•i•ty
con•gen•i•tal
con•ger eel
con•gest
con•ges•tion
con•glom•er•ate
con•glom•er•a•tion
con•grat•u•late
con•grat•u•la•tion
con•grat•u•la•to•ry
con•gre•gate
con•gre•ga•tion
con•gre•ga•tion•al
con•gress
con•gres•sio•nal
con•gress•man
con•gress•wom•an
con•gru•ence
con•gru•ent
con•gru•ity
con•gru•ous
con•ic
con•i•cal

co·ni·fer
co·nif·er·ous
con·jec·tur·al
con·jec·ture
con·ju·gal
con·ju·gate
con·ju·ga·tion
con·junc·tion
con·junc·ti·va
con·junc·ture
con·jure
con·jur·er
con·nect
con·nect·ed·ly
Con·nect·i·cut
con·nec·tion
con·nec·tive
con·nec·tor
con·niv·ance
con·nive
con·nois·seur
con·no·ta·tion
con·no·ta·tive
con·note
con·nu·bi·al
con·quer
con·quered
con·quer·ing
con·quer·or
con·quest
con·san·guin·e·ous
con·san·guin·i·ty
con·science
con·sci·en·tious

con·scious
con·scious·ness
con·script
con·scrip·tion
con·se·crate
con·se·cra·tion
con·sec·u·tive
con·sen·sus
con·sent
con·se·quence
con·se·quent
con·se·quen·tial
con·se·quent·ly
con·ser·va·tion
con·ser·va·tism
con·ser·va·tive
con·ser·va·to·ry
con·serve
con·sid·er
con·sid·er·able
con·sid·er·ate
con·sid·er·ation
con·sid·ered
con·sign
con·sign·ee
con·sign·ment
con·sign·or
con·sist
con·sis·ten·cy
con·sis·tent
con·sis·to·ry
con·so·la·tion
con·so·la·to·ry
con·sole

con·sol·i·date
con·sol·i·da·tion
con·som·mé
con·so·nance
con·so·nant
con·so·nan·tal
con·sort
con·sor·tium
con·spec·tus
con·spic·u·ous
con·spir·a·cy
con·spir·a·tor
con·spire
con·sta·ble
con·stab·u·lary
con·stan·cy
con·stant
con·stel·la·tion
con·ster·na·tion
con·sti·pate
con·stit·u·en·cy
con·stit·u·ent
con·sti·tute
con·sti·tu·tion
con·sti·tu·tion·al
con·sti·tu·tion·al·i·ty
con·sti·tu·tion·al·ly
con·strain
con·straint
con·strict
con·stric·tion
con·stric·tor
con·struct

con•struc•tion
con•struc•tion•ist
con•struc•tive
con•strue
con•strued
con•stru•ing
con•sul (government
    official; cf. *council,*
    counsel)
con•sul•ar
con•sul•ate
con•sult
con•sul•tant
con•sul•ta•tion
con•sul•ta•tive
con•sume
con•sum•ed•ly
con•sum•mate
con•sum•ma•tion
con•sump•tion
con•sump•tive
con•tact
con•ta•gion
con•ta•gious
con•tain•er
con•tain•ment
con•tam•i•nant
con•tam•i•nate
con•tam•i•na•tion
con•tem•plate
con•tem•pla•tion
con•tem•pla•tive
con•tem•po•ra•
    ne•ous

con•tem•po•rary
con•tempt
con•tempt•ible
con•temp•tu•ous
con•tend
con•ten•tion
con•ten•tious
con•tent•ment
con•test
con•tes•tant
con•tes•ta•tion
con•text
con•tex•tu•al
con•tex•ture
con•ti•gu•ity
con•tig•u•ous
con•ti•nence
con•ti•nent
con•ti•nen•tal
con•tin•gen•cy
con•tin•gent
con•tin•u•al
con•tin•u•ance
con•tin•u•a•tion
con•tin•ue
con•tinu•ing
con•ti•nu•ity
con•tin•u•ous
con•tin•u•um
con•tort
con•tor•tion
con•tor•tion•ist
con•tour
con•tra•band

con•tra•bass
con•tract
con•trac•tion
con•trac•tor
con•tra•dict
con•tra•dic•tion
con•tra•dic•to•ri•ly
con•tra•dic•to•ry
con•tra•dis•tinc•tion
con•tra•in•di•cate
con•tral•to
con•trap•tion
con•tra•pun•tal
con•trari•ness
con•trari•wise
con•trary
con•trast
con•tra•vene
con•tra•ven•tion
con•tre•danse
con•tre•temps
con•trib•ute
con•tri•bu•tion
con•trib•u•tor
con•trib•u•to•ry
con•trite
con•tri•tion
con•triv•ance
con•trive
con•trol
con•trol•la•ble
con•trolled
con•trol•ler
con•trol•ling

con•tro•ver•sial
con•tro•ver•sy
con•tro•vert
con•tu•ma•cious
con•tu•ma•cy
con•tu•me•li•ous
con•tume•ly
con•tuse
con•tu•sion
co•nun•drum
con•va•lesce
con•va•les•cence
con•va•les•cent
con•va•lesc•ing
con•vec•tion
con•vene
con•ve•nience
con•ve•nient
con•vent
con•ven•ti•cle
con•ven•tion
con•ven•tion•al
con•ven•tion•al•i•ty
con•ven•tu•al
con•verge
con•ver•gence
con•ver•sant
con•ver•sa•tion
con•ver•sa•tion•al
con•ver•sa•tion•al•
   ist
con•verse
con•ver•sion
con•vert

con•vert•er
con•vert•ibil•i•ty
con•vert•ible
con•vex
con•vex•i•ty
con•vey
con•vey•ance
con•vict
con•vic•tion
con•vince
con•vinc•ing•ly
con•viv•ial
con•viv•i•al•i•ty
con•vo•ca•tion
con•voke
con•vo•lu•tion
con•vol•vu•lus
con•voy
con•voy•ing
con•vulse
con•vul•sion
con•vul•sive
cook•ery
cook•out n.
cool•ant
cool•er
coo•lie (laborer; cf.
   collie, coolly)
cool•ly (coldly; cf.
   collie, coolie)
co–op
coo•per
coo•per•age
co•op•er•ate

co•op•er•a•tion
co•op•er•a•tive
co–opt
co•or•di•nate
Co•per•ni•can
copi•er
co•pi•lot
co•pi•ous
cop•per
cop•per•as
cop•per•head
cop•per•plate
cop•per•smith
cop•pice
co•pra
cop•u•late
copy•book
copy•cat
copy•hold•er
copy•ing
copy•ist
copy•right
co•que•try
co•quette
cor•al (pink; cf. *choral,*
   chorale, corral)
cor•al•line
cord (string; cf. *chord*)
cord•age
cor•dial
cor•dial•i•ty
cord•ite
cor•don
cor•do•van

cor·du·roy

core (center; cf. *corps*, *corpse*)

co·re·spon·dent (legal term; cf. *correspondent*)

co·ri·an·der

Co·rin·thi·an

cork·screw

cork·wood

cor·mo·rant

corn bor·er

corn bread

corn·cob

corn·crib

cor·nea

cor·ner

cor·ner·stone

cor·ner·wise

cor·net

cor·net·ist

corn–fed

corn·field

corn·flakes

corn·flow·er

cor·nice

corn·meal

corn pone

corn·stalk

corn·starch

corn sug·ar

cor·nu·co·pia

co·rol·la

cor·ol·lary

co·ro·na

cor·o·nach

cor·o·nary

cor·o·na·tion

cor·o·ner

cor·o·net

cor·po·ral

cor·po·rate

cor·po·ra·tion

cor·po·ra·tive

cor·po·re·al

corps (group of people; cf. *core*, *corpse*)

corpse (body; cf. *core*, *corps*)

cor·pu·lence

cor·pu·lent

cor·pus

cor·pus·cle

cor·rade

cor·ral (animal pen; cf. *choral*, *chorale*, *coral*)

cor·rect

cor·rec·tion

cor·rec·tive

cor·rec·tor

cor·re·late

cor·re·la·tion

cor·rel·a·tive

cor·re·spond

cor·re·spon·dence (letters; cf. *correspondents*)

cor·re·spon·dent (writer of letters; cf. *corespondent*)

cor·re·spon·dents (writers of letters; cf. *correspondence*)

cor·ri·dor

cor·rob·o·rate

cor·rob·o·ra·tion

cor·rob·o·ra·tive

cor·rode

cor·ro·sion

cor·ro·sive

cor·ru·gate

cor·ru·ga·tion

cor·rupt

cor·rupt·ible

cor·rup·tion

cor·sage

cor·sair

corse (corpse; cf. *coarse*, *course*)

corse·let

cor·set

cor·tege

cor·ti·sone

co·run·dum

cor·us·cate

cor·us·ca·tion

cor·vette

co·ry·za

cos·met·ic

cos·me·tol·o·gist

cos·me·tol·o·gy

cos·mic
cos·mog·o·ny
cos·mol·o·gy
cos·mo·naut
cos·mo·pol·i·tan
cos·mop·o·lite
cos·mos
cos·sack
cost–ef·fec·tive
cost·li·ness
cost–plus
cos·tume
cos·tum·er
co·te·rie
co·ter·mi·nous
co·til·lion
cot·tage
cot·ton
cot·ton·tail
cot·ton·wood
cou·gar
cou·lomb
coun·cil (assembly; cf. consul, counsel)
coun·cil·man
coun·cil·or
coun·cil·wom·an
coun·sel (advice; cf. consul, council)
coun·seled
coun·sel·ing
coun·sel·or
count·down n.
coun·te·nance

count·er
coun·ter·act
coun·ter·bal·ance
coun·ter·claim
coun·ter·clock·wise
coun·ter·feit
coun·ter·feit·er
coun·ter·foil
coun·ter·ir·ri·tant
coun·ter·mand
coun·ter·march
coun·ter·mea·sure
coun·ter·mine
coun·ter·pane
coun·ter·part
coun·ter·point
coun·ter·pro·duc·tive
coun·ter·rev·o·lu·tion
coun·ter·sign
coun·ter·spy
coun·ter·ten·or
coun·ter·top
coun·ter·weight
count·ess
count·ing·house
count·less
coun·try
coun·try·man
coun·try·seat
coun·try·side
coun·try·wom·an
coun·ty

coup d'état
cou·pé or coupe
cou·ple
cou·pler
cou·plet
cou·pling
cou·pon
cour·age
cou·ra·geous
cou·ri·er
course (way; cf. coarse, corse)
cour·te·ous
cour·te·san
cour·te·sy
court·house
court·ier
court·li·ness
court·ly
court–mar·tial
court·room
court·ship
court·yard
cous·in
cous·in–ger·man
cou·tu·ri·er
cov·e·nant
Cov·en·try
cov·er
cov·er·age
cov·er·all
cov·er charge
cov·er·let
co·vert

cov•er•ture

cov•et•ous

cov•ey

cow•ard (frightened;
   cf. *cowered*)

cow•ard•ice

cow•ard•li•ness

cow•ard•ly

cow•bell

cow•boy

cow•catch•er

cow•ered (crouched;
   cf. *coward*)

cow•girl

cow•hand

cow•hide

cow•lick

cowl•ing

co•work•er

cow•pea

cow•pox

cow•punch•er

cow•slip

cox•comb

cox•swain

coy•ly

coy•ote

co•zi•ly

co•zi•ness

co•zy

crab ap•ple

crabbed

crab•bing

crab•grass

crack•brained

crack down v.

crack•down n.

crack•er

crack•er•jack

crack•le

crack•le•ware

crack•pot

cracks•man

cra•dle

craft•i•ly

crafts•man

crafts•wom•an

cram

crammed

cram•ming

cran•ber•ry

cra•ni•al

cra•ni•um

crank•case

crank•i•ness

crank•pin

crank•shaft

cranky

cran•ny

cra•ter

cra•vat

cra•ven

craw•fish

cray•on

cra•zi•ly

cra•zi•ness

cra•zy

creak (sound; cf. *creek*,
   crick)

cream•ery

cream•i•ness

cream puff

cre•ate

cre•ation

cre•ative

cre•ator

crea•ture

cre•dence

cre•den•tial

cre•den•za

cred•i•bil•i•ty

cred•i•ble (believable;
   cf. *creditable*,
   credulous)

cred•it

cred•it•able
   (estimable; cf.
   credible, credulous)

cred•it card

cred•i•tor

cred•it rat•ing

cre•do

cred•u•lous (gullible;
   cf. *credible*,
   creditable)

creek (water; cf. *creak*,
   crick)

creep•i•ness

creepy

cre•mate
cre•ma•tion
cre•ma•to•ry
Cre•mo•na
cre•ole
cre•o•sote
crepe
cre•pus•cu•lar
cre•scen•do
cres•cent
crest•fall•en
cre•tin
cre•tonne
cre•vasse
crev•ice
crews (sailors; cf. *cruise, cruse*)
crib
crib•bage
cribbed
crib•bing
crick (cramp; cf. *creak, creek*)
crick•et
cried
cri•er
Cri•me•an
crim•i•nal
crim•i•nal•i•ty
crim•i•nal•ly
crim•i•nol•o•gy
crim•son
cringe

cring•ing
crin•kle
crin•o•line
crip•ple
crip•pled
crip•pling
cri•ses pl.
cri•sis sing.
criss•cross
cri•te•ria pl.
cri•te•ri•on sing.
crit•ic
crit•i•cal
crit•i•cism
crit•i•cize
cri•tique
cro•chet
crock•ery
croc•o•dile
cro•cus
crook•ed•ness
croon•er
crop
cropped
crop•ping
cro•quet (game)
cro•quette (food)
cro•sier
cross•bar
cross•bow
cross–coun•try
cross•cut
cross–ex•am•ine

cross–eyed
cross–grained
cross hair
cross•hatch
cross•ing
cross•over
cross–ques•tion
cross–ref•er•ence
cross•road
cross sec•tion
cross–stitch
cross•walk
cross•wise
cross•word puz•zle
crotch•et
crotch•ety
crou•pi•er
crou•ton
crow•bar
cru•cial
cru•ci•ble
cru•ci•fix
cru•ci•fix•ion
cru•ci•form
cru•ci•fy
cru•di•ty
cru•el
cru•el•ly
cru•el•ty
cru•et
cruise (sail; cf. *crews, cruse*)
cruis•er

crul•ler

crum•ble (break; cf. *crumple*)

crum•bling

crum•pet

crum•ple (wrinkle; cf. *crumble*)

crum•pling

crup•per

cru•sade

cruse (small cup; cf. *crews, cruise*)

crus•ta•ceous

crux

cry *(cried, cries)*

cry•ing

cryo•bi•ol•o•gy

cryo•gen

cryo•gen•ics

crypt

crypt•anal•y•sis

cryp•tic

cryp•to•gram

crys•tal

crys•tal•line

crys•tal•li•za•tion

crys•tal•lize

cu•bic

cu•bi•cal adj.

cu•bi•cle n.

cu•bit

cuck•old

cuck•oo

cu•cum•ber

cud•dle

cud•gel

cud•geled

cud•gel•ing

cue (signal; cf. *queue*)

cui•rass

cui•sine

cul–de–sac

cu•li•nary

cul•mi•nate

cul•mi•na•tion

cul•pa•bil•i•ty

cul•pa•ble

cul•prit

cul•ti•vate

cul•ti•va•tion

cul•ti•va•tor

cul•tur•al

cul•ture

cul•vert

cum•ber•some

cum•brous

cum•mer•bund

cu•mu•la•tive

cu•mu•lus

cu•ne•i•form

cun•ning•ly

cup•bear•er

cup•board

cu•pel

cup•ful

cu•pid•i•ty

cu•po•la

cur•able

cu•ra•cao

cu•ra•re

cu•rate

cu•ra•tive

cu•ra•tor

curb•stone

cur•dle

cu•rette

cur•few

cu•rio

cu•ri•os•i•ty

cu•ri•ous

curli•cue

curl•i•ness

cur•rant (berry)

cur•rent (prevalent)

cur•ric•u•la pl.

cur•ric•u•lum sing.

cur•ried

cur•ry

cur•ry•comb

cur•sive

cur•sor

cur•so•ri•ly

cur•so•ry

cur•tail

cur•tain

cur•tain call

cur•va•ture

curve

cur•vi•lin•ear

cush·ion
cus·pi·dor
cus·tard
cus·to·di·al
cus·to·di·an
cus·to·dy
cus·tom
cus·tom·ary
cus·tom·er
cus·tom·house
cut–and–dry
cut·away
cut·back
cu·ti·cle
cut·lass
cut·lery
cut·let
cut off v.
cut·off n.
cut·out n., adj.

cut·purse
cut–rate
cut·throat
cut·ting
cut·tle·fish
cut up v.
cut·up n.
cut·wa·ter
cut·worm
cy·an·a·mide
cy·an·ic
cy·a·nide
cy·ano·gen
cy·a·no·sis
cy·ber·net·ics
cy·cla·mate
cy·cle
cy·cli·cal
cy·cloid
cy·clone

cy·clo·pe·dia
cy·clops
cy·clo·ra·ma
cy·clo·tron
cyg·net
cyl·in·der
cy·lin·dri·cal
cym·bal (musical; cf.
   symbol)
cyn·ic
cyn·i·cal
cyn·i·cism
cy·no·sure
cy·press
cyst
cys·tic
cys·toid
czar
cza·ri·na
Czech

D

dab·ble
da ca·po
dachs·hund
Da·cron
dac·tyl
daf·fo·dil
dag·ger

da·guerre·o·type
dahl·ia
dai·lies
dai·ly
dain·ti·ly
dain·ti·ness
dain·ty

dairy (for milk; cf.
   diary)
dairy·maid
dairy·man
da·is
dai·sy
dai·sy wheel

dal•li•ance
dal•ma•tian
dam•age
dam•a•scene
dam•ask
dammed (blocked; cf. *damned*)
dam•ming
dam•na•ble
dam•na•tion
damned (cursed; cf. *dammed*)
damned•est
damn•ing
Dam•o•cles
damp•en
damp•er
dam•sel
dance
dan•de•li•on
dan•dle
dan•dling
dan•druff
dan•ger
dan•ger•ous
dan•gle
Dan•ish
dan•seuse
dare•dev•il
dark•en
dark horse
dar•kle
dark•ness
dark•room

dar•ling
Dar•win•ian
dash•board
das•tard•ly
da•ta (sing.: *datum*)
da•ta file
date
dat•ing
da•tum (pl.: *data*)
daugh•ter
daugh•ter-in-law
daunt•less•ly
dau•phin
dav•en•port
da•vit
daw•dle
daw•dling
day•bed
day•book
day•break
day camp
day-care
day coach
day•dream
day•flow•er
day la•bor
day•light
day•room
day school
day•star
day•time
day-to-day
daz•zle
daz•zling

dea•con
dead•beat
dead•en
dead•eye
dead•fall
dead•head
dead heat
dead•light
dead•line
dead•li•ness
dead•lock
dead•weight
dead•wood
deaf-mute
deal
dealt
dear (beloved; cf. *deer*)
dearth
death•bed
death ben•e•fit
death•blow
death•less
death•ly
death mask
death's-head
death war•rant
death•watch
de•ba•cle
de•bar•ka•tion
de•base
de•bat•able
de•bate
de•bauch
de•bauch•ery

de•ben•ture
de•bil•i•tate
de•bil•i•ty
deb•it (bookkeeping entry; cf. *debt*)
deb•o•nair
de•brief•ing
de•bris
debt (obligation; cf. *debit*)
debt•or
de•but
deb•u•tante
de•cade
dec•a•dence
dec•a•dent
de•caf•fein•at•ed
deca•gon
de•cal•co•ma•nia
deca•logue
de•camp
de•cant
de•cant•er
de•cap•i•tate
de•cath•lon
de•cay
de•cease
de•ceased (dead; cf. *diseased*)
de•ce•dent
de•ceit•ful
de•ceive
De•cem•ber
de•cem•vir

de•cen•cy
de•cent (proper; cf. *descent, dissent*)
de•cen•tral•ize
de•cep•tion
de•cep•tive
deci•bel
de•cide
de•cid•ed
de•cid•u•ous
dec•i•mal
dec•i•mate
deci•me•ter
de•ci•pher
de•ci•sion
de•ci•sive
deck chair
de•claim
dec•la•ma•tion
dec•lam•a•to•ry
dec•la•ra•tion
de•clar•a•tive
de•clare
de•clen•sion
dec•li•na•tion
de•cline
de•cliv•i•ty
de•coc•tion
dé•col•le•té
de•com•pose
de•com•po•si•tion
de•con•tam•i•nate
dec•o•rate
dec•o•ra•tion

dec•o•ra•tive
dec•o•ra•tor
dec•o•rous
de•co•rum
de•coy
de•coyed
de•coy•ing
de•crease
de•cree (law; cf. *degree*)
de•cree•ing
de•crep•it
de•cre•scen•do
de•cry
ded•i•cate
ded•i•ca•tion
de•duce
de•duc•ible
de•duc•ing
de•duct•ible
de•duc•tion
de•duc•tive
deep•en
deep–root•ed
deep–seat•ed
deer (animal; cf. *dear*)
deer•hound
deer•skin
de–es•ca•la•tion
de•face
de fac•to
de•fal•cate
de•fal•ca•tion
def•a•ma•tion

de·fam·a·to·ry
de·fame
de·fault
de·fault·er
de·feat
de·fect
de·fec·tion
de·fec·tive
de·fec·tor
de·fend
de·fen·dant
de·fense
de·fen·si·ble
de·fen·sive
de·fer
def·er·ence (respect;
  cf. *difference*)
def·er·en·tial
  (respectful; cf.
  differential)
de·fer·ment
de·fer·ra·ble
de·ferred
de·fer·ring
de·fi·ance
de·fi·ant
de·fi·cien·cy
de·fi·cient
def·i·cit
de·fied
de·file
de·fin·able
de·fine

de·fine·ment
def·i·nite (clear; cf.
  definitive)
def·i·ni·tion
de·fin·i·tive (final; cf.
  definite)
de·flate
de·fla·tion
de·flect
de·flec·tion
de·fo·li·ant
de·fo·li·ate
de·fo·li·a·tion
de·form
de·for·ma·tion
de·for·mi·ty
de·fraud
de·fray
de·frayed
de·funct
de·fy
de·fy·ing
de·gen·er·a·cy
de·gen·er·ate
de·gen·er·a·tion
deg·ra·da·tion
de·grade
de·gree (from college;
  cf. *decree*)
de·gree–day
de·hu·mid·i·fy
de·hy·drate
de·i·fi·ca·tion

deign
de·ist
de·i·ty
de·ject·ed
de·jec·tion
de ju·re
deka·gram
Del·a·ware
de·lay
de·layed
de·lay·ing
de·lec·ta·ble
de·lec·ta·tion
del·e·gate
del·e·ga·tion
de·lete
del·e·te·ri·ous
de·le·tion
delft·ware
de·lib·er·ate
de·lib·er·a·tion
de·lib·er·a·tive
del·i·ca·cies
del·i·ca·cy
del·i·cate
del·i·ca·tes·sen
de·li·cious
de·light
de·light·ful
de·lin·eate
de·lin·ea·tion
de·lin·ea·tor
de·lin·quen·cy

de·lin·quent
del·i·quesce
del·i·ques·cent
de·lir·i·ous
de·lir·i·um
de·liv·er
de·liv·er·ance
de·liv·er·ies
de·liv·ery
de·lude
del·uge
de·lu·sion
de·luxe
delve
de·mag·ne·tize
dem·a·gogue
de·mand
de·mar·ca·tion
de·mean
de·mean·or
de·ment·ed
de·men·tia
de·mer·it
de·mesne
demi·god
demi·john
de·mil·i·ta·rize
demi·monde
de·mise
demi·tasse
de·mo·bi·lize
de·moc·ra·cy
dem·o·crat

dem·o·crat·ic
de·mog·ra·pher
de·mo·graph·ic
de·mog·ra·phy
de·mol·ish
de·mo·li·tion
de·mon
de·mon·e·ti·za·tion
de·mon·e·tize
de·mon·stra·ble
dem·on·strate
dem·on·stra·tion
dem·on·stra·tive
dem·on·stra·tor
de·mor·al·ize
de·mount·able
de·mur (delay)
de·mure (modest)
de·mur·rage
de·murred
de·mur·rer
de·mur·ring
de·na·ture
de·ni·al
de·nied
den·im
den·i·zen
de·nom·i·na·tion
de·nom·i·na·tor
de·note
de·noue·ment
de·nounce
den·si·ty

den·tal
den·ti·frice
den·tist
den·tist·ry
den·ture
de·nude
de·nun·ci·a·tion
de·nun·ci·a·to·ry
de·ny
de·odor·ant
de·odor·ize
de·part
de·part·ment
de·part·men·tal
de·par·ture
de·pend·able
de·pen·den·cy
de·pen·dent
de·pict
de·pic·tion
de·pil·a·to·ry
de·plane
de·plete
de·ple·tion
de·plor·able
de·plore
de·ploy
de·po·nent
de·pop·u·late
de·port·able
de·por·ta·tion
de·port·ment
de·pose

de•pos•it
de•pos•i•tary
de•po•si•tion
de•pos•i•to•ry
de•pot
de•pra•va•tion
  (corruption; cf.
  deprivation)
de•prave
de•prav•i•ty
dep•re•cate
dep•re•ca•tion
dep•re•ca•to•ry
de•pre•ci•ate
de•pre•ci•a•tion
dep•re•da•tion
de•press
de•pressed
de•pres•sion
de•pri•va•tion (loss;
  cf. *depravation*)
de•prive
dep•u•ta•tion
de•pute
dep•u•tize
dep•u•ty
de•rail
de•range
de•range•ment
de•reg•u•la•tion
der•e•lict
der•e•lic•tion
de•ride
de•ri•sion

de•ri•sive
de•ri•so•ry
der•i•va•tion
de•riv•a•tive
de•rive
der•ma•tol•o•gist
der•ma•tol•o•gy
der•o•ga•tion
de•rog•a•to•ry
der•rick
der•vish
des•cant
de•scend
de•scen•dant
de•scent (going down;
  cf. *decent, dissent*)
de•scrib•able
de•scribe
de•scrip•tion
de•scrip•tive
des•e•crate
des•e•cra•tion
de•seg•re•gate
de•sen•si•tize
des•ert n. (dry
  country; cf. *dessert*)
de•sert v. (leave; cf.
  dessert)
de•ser•tion
de•serve
de•served•ly
de•serv•ing
des•ic•cate
des•ic•ca•tion

des•ic•ca•tor
de•sid•er•a•ta pl.
de•sid•er•a•tum
  sing.
de•sign
des•ig•nate
des•ig•na•tion
de•sign•ed•ly
des•ig•nee
de•sign•er
de•sir•abil•i•ty
de•sir•able
de•sire
de•sir•ous
de•sist
Des Moines Iowa
des•o•late
des•o•la•tion
de•spair
des•per•a•do sing.
des•per•a•does pl.
des•per•ate (hopeless;
  cf. *disparate*)
des•per•a•tion
de•spi•ca•ble
de•spise
de•spite
de•spoil
de•spond
de•spon•den•cy
de•spon•dent
des•pot
des•pot•ic
des•pot•i•cal•ly

des•po•tism
des•sert (food; cf. *desert*)
des•sert•spoon
des•ti•na•tion
des•tine v.
des•ti•nies
des•ti•ny
des•ti•tute
des•ti•tu•tion
de•stroy
de•struc•ti•ble
de•struc•tion
de•struc•tive
de•sue•tude
des•ul•to•ry
de•tach
de•tach•ment
de•tail
de•tain
de•tect
de•tect•able
de•tec•tion
de•tec•tive
de•tec•tor
de•ten•tion
de•ter
de•ter•gent
de•te•ri•o•rate
de•te•ri•o•ra•tion
de•ter•min•able
de•ter•mi•nant
de•ter•mi•nate
de•ter•mi•na•tion

de•ter•mine
de•ter•min•ism
de•terred
de•ter•rent
de•ter•ring
de•test
de•test•able
de•tes•ta•tion
de•throne
det•i•nue
det•o•nate
det•o•na•tion
det•o•na•tor
de•tract
de•trac•tion
det•ri•ment
det•ri•men•tal
dev•as•tate
dev•as•ta•tion
de•vel•op
de•vel•oped
de•vel•op•er
de•vel•op•ing
de•vel•op•ment
de•vi•ate
de•vi•a•tion
de•vice n. (invention; cf. *devise*)
dev•il•fish
dev•il•ish
dev•il•ment
de•vi•ous
de•vise v. (invent; cf. *device*)

de•void
de•volve
de•vote
dev•o•tee
de•vo•tion
de•vo•tion•al
de•vour
de•vout
dew•ber•ry
dew•drop
dew•lap
dew point
dewy
dex•ter
dex•ter•i•ty
dex•ter•ous
dex•trose
dhow
di•a•be•tes
di•a•bet•ic
di•a•ble•rie
di•a•bol•ic
di•a•bol•i•cal
di•ab•o•lism
di•a•crit•i•cal
di•a•dem
di•aer•e•sis
di•ag•nose
di•ag•no•sis
di•ag•nos•tic
di•ag•nos•ti•cian
di•ag•o•nal
di•a•gram
di•a•gram•mat•ic

di•al
di•a•lect
di•a•lec•tic
di•a•lec•ti•cal
di•aled
di•al•ing
di•a•logue
di•al•y•sis
di•am•e•ter
di•a•met•ric
di•a•mond
di•a•per
di•aph•a•nous
di•a•phragm
di•ar•rhea
di•a•ry (journal; cf.
    dairy)
dia•ton•ic
di•a•tribe
di•chot•o•my
dic•ta (sing.: *dictum*)
Dic•ta•phone
dic•tate
dic•ta•tion
dic•ta•tor
dic•ta•to•ri•al
dic•tion
dic•tio•nar•ies
dic•tio•nary
dic•tum (pl.: *dicta*)
di•dac•tic
died (perished; cf.
    dyed)
die–hard adj.

die•hard n.
di•elec•tric
die•mak•er
di•er•e•sis
die•sel
die•sink•er
di•et
di•etary
di•etet•ic
di•etet•ics
di•eti•tian
dif•fer
dif•fer•ence
    (unlikeness; cf.
    deference)
dif•fer•ent
dif•fer•en•tial
    (change; cf.
    deferential)
dif•fer•en•ti•ate
dif•fer•en•ti•a•tion
dif•fi•cult
dif•fi•cul•ties
dif•fi•cul•ty
dif•fi•dence
dif•fi•dent
dif•frac•tion
dif•fuse
dif•fu•sion
di•gest
di•gest•ible
di•ges•tion
di•ges•tive
dig•it

dig•i•tal
dig•i•tal•is
dig•ni•fied
dig•ni•fy
dig•ni•tary
dig•ni•ty
di•gress
di•gres•sion
di•lap•i•date
di•lap•i•dat•ed
di•lap•i•da•tion
di•la•ta•tion
di•late
di•la•tion
dil•a•to•ri•ness
dil•a•to•ry
di•lem•ma
dil•et•tante
dil•i•gence
dil•i•gent
di•lute
di•lu•tion
di•men•sion
di•min•ish
di•min•u•en•do
dim•i•nu•tion
di•min•u•tive
dim•i•ty
dim•mer
dim•ness
dim•out
dim•ple
dim•wit n.
dim–wit•ted adj.

di•nar (coin)
din•er (eater)
di•nette
din•ghy (boat)
din•gy (dull)
din•ner
din•ner bell
din•ner cloth
din•ner fork
din•ner jack•et
din•ner ta•ble
din•ner•ware
di•no•saur
di•oc•e•san
di•o•cese
di•ode
di•ora•ma
diph•the•ria
diph•thong
di•plo•ma
di•plo•ma•cy
dip•lo•mat
dip•lo•mat•ic
dip•per
dip•so•ma•nia
di•rect
di•rec•tion
di•rec•tive
di•rect•ly
di•rec•tor
di•rec•tor•ate
di•rec•tor•ship
di•rec•to•ry
dire•ful

dirge
di•ri•gi•ble
dirndl
dirt•i•ly
dirt•i•ness
dirty
dis•abil•i•ty
dis•able
dis•abuse
dis•ad•van•tage
dis•ad•van•ta•geous
dis•af•fect•ed
dis•af•fec•tion
dis•agree
dis•agree•able
dis•agree•ment
dis•al•low
dis•al•low•ance
dis•ap•pear
dis•ap•pear•ance
dis•ap•point
dis•ap•point•ment
dis•ap•pro•ba•tion
dis•ap•prov•al
dis•ap•prove
dis•ar•ma•ment
dis•ar•range
dis•ar•ray
dis•ar•tic•u•late
dis•as•sem•ble (take
   apart; cf. *dissemble*)
dis•as•so•ci•ate
di•sas•ter
di•sas•trous

dis•avow
dis•avow•al
dis•band
dis•bar
dis•bar•ring
dis•be•lief
dis•be•lieve
dis•be•liev•er
dis•burse (pay out; cf.
   disperse)
dis•burse•ment
dis•card
dis•cern
dis•cern•ible
dis•cern•ment
dis•charge
dis•ci•ple
dis•ci•pli•nar•i•an
dis•ci•plin•ary
dis•ci•pline
dis•claim
dis•claim•er
dis•close
dis•clo•sure
dis•co
dis•cog•ra•phy
dis•col•or
dis•col•or•ation
dis•com•fit (balk; cf.
   discomfort)
dis•com•fi•ture
dis•com•fort
   (uneasiness; cf.
   discomfit)

dis•com•pose
dis•com•po•sure
dis•con•cert
dis•con•nect
dis•con•so•late
dis•con•tent
dis•con•tent•ment
dis•con•tin•u•ance
dis•con•tin•ue
dis•con•tin•u•ous
dis•cord
dis•cor•dance
dis•cor•dant
dis•co•theque
dis•count
dis•cour•age
dis•cour•age•ment
dis•course
dis•cour•te•ous
dis•cour•te•sy
dis•cov•er
dis•cov•er•er
dis•cov•ery
dis•cred•it
dis•cred•it•able
dis•creet (prudent; cf. *discrete*)
dis•crep•an•cy
dis•crete (separate; cf. *discreet*)
dis•cre•tion
dis•cre•tion•ary
dis•crim•i•nate
dis•crim•i•na•tion

dis•crim•i•na•to•ry
dis•cur•sive
dis•cus (athletic term)
dis•cuss (talk about)
dis•cus•sion
dis•dain
dis•dain•ful
dis•ease
dis•eased (sick; cf. *deceased*)
dis•em•bar•ka•tion
dis•em•bar•rass
dis•em•bow•el
dis•en•chant•ment
dis•en•gage
dis•en•tan•gle
dis•es•teem
dis•fa•vor
dis•fig•ure
dis•fig•ure•ment
dis•fran•chise
dis•gorge
dis•grace
dis•grace•ful
dis•grun•tle
dis•guise
dis•gust
dis•ha•bille
dis•har•mon•ic
dish•cloth
dish•heart•en
di•shev•el
di•shev•el•ling
dish•mop

dis•hon•est
dis•hon•or
dis•hon•or•able
dish•pan
dish•rag
dish tow•el
dish•wash•er
dish•wa•ter
dis•il•lu•sion
dis•in•cen•tive
dis•in•cli•na•tion
dis•in•fect
dis•in•fec•tant
dis•in•fes•ta•tion
dis•in•gen•u•ous
dis•in•her•it
dis•in•te•grate
dis•in•te•gra•tion
dis•in•ter•est•ed
dis•join
dis•junc•tion
dis•junc•tive
disk drive
dis•kette
dis•like
dis•lo•cate
dis•lo•ca•tion
dis•lodge
dis•loy•al
dis•loy•al•ty
dis•mal
dis•man•tle
dis•man•tling
dis•mast

dis•may
dis•mem•ber
dis•miss
dis•miss•al
dis•mount
dis•obe•di•ence
dis•obe•di•ent
dis•obey
dis•obeyed
dis•oblige
dis•or•der
dis•or•dered
dis•or•der•ly
dis•or•ga•ni•za•tion
dis•or•ga•nize
dis•own
dis•par•age
dis•par•age•ment
dis•pa•rate (different;
   cf. *desperate*)
dis•par•i•ty
dis•pas•sion•ate
dis•patch
dis•patch•er
dis•pel
dis•pelled
dis•pel•ling
dis•pen•sa•ry
dis•pen•sa•tion
dis•pense
dis•pers•al
dis•perse (scatter; cf.
   disburse)
dis•pers•ible

dis•per•sion
dispir•it
dis•place
dis•place•ment
dis•play
dis•play word
   pro•ces•sor
dis•please
dis•plea•sure
dis•port
dis•pos•able
dis•pos•al
dis•pose
dis•po•si•tion
dis•pos•sess
dis•proof
dis•pro•por•tion
dis•pro•por•tion•ate
dis•prove
dis•put•able
dis•pu•tant
dis•pu•ta•tion
dis•pu•ta•tious
dis•pute
dis•qual•i•fi•ca•tion
dis•qual•i•fy
dis•qui•si•tion
dis•re•gard
dis•re•pair
dis•rep•u•ta•ble
dis•re•pute
dis•re•spect
dis•re•spect•ful
dis•robe

dis•rupt
dis•rup•tion
dis•rup•tive
dis•sat•is•fac•tion
dis•sat•is•fied
dis•sect
dis•sec•tion
dis•sem•ble (disguise;
   cf. *disassemble*)
dis•sem•i•nate
dis•sen•sion
dis•sent (disagreement;
   cf. *decent, descent*)
dis•sent•er
dis•sen•tient
dis•ser•ta•tion
dis•ser•vice
dis•si•dence
dis•si•dent
dis•sim•i•lar
dis•sim•i•lar•i•ty
dis•sim•i•la•tion
dis•sim•u•late
dis•si•pate
dis•si•pat•ed
dis•si•pa•tion
dis•so•ci•ate
dis•so•ci•a•tion
dis•sol•u•ble
dis•so•lute
dis•so•lu•tion
dis•solve
dis•so•nance
dis•so•nant

dis•suade
dis•sua•sion
dis•taff
dis•tance
dis•tant
dis•taste
dis•taste•ful
dis•tem•per
dis•tend
dis•ten•sion
dis•tich
dis•till
dis•til•late
dis•til•la•tion
dis•till•er
dis•till•ery
dis•tinct
dis•tinc•tion
dis•tinc•tive
dis•tinc•tive•ly
dis•tinc•tive•ness
dis•tin•guish
dis•tort
dis•tor•tion
dis•tract
dis•trac•tion
dis•traught
dis•tress
dis•trib•ut•able
dis•trib•ute
dis•tri•bu•tion
dis•trib•u•tor
dis•trict

Dis•trict of
   Co•lum•bia
dis•trust
dis•trust•ful
dis•turb
dis•tur•bance
dis•union
dis•use
dit•to
di•ur•nal
di•va
di•van
div•er
di•verge
di•ver•gence
di•ver•gent
di•vers (various)
di•verse (different)
di•ver•si•fi•ca•tion
di•ver•si•fy
di•ver•sion
di•ver•si•ty
di•vert
di•vest
di•vide
div•i•dend
div•i•na•tion
di•vine
di•vin•i•ty
di•vis•i•bil•i•ty
di•vi•sion
di•vorce
div•ot

di•vulge
diz•zi•ly
diz•zi•ness
diz•zy
doc•ile
do•cil•i•ty
dock•et
dock•hand
dock•side
dock•yard
doc•tor
doc•tor•al
doc•tor•ate
doc•tri•naire
doc•trin•al
doc•trine
doc•u•ment
doc•u•men•ta•ry
doc•u•men•ta•tion
dodge
doe (deer; cf. *dough*)
doe•skin
dog•ber•ry
dog•cart
dog•catch•er
dog col•lar
dog days
doge
dog–eared
dog•fight
dog•fish
dog•ged
dog•ger•el

dog•house

dog•ma

dog•mat•ic

dog•mat•i•cal

dog•ma•tism

dog•ma•tize

do–good•er

dog pad•dle n.

dog–pad•dle v.

dog rose

dog tag

dog•tooth

dog•trot

dog•watch

dog•wood

doi•lies

doi•ly

dol•drums

dole•ful

dol•lar

dol•man (cloak)

dol•men (monument)

do•lor

do•lor•ous

dol•phin

do•main

Domes•day Book

do•mes•tic

do•mes•ti•cate

do•mes•tic•i•ty

do•mi•cile

dom•i•nant

dom•i•nate

dom•i•na•tion

dom•i•neer•ing

Do•min•i•can

do•mi•nie

do•min•ion

dom•i•no sing.

dom•i•noes pl.

do•nate

do•na•tion

done (finished; cf. *dun*)

don•jon

don•key

don•key•work

do•nor

don't

dooms•day

door•jamb

door•keep•er

door•knob

door•man

door•mat

door•nail

door•plate

door prize

door•sill

door•step

door•stop

door–to–door

door•way

door•yard

dor•mant

dor•mer

dor•mi•to•ry

dor•mouse

dor•sal

dos•age

dos•sier

dot•age

dot•ard

dot ma•trix

dou•ble

dou•ble–deal•er

dou•ble–deal•ing

dou•ble–deck•er

dou•ble en•try n.

dou•ble–en•try adj.

dou•ble–faced

dou•ble–park

dou•ble–quick

dou•blet

dou•ble take

dou•ble–talk n.

dou•ble•think

dou•ble time n.

dou•ble–time v.

dou•bloon

doubt•ful

doubt•less

dough (bread; cf. *doe*)

dough•boy

dough•nut

dove•cote

dove•tail

dow•a•ger

dowd•i•ness

dowdy

dow•el

dow•eled

dow•el•ing

dow•er

down–and–out adj., n.

down–and–out•er n.

down•beat

down•cast

down•fall

down•grade

down•heart•ed

down•hill

down•pour

down•range

down•right

down•spout

down•stage

down•stairs

down•state

down•stream

down•stroke

down•swing

down•time

down–to–earth

down•town

down•trend

down•trod•den

down•turn

down•ward

down•wind

downy

dow•ry

dox•ol•o•gy

doy•en

doz•en

drab

drab•ber

drab•best

drach•ma

dra•co•ni•an

draft (draw; cf. *draught, drought*)

draft•er

draft horse

draft•i•ness

drafts•man

drag

dragged

drag•ging

drag•line

drag•net

drag•o•man

drag•on

drag•on•et

drag•on•fly

dra•goon

drag•rope

drain•age

drain•er

drain•pipe

dra•mat•ic

dra•ma•tist

dra•ma•tize

dra•ma•tur•gy

drap•ery

dras•tic

draught (drink; cf. *draft, drought*)

draw•back n.

draw•bar

draw•bridge

draw•ee

draw•er

drawn•work

draw•string

dray•age

dray•man

dread•ful

dread•nought

dream•i•ly

dream•i•ness

dream•land

dreamy

drea•ri•ly

drea•ri•ness

drea•ry

dress•er

dress•i•ness

dress•ing room

dress•mak•er

drib•ble

drib•bling

drift•wood

drill

dril•ling n.

drill•mas•ter

drill press

drink•able

drip

drip–dry

dripped

drip•ping

drive–in n.

driv•el

driv•er

drive•way

driz•zle

droll•ery

drom•e•dary

drop

drop cur•tain

drop•head

drop–kick v.

drop•kick n.

drop leaf

drop let•ter n.

drop•light

drop•out n.

dropped

drop•per

drop•ping

drop•sy

drought (dryness; cf. draft, draught)

drowsy

drudg•ery

drug

drugged

drug•ging

drug•gist

drug•store

drum

drum•beat

drum•fire

drum ma•jor•ette

drummed

drum•mer

drum•ming

drum•roll

drum•stick

drunk•ard

drunk•en

drunk•o•me•ter

dry (dried, dries)

dry•ad

dry cell

dry–clean v.

dry clean•ing n.

dry dock n.

dry–dock v.

dry goods

dry ice

dry•ly

dry•ness

dry•point

dry rot n.

dry–rot v.

dry run

dry–shod

du•al (twofold; cf. duel)

du•bi•ety

du•bi•ous

du•cal

duc•at

duch•ess

duchy

duck•board

duck•ling

duck•pin

duck soup

duc•tile

dud•geon

du•el (combat; cf. dual)

du•eled

du•el•ing

du•el•ist

du•et

du•gong

dug•out

duke•dom

dul•cet

dul•ci•mer

dull•ard

dull•ness

dul•ly

du•ly

dumb•bell

dumb•wait•er

dum•my

dump•ling

dun (demand for payment; cf. done)

dune bug•gy

dun•ga•ree

dun•geon

dun•nage

duo•dec•i•mal

duo•dec•i•mo

du•o•de•nal

du•o•de•num

du•plex

du•pli•cate

du•pli•ca•tion
du•pli•ca•tor
du•plic•i•ty
du•ra•bil•i•ty
du•ra•ble
du•rance
du•ra•tion
dur•bar
du•ress
dur•ing
dusky
dust•bin
dust bowl
dust•cloth
dust•cov•er
dust•heap
dust•i•ness
dust jack•et
dust•less
dust•man

dust mop
dust•pan
dust•proof
dust•rag
dust storm
dust•up
dusty
Dutch ov•en
Dutch treat
du•te•ous
du•ti•able
du•ti•ful
du•ty
dwarf•ish
dwell•ing
dwin•dle
dwin•dling
dyed (colored; cf. *died*)
dye•ing (coloring)

dye•stuff
dye•wood
dy•ing (expiring)
dy•nam•ic
dy•na•mite
dy•na•mo
dy•na•mom•e•ter
dy•nast
dy•nas•tic
dy•nas•ty
Dy•nel
dys•en•tery
dys•func•tion
dys•lex•ia
dys•pep•sia
dys•pep•tic
dys•pho•ria
dys•tro•phy
dys•uria

ea•ger
ea•gle
ea•gre
ear•ache
ear•drop
ear•drum
ear•li•er
ear•li•est

ear•ly
ear•mark
earn (gain; cf. *urn*)
ear•nest
earn•ings
ear•phone
ear•ring
ear•shot

ear•split•ting
earth•born
earth•bound
earth•en•ware
earth•li•ness
earth•ly
earth•quake
earth•ward

earth•work
earth•worm
ear•wax
ear•wig
ea•sel
ease•ment
eas•i•er
eas•i•est
eas•i•ly
Eas•ter
east•ern
east•ward
easy•go•ing
eat•able
ebb
ebbed
ebb•ing
eb•o•ny
ebul•lient
eb•ul•li•tion
ec•cen•tric
ec•cen•tric•i•ty
ec•chy•mo•sis
ec•cle•si•as•ti•cal
ech•e•lon
echo
ech•oes
éclair
eclec•tic
eclipse
eco•log•i•cal
ecol•o•gist
ecol•o•gy
eco•nom•ic

eco•nom•i•cal
econ•o•mist
econ•o•mize
econ•o•my
ec•sta•sy
ec•stat•ic
ec•u•men•i•cal
ec•ze•ma
ed•dy
edel•weiss
ede•ma
edge•ways
edg•i•ness
edg•ing
ed•i•ble
edict
ed•i•fi•ca•tion
ed•i•fice
ed•i•fy
Edin•burg Tex.
Ed•in•burgh Scotland
ed•it
ed•it•ing
edi•tion (printing; cf. *addition*)
ed•i•tor
ed•i•to•ri•al
ed•i•to•ri•al•ize
ed•u•ca•ble
ed•u•cate
ed•u•ca•tion•al
ed•u•ca•tive
ed•u•ca•tor
ef•face

ef•face•ment
ef•fect (result; cf. *affect*)
ef•fec•tive
ef•fec•tu•al
ef•fec•tu•ate
ef•fem•i•nate
ef•fer•vesce
ef•fer•ves•cent
ef•fete
ef•fi•ca•cious
ef•fi•ca•cy
ef•fi•cien•cy
ef•fi•cient
ef•fi•gy
ef•flo•res•cent
ef•flu•ent (cf. *affluent*)
ef•flu•vi•um
ef•fort
ef•fron•tery
ef•ful•gence
ef•fu•sion
ef•fu•sive
egg•head
egg•nog
egg•plant
ego
ego•ism
ego•ist
ego•tism
ego•tist
egre•gious
egress
ei•der

eight
ei·ther
ejac·u·late
ejac·u·la·tion
eject
ejec·tion
elab·o·rate
elab·o·ra·tion
élan
elapse (pass; cf. *lapse*)
elas·tic
elas·tic·i·ty
elat·ed·ly
ela·tion
el·bow·room
el·der
el·der·ber·ry
el·dest
elect
elec·tion
elec·tion·eer
elec·tive
elec·tor
elec·tor·al
elec·tor·ate
elec·tric
elec·tri·cal
elec·tri·cian
elec·tric·i·ty
elec·tri·fi·ca·tion
elec·tri·fied
elec·tri·fy
elec·tro·cute

elec·trode
elec·trol·y·sis
elec·tro·lyte
elec·tro·mag·net
elec·tro·me·chan·i·cal
elec·tron
elec·tron·ic
elec·tron·ic mail
elec·tron·ic type·writ·er
elec·tro·plate
elec·tro·scope
elec·tro·stat·ic print·er
elec·tro·type
el·ee·mo·sy·nary
el·e·gance
el·e·gant
ele·gi·ac
el·e·gy
el·e·ment
el·e·men·tal
el·e·men·ta·ry
el·e·phant
el·e·phan·ti·a·sis
el·e·phan·tine
el·e·vate
el·e·va·tor
elf (pl.: *elves*)
elic·it (draw out; cf. *illicit*)
elide

el·i·gi·bil·i·ty
el·i·gi·ble (qualified; cf. *illegible*)
elim·i·nate
elim·i·na·tion
eli·sion
elite
elix·ir
Eliz·a·be·than
el·lipse
el·lip·sis
el·lip·tic
el·lip·ti·cal
el·o·cu·tion
el·o·cu·tion·ist
elon·gate
elon·ga·tion
elope
el·o·quence
el·o·quent
else·where
elu·ci·date
elu·ci·da·tion
elude (escape; cf. *allude*)
elu·sive (evasive; cf. *illusive*)
elves (sing.: *elf*)
ema·ci·ate
ema·ci·a·tion
em·a·nate
em·a·na·tion
eman·ci·pate

eman·ci·pa·tion
eman·ci·pa·tor
emas·cu·late
em·balm
em·bank·ment
em·bar·go
em·bar·goes
em·bar·rass
em·bar·rass·ment
em·bas·sy
em·bel·lish
em·bez·zle
em·bit·ter
em·bla·zon
em·blem
em·blem·at·ic
em·bodi·ment
em·body
em·bold·en
em·bo·lism
em·boss
em·bou·chure
em·brace
em·bra·sure
em·broi·dery
em·broil
em·bryo
em·bry·on·ic
emend (correct; cf. *amend*)
emen·da·tion
em·er·ald
emerge

emer·gence
emer·gen·cy
emer·gent
emer·i·tus
emet·ic
em·i·grant (outgoing; cf. *immigrant*)
em·i·grate
em·i·gra·tion
émi·gré
em·i·nence
em·i·nent (prominent; cf. *imminent*)
emir
em·is·sary
emis·sion
emit
emit·ted
emit·ting
emol·lient
emol·u·ment
emo·tion
emo·tion·al
em·per·or
em·pha·ses pl.
em·pha·sis sing.
em·pha·size
em·phat·ic
em·pire
em·pir·ic
em·pir·i·cal
em·ploy
em·ploy·abil·i·ty

em·ploy·able
em·ploy·ee
em·ploy·er
em·ploy·ment
em·po·ri·um
em·pow·er
em·press n.
emp·ty
emp·ty–head·ed
em·py·ema
em·py·re·an
emu
em·u·late
em·u·la·tion
em·u·lous
emul·si·fy
emul·sion
en·able
en·act
en·act·ment
enam·el
enam·eled
enam·el·ing
enam·el·ware
en·am·or
en·camp·ment
en·caus·tic
en·ceinte
en·chant·er
en·chant·ing
en·chant·ment
en·chant·ress
en·cir·cle

en·clave
en·clit·ic
en·close
en·clo·sure
en·co·mi·as·tic
en·co·mi·um
en·com·pass
en·core
en·coun·ter
en·cour·age
en·cour·age·ment
en·cour·ag·ing
en·croach
en·croach·ment
en·cum·ber
en·cum·brance
en·cyc·li·cal
en·cy·clo·pe·dia
en·dan·ger
en·dear
en·dear·ment
en·deav·or
en·dem·ic
end·ing
en·dive
end·less
end·long
end man
end·most
en·dorse
en·dorse·ment
en·dow
en·dow·ment
end prod·uct

end ta·ble
en·dur·able
en·dur·ance
en·dure
en·dur·ing
end·ways
en·e·ma
en·e·mies pl.
en·e·my sing.
en·er·get·ic
en·er·gize
en·er·giz·er
en·er·gy
en·er·vate v.
ener·vate adj.
en·er·va·tion
en·fee·ble
en·fet·ter
en·fold
en·force
en·force·able
en·force·ment
en·forc·er
en·fran·chise
en·fran·chise·ment
en·gage
en·gaged
en·gage·ment
en·gag·ing
en·gen·der
en·gine
en·gi·neer
en·gi·neer·ing
En·glish

En·glish·man
En·glish·wom·an
en·graft
en·grave
en·grav·er
en·grav·ing
en·gross
en·gross·ing
en·gross·ment
en·gulf
en·hance
en·hance·ment
enig·ma
enig·mat·ic
en·join
en·joy
en·joy·ably
en·joy·ment
en·lace
en·large
en·large·ment
en·light·en
en·light·en·ment
en·list
en·list·ment
en·liv·en
en·mi·ty
en·nui
enor·mi·ty
enor·mous
enough
en·rage
en·rap·ture
en·rich

en·rich·ment
en·robe
en·roll
en·rolled
en·roll·ing
en·roll·ment
en route
en·sconce
en·sem·ble
en·shrine
en·shroud
en·sign
en·slave
en·slave·ment
en·snare
en·sue
en·sure
en·tab·la·ture
en·tail
en·tail·ment
en·tan·gle
en·tan·gle·ment
en·ter
en·ter·prise
en·ter·pris·ing
en·ter·tain
en·ter·tain·er
en·ter·tain·ment
en·thrall
en·throne
en·thuse
en·thu·si·asm
en·thu·si·ast
en·thu·si·as·tic

en·thu·si·as·ti·cal·ly
en·tice
en·tice·ment
en·tire
en·tire·ty
en·ti·tle
en·ti·ty
en·tomb
en·tomb·ment
en·to·mol·o·gy
   (insects; cf. *etymology*)
en·tou·rage
en·trails
en·train
en·trance
en·trant
en·trap
en·treat
en·treat·ies
en·treaty
en·tree
en·tre·pre·neur
en·tre·pre·neur·ial
en·tre·pre·neur·
   ship
en·try·way
en·twine
enu·mer·ate
enu·mer·a·tion
enu·mer·a·tor
enun·ci·ate
enun·ci·a·tion
enun·ci·a·tor
en·vel·op v.

en·ve·lope n.
en·vel·oped
en·vel·op·ment
en·ven·om
en·vi·able
en·vi·ably
en·vied
en·vi·ous
en·vi·ron
en·vi·ron·ment
en·vi·ron·men·tal·ly
en·vis·age
en·vi·sion
en·voy
en·vy
en·zyme
Eo·lith·ic
ep·au·let
ephem·er·al
ep·ic (poem; cf. *epoch*)
ep·i·cal
ep·i·cure
ep·i·cu·re·an
ep·i·dem·ic
epi·der·mal
epi·der·mic
epi·der·mis
ep·i·gram (witty
   saying; cf. *epigraph,*
   epitaph, epithet)
ep·i·graph (motto; cf.
   epigram, epitaph,
   epithet)
ep·i·graph·ic

ep·i·lep·sy
ep·i·lep·tic
ep·i·logue
epiph·a·ny
epis·co·pal
Epis·co·pa·lian
ep·i·sode
ep·i·sod·ic
ep·i·sod·i·cal
epis·tle
epis·to·lary
ep·i·taph (inscription; cf. *epigram, epigraph, epithet*)
ep·i·thet (curse; cf. *epigram, epigraph, epitaph*)
epit·o·me
epit·o·mize
ep·och (era; cf. *epic*)
ep·och·al
ep·oxy
equa·bil·i·ty
equa·ble
equal
equaled
equal·ing
equal·i·ty
equal·ize
equal·iz·er
equal·ly
equa·nim·i·ty
equa·tion
equa·tor

equa·to·ri·al
eques·tri·an
equi·an·gu·lar
equi·dis·tant
equi·lat·er·al
equi·lib·ri·um
equi·noc·tial
equi·nox
equip
equip·ment
equipped
equip·ping
eq·ui·ta·ble
eq·ui·ty
equiv·a·lence
equiv·a·lent
equiv·o·cal
equiv·o·cate
equiv·o·ca·tion
equiv·o·ca·tor
era
erad·i·ca·ble
erad·i·cate
erad·i·ca·tion
erad·i·ca·tive
erad·i·ca·tor
eras·able (can be erased; cf. *irascible*)
erase
eras·er
era·sure
erect
erec·tion
er·go

er·mine
ero·sion
ero·sive
erot·ic
err
er·rand
er·rant
er·rant·ry
er·ra·ta pl.
er·rat·ic
er·ra·tum sing.
er·ro·ne·ous
er·ror
erst·while
eruct
eruc·ta·tion
er·u·dite
er·u·di·tion
erupt (break out; cf. *irrupt*)
erup·tion
erup·tive
es·ca·late
es·ca·la·tor
es·ca·pade
es·cape
es·cape·ment
es·cap·ism
es·ca·role
es·cheat
es·chew
es·chew·al
es·cort
es·cri·toire

es•crow
es•cutch•eon
Es•ki•mo
esoph•a•gus
es•o•ter•ic
es•pe•cial
Es•pe•ran•to
es•pi•o•nage
es•pla•nade
es•pous•al
es•pouse
espres•so
es•prit
es•py
es•quire
es•say (try; cf. *assay*)
es•say•ist
es•sence
es•sen•tial
es•sen•ti•al•i•ty
es•tab•lish
es•tab•lish•ment
es•tate
es•teem
es•ti•ma•ble
es•ti•mate
es•ti•ma•tion
es•top
es•topped
es•top•pel
es•trange
es•trange•ment
es•tu•ary
et cet•era

etch•ing
eter•nal
eter•ni•ty
ether
ethe•re•al
ethe•re•al•ize
ether•iza•tion
eth•i•cal
eth•ics
Ethi•o•pi•an
eth•nic
eth•ni•cal
eth•yl
eth•yl•ene
et•i•quette
et•y•mo•log•i•cal
et•y•mol•o•gy
(words; cf.
entomology)
eu•chre
eu•clid•e•an
eu•lo•gies
eu•lo•gize
eu•lo•gy
eu•phe•mism
eu•phe•mis•tic
eu•phe•mize
eu•pho•ni•ous
eu•pho•ny
Eu•ro•pe•an
eu•tro•phi•ca•tion
evac•u•ate
evac•u•a•tion
evade

eval•u•ate
eval•u•a•tion
ev•a•nes•cence
evan•gel•i•cal
evan•ge•lism
evan•ge•list
evan•ge•lis•tic
evan•ge•lize
evap•o•rate
evap•o•ra•tion
evap•o•ra•tive
eva•sion
eva•sive
even
even•fall
even•hand•ed
eve•ning (time)
even•ing (smoothing)
even•ness
even•song
event
event•ful
even•tide
even•tu•al
even•tu•al•i•ty
even•tu•al•ly
even•tu•ate
ev•er•green
ev•er•last•ing
ev•er•more
evert
ev•ery•body
ev•ery•day
ev•ery•place

ev•ery•thing
ev•ery•where
evict
evic•tion
ev•i•dence
ev•i•dent
ev•i•den•tial
ev•i•den•tia•ry
evil•ly
evince
evis•cer•ate
evo•ca•ble
evo•ca•tion
evoc•a•tive
evo•ca•tor
evoke
evo•lu•tion
evo•lu•tion•ary
evolve
evul•sion
ewe (sheep; cf. *yew*, *you*)
ex•ac•er•bate
ex•ac•er•ba•tion
ex•act
ex•act•ing
ex•ac•ti•tude
ex•act•ly
ex•act•ness
ex•ag•ger•ate
ex•ag•ger•a•tion
ex•ag•ger•a•tor
ex•alt
ex•al•ta•tion

ex•am•i•na•tion
ex•am•ine
ex•am•ple
ex•as•per•ate
ex•as•per•a•tion
Ex•cal•i•bur
ex•ca•vate
ex•ca•va•tion
ex•ca•va•tor
ex•ceed (surpass; cf. *accede*)
ex•ceed•ing
ex•cel
ex•celled
ex•cel•lence
ex•cel•len•cy
ex•cel•lent
ex•cel•ling
ex•cel•si•or
ex•cept (exclude; cf. *accept*)
ex•cept•ing
ex•cep•tion
ex•cep•tion•able
ex•cep•tion•al
ex•cerpt
ex•cess (surplus; cf. *access*)
ex•ces•sive
ex•change
ex•che•quer
ex•cis•able
ex•cise
ex•ci•sion

ex•cit•abil•i•ty
ex•cit•able
ex•ci•ta•tion
ex•cite
ex•cite•ment
ex•cit•ing
ex•claim
ex•cla•ma•tion
ex•clam•a•to•ry
ex•clude
ex•clu•sion
ex•clu•sive
ex•com•mu•ni•cate
ex•com•mu•ni•ca•tion
ex•co•ri•ate
ex•crete
ex•cre•tion
ex•cru•ci•ate
ex•cru•ci•a•tion
ex•cul•pate
ex•cul•pa•tion
ex•cul•pa•to•ry
ex•cur•sion
ex•cur•sive
ex•cus•able
ex•cuse
ex•e•crate
ex•e•cra•tion
ex•e•cute
ex•e•cu•tion
ex•e•cu•tion•er
ex•ec•u•tive
ex•ec•u•tor

ex•ec•u•trix fem.
ex•e•ge•sis
ex•em•plar
ex•em•pla•ry
ex•em•pli•fi•ca•tion
ex•em•pli•fy
ex•empt
ex•emp•tion
ex•er•cise (exertion; cf. *exorcise*)
ex•ert (exercise; cf. *exsert*)
ex•er•tion
ex•e•unt
ex•hal•ant
ex•ha•la•tion
ex•hale
ex•haust
ex•haust•er
ex•haust•ible
ex•haus•tion
ex•haus•tive
ex•hib•it
ex•hi•bi•tion
ex•hi•bi•tion•er
ex•hib•i•tive
ex•hib•i•tor
ex•hib•i•to•ry
ex•hil•a•rant
ex•hil•a•rate
ex•hil•a•ra•tion
ex•hil•a•ra•tive
ex•hort
ex•hor•ta•tion

ex•hu•ma•tion
ex•hume
ex•i•gen•cies
ex•i•gen•cy
ex•ile
ex•ist
ex•is•tence
ex•is•tent
ex•is•ten•tial•ism
ex•it
ex•o•dus
ex•of•fend•er
ex•on•er•ate
ex•on•er•a•tion
ex•on•er•a•tive
ex•o•ra•ble
ex•or•bi•tant
ex•or•cise (expel; cf. *exercise*)
ex•o•ter•ic
ex•ot•ic
ex•pand
ex•panse
ex•pan•si•ble
ex•pan•sion
ex•pan•sive
ex par•te
ex•pa•ti•ate
ex•pa•tri•ate
ex•pa•tri•a•tion
ex•pect
ex•pec•tan•cy
ex•pec•tant
ex•pec•ta•tion

ex•pec•to•rant
ex•pec•to•rate
ex•pec•to•ra•tion
ex•pe•di•en•cy
ex•pe•di•ent
ex•pe•di•ent•ly
ex•pe•dite
ex•pe•di•tion
ex•pe•di•tion•ary
ex•pe•di•tious
ex•pel
ex•pelled
ex•pel•ling
ex•pend•able
ex•pen•di•ture
ex•pense
ex•pen•sive
ex•pe•ri•ence
ex•pe•ri•enced
ex•per•i•ment
ex•per•i•men•tal
ex•per•i•men•ta•tion
ex•pert•ly
ex•pert•ness
ex•pi•a•ble
ex•pi•ate
ex•pi•a•tion
ex•pi•a•to•ry
ex•pi•ra•tion
ex•pire
ex•plain•able
ex•pla•na•tion
ex•plan•a•to•ry

ex•ple•tive
ex•pli•ca•ble
ex•plic•it
ex•plode
ex•ploit
ex•ploi•ta•tion
ex•plo•ra•tion
ex•plor•a•to•ry
ex•plore
ex•plor•er
ex•plo•sion
ex•plo•sive
ex•po•nent
ex•port
ex•port•able
ex•por•ta•tion
ex•port•er
ex•pose v.
ex•po•sé n.
ex•posed
ex•pos•er
ex•po•si•tion
ex•pos•i•tive
ex•pos•i•to•ry
ex post fac•to
ex•pos•tu•la•tion
ex•po•sure
ex•pound
ex•press
ex•press•age
ex•press•ible
ex•pres•sion
ex•pres•sive
ex•press•ly

ex•press•man
ex•press•way
ex•pul•sion
ex•pul•sive
ex•punge
ex•pur•gate
ex•pur•ga•tion
ex•pur•ga•to•ry
ex•qui•site
ex•sert (protrude; cf. *exert*)
ex•sert•ed
ex•tant (existing; cf. *extent*)
ex•tem•po•ra•ne•ous
ex•tem•po•rary
ex•tem•po•re
ex•tem•po•rize
ex•tend
ex•ten•si•ble
ex•ten•sion
ex•ten•sive
ex•tent (degree; cf. *extant*)
ex•ten•u•ate
ex•ten•u•a•tion
ex•te•ri•or
ex•ter•mi•nate
ex•ter•mi•na•tion
ex•ter•mi•na•tor
ex•ter•mi•na•to•ry
ex•ter•nal
ex•ter•nal•ize

ex•ter•nal•ly
ex•tinct
ex•tinc•tion
ex•tin•guish•able
ex•tir•pate
ex•tol
ex•tolled
ex•tol•ling
ex•tort
ex•tor•tion
ex•tra
ex•tract
ex•tract•able
ex•trac•tion
ex•trac•tive
ex•trac•tor
ex•tra•cur•ric•u•lar
ex•tra•dit•able
ex•tra•dite
ex•tra•di•tion
ex•tral•i•ty
ex•tra•mar•i•tal
ex•tra•mu•ral
ex•tra•ne•ous
ex•traor•di•nari•ly
ex•traor•di•nary
ex•trap•o•late
ex•tra•sen•so•ry
ex•tra•ter•ri•to•ri•al
ex•tra•ter•ri•to•ri•al•i•ty
ex•trav•a•gance
ex•trav•a•gant
ex•trav•a•gan•za

ex·trav·a·sa·tion
ex·treme
ex·trem·ist
ex·trem·i·ty
ex·tri·ca·ble
ex·tri·cate
ex·tri·ca·tion
ex·trin·sic
ex·tro·vert
ex·trude
ex·tru·sion
ex·u·ber·ance
ex·u·ber·ant
ex·u·da·tion
ex·ude

ex·ult
ex·ul·ta·tion
eye·ball
eye·bright
eye·brow
eye·cup
eyed
eye·drop·per
eye·ful
eye·glass
eye·hole
eye·ing
eye·lash
eye·let (decorative hole; cf. *islet*)

eye·le·teer
eye·lid
eye–open·er
eye·piece
eye·sight
eye·sore
eye·spot
eye·strain
eye·strings
eye·tooth
eye·wash
eye·wink
eye·wit·ness
ey·rie

fa·ble
fa·bled
fab·ric
fab·ri·cate
fab·ri·ca·tion
fab·u·lous
fa·cade
face·down adv.
face–hard·en
face–lift·ing
fac·er
fac·et (of diamond; cf. *faucet*)

fa·ce·tious
face–to–face
fa·cial
fac·ile
fa·cil·i·tate
fa·cil·i·ties
fa·cil·i·ty
fac·ing
fac·sim·i·le
fac·tion
fac·tion·al
fac·tious (partisan; cf. *factitious, fictitious*)

fac·ti·tious (artificial; cf. *factious, fictitious*)
fac·tor
fac·to·ri·al
fac·tor·ize
fac·to·ry
fac·tu·al
fac·ul·ta·tive
fac·ul·ties
fac·ul·ty
fad
fade
fag·ot

Fahr·en·heit
fa·ience
fail–safe
fail·ure
faint (weak; cf. *feint*)
faint·heart·ed
faint·ish
faint·ly
fair (just; cf. *fare*)
fair·ground
fair·ly
fair–mind·ed
fair·ness
fair–spo·ken
fair trade n.
fair–trade v.
fair·way
fair–weath·er adj.
fairy
fairy·land
fairy tale n.
fairy–tale adj.
faith·ful
faith·less
fak·er
fa·kir
fal·con
fal·la·cious
fal·la·cy
fal–lal
fall·en
fal·li·bil·i·ty
fal·li·ble
fall·ing

fall·ing–out
fall out v.
fall·out n.
fal·low
false·hood
false·ly
false·ness
fal·set·to
fal·si·fi·ca·tion
fal·si·fi·er
fal·si·fy
fal·si·ty
fal·ter
fa·mil·iar
fa·mil·iar·i·ty
fa·mil·iar·ize
fa·mil·iar·ly
fam·i·lies
fam·i·ly
fam·ine
fam·ish
fa·mous
fa·nat·ic
fa·nat·i·cal
fa·nat·i·cism
fan·ci·er
fan·ci·ful
fan·cy
fan·cy–free
fan·cy·work
fan·fare
fan·light
fanned
fan·ning

fan·tail
fan·ta·sia
fan·ta·size
fan·tas·tic
fan·tas·ti·cal
fan·ta·sy
far·ad
far·a·day
far·a·way
farce
far·ci·cal
fare (price; cf. *fair*)
fare·well
far·fetched
fa·ri·na
far·i·na·ceous
farm·er
farm·hand
farm·house
farm·ing
farm·land
farm·stead
farm·yard
far–off
far–out
far·ra·go
far–reach·ing
far·row
far·see·ing
far·sight·ed
far·ther (at greater
    distance; cf. *further*)
far·ther·most
far·thest

far·thing
fas·cia
fas·ci·nate
fas·ci·na·tion
fas·ci·na·tor
fas·cism
fash·ion·able
fas·ten·er
fas·ten·ing
fas·tid·i·ous
fas·ti·gi·ate
fas·ti·gi·at·ed
fast·ness
fa·tal·ist
fa·tal·is·tic
fa·tal·i·ty
fa·tal·ly
fate (destiny; cf. *fete*)
fat·ed
fate·ful
fa·ther
fa·ther·hood
fa·ther–in–law
fa·ther·land
fa·ther·less
fa·ther·like
fa·ther·ly
fath·om
fath·om·able
fath·om·less
fa·tigue
fat·ten
fat·ty
fa·tu·ity

fat·u·ous
fau·cet (for water; cf. *facet*)
fault·i·ly
fault·i·ness
fault·less
faulty
faun (deity; cf. *fawn*)
faux pas
fa·vor·able
fa·vored
fa·vor·er
fa·vor·ite
fa·vor·it·ism
fawn (deer; cf. *faun*)
faze
fe·al·ty
fear·ful
fear·less
fear·some
fea·si·bil·i·ty
fea·si·bil·i·ty study
fea·si·ble
feat (deed; cf. *feet*)
feath·er·bed·ding
feath·er·brained
feath·ered
feath·er·edge
feath·er·head·ed
feath·er·stitch
feath·er·weight
feath·ery
fea·ture
fea·tured

fea·ture·less
feb·ri·fuge
Feb·ru·ary
fe·cund
fe·cun·di·ty
fed·er·al·ism
fed·er·al·ist
fed·er·al·iza·tion
fed·er·al·ize
fed·er·ate
fed·er·a·tion
fee·ble
fee·ble·mind·ed
feed·back
feed·er
feed·stuff
feel·er
feel·ing
feet (pl. of *foot*; cf. *feat*)
feign
feigned
feint (trick; cf. *faint*)
feld·spar
fe·lic·i·tate
fe·lic·i·ta·tion
fe·lic·i·tous
fe·lic·i·ty
fe·line
fel·low·ship
fel·on
fe·lo·ni·ous
fel·o·ny
felt·ing
fe·male

fem•i•nine
fem•i•nin•i•ty
fem•i•nism
fem•i•ni•za•tion
fe•mur
fence
fence•less
fenc•er
fenc•ing
fend•er
fen•es•tra•tion
fer•ment
fer•ment•able
fer•men•ta•tion
fern•ery
fe•ro•cious
fe•roc•i•ty
fer•ret
fer•ri•age
fer•ried
Fer•ris wheel
fer•rous
fer•rule (metal ring; cf. *ferule*)
fer•ry•boat
fer•tile
fer•til•i•ty
fer•til•iza•tion
fer•til•ize
fer•til•iz•er
fer•ule (rod; cf. *ferrule*)
fer•vent
fer•vid

fer•vor
fes•cue
fes•tal
fes•ter
fes•ti•val
fes•tive
fes•tiv•i•ty
fes•toon
fetch•ing
fete (festival; cf. *fate*)
fe•tish•ism
fet•lock
fet•ter
fet•tle
fe•tus
feu•dal•ism
feu•dal•ize
feu•dal•ly
feu•da•to•ry
feud•ist
feuil•le•ton
fe•ver
fe•ver•ish
fe•ver•weed
fey
fi•an•cé mas.
fi•an•cée fem.
fi•as•co
fi•at
fi•ber•board
fi•ber•glass
fi•ber–op•tics
fi•brous
fib•u•la

fiche (microfilm)
fick•le
fic•tion
fic•tion•al
fic•ti•tious (imaginary; cf. *factious, factitious*)
fid•dle
fid•dler
fid•dle•stick
fi•del•i•ty
fidg•ety
fi•du•cia•ry
field corn
field day
field•er
field glass
field goal
field house
field•piece
fiend•ish
fierce
fi•ery
fi•es•ta
fif•teen
fif•ti•eth
fif•ty
fif•ty–fif•ty
fig•ment
fig•u•ra•tive
fig•ure
fig•ured
fig•ure•head
fig•u•rine
fil•a•ment

fil•a•ture
fil•bert
fil•ial
fil•i•bus•ter
fil•i•gree
fil•ing
Fil•i•pi•no
fill•er
fil•let
fill•ing
film•strip
fil•ter (strainer; cf. *philter*)
filth•i•ness
filthy
fil•tra•tion
fi•nal
fi•na•le
fi•nal•ist
fi•nal•i•ty
fi•nal•ly
fi•nance
fi•nan•cial
fi•nan•cier
find•er
find•ing
fine•ly
fine•ness
fin•ery
fine•spun
fi•nesse
fine–tune
fin•ger
fin•ger bowl

fin•ger•print
fin•ger•tip
fin•i•cal
fin•icky
fi•nis
fin•ish
fin•ished
fin•ish•er
fi•nite
fir (tree; cf. *fur*)
fire ant
fire•arm
fire•ball
fire•bird
fire blight
fire•boat
fire•box
fire•brand
fire•break
fire•brick
fire•bug
fire•clay
fire•crack•er
fire–cured
fire•damp
fire•dog
fire–eat•er
fire fight•er
fire•fly
fire•house
fire irons
fire•light
fire•man
fire•place

fire•plug
fire•pow•er
fire•proof
fire sale
fire screen
fire•side
fire•stone
fire tow•er
fire•trap
fire wall
fire•wa•ter
fire•wom•an
fire•wood
fire•work
fir•ing
fir•kin
firm•ly
firm•ness
first•born
first class n.
first–class adj., adv.
first–de•gree burn
first•hand
first–rate
fis•cal (financial; cf. *physical*)
fish•er
fish•er•man
fish•ery
fish•hook
fish•ing
fish•mong•er
fish•plate
fish stick

fish sto·ry
fish·tail
fishy
fis·sion
fis·sion·able
fis·sure
fist·ic
fist·i·cuffs
fit·ful
fit·ness
fit·ted
fit·ting
five·fold
fix·able
fix·ate
fix·a·tion
fix·a·tive
fixed
fix·ing
fix·ture
fiz·zle
flab·ber·gast
flab·bi·ness
flab·by
flac·cid
fla·con
flag·el·late
flag·el·la·tion
flag·ging
flag·man
flag·on
flag·pole
fla·gran·cy
fla·grant

flag·ship
flag·staff
flag·stone
flail
flair (aptitude; cf. *flare*)
flaky
flam·boy·ant
flame·out
flame·proof
fla·min·go
flam·ma·ble
fla·neur
flan·nel
flan·nel·ette
flap·jack
flapped
flap·per
flap·ping
flare (torch; cf. *flair*)
flare–up
flash·back
flash·board
flash·bulb
flash card
flash flood
flash·i·ly
flash·i·ness
flash·ing
flash·light
flash point
flashy
flat·boat
flat·car
flat·foot n.

flat–foot·ed
flat·iron
flat·ten
flat·ter
flat·ter·er
flat·tery
flat·top
flat·u·lent
flat·ware
flat·work
flaunt
fla·vor·ful
fla·vor·ing
flax·seed
flaxy
flea (insect; cf. *flee*)
flea·bite
flea–bit·ten
fledg·ling
flee (escape; cf. *flea*)
flee·ing
flesh·i·ness
flesh·ly
flesh·pots
fleshy
flew (did fly; cf. *flu*,
    flue)
flex·i·bil·i·ty
flex·i·ble
flick·er
fli·er
flight at·ten·dant
flight deck
flight·i·ness

flight pay
flim•flam
flim•si•ly
flim•si•ness
flim•sy
flin•ders
flint glass
flint•i•ness
flinty
flip–flop
flip•pan•cy
flip•pant
flipped
flip•per
flip•ping
flip side
flir•ta•tion
flir•ta•tious
flitch
flit•ter
fliv•ver
float•ing
floc•cu•lent
floe (ice; cf. *flow*)
flood•gate
flood•light
flood•wa•ter
floor•board
floor•ing
floor lamp
floor•walk•er
flop•house
flop•ping
flop•py

flop•py disk
flop•py dis•kette
flo•ral
flo•res•cence
flo•res•cent
flo•ri•cul•ture
flor•id
Flor•i•da
flo•rin
flo•ta•tion
flo•til•la
flot•sam
flounce
flounc•ing
floun•der
flour (bread; cf. *flower*)
flour•ish
floury
flow (of water; cf. *floe*)
flow•chart
flow•er (blossom; cf. *flour*)
flow•er•pot
flow•ery
flown
flu (influenza; cf. *flew*, *flue*)
fluc•tu•ate
fluc•tu•a•tion
flue (chimney; cf. *flew*, *flu*)
flu•en•cy
flu•ent
fluff•i•ness

fluffy
flu•id
flu•id•ex•tract
flu•id•i•ty
flu•id•ounce
flu•o•res•cent
flu•o•ri•date
flu•o•ri•da•tion
flu•o•ride
flu•o•rine
flu•o•ro•scope
flur•ry
flut•ter
flut•tery
flux
fly•blown
fly–boy
fly•by
fly–by–night
fly•catch•er
fly•er
fly•ing
fly•leaf
fly•pa•per
fly•speck
fly•wheel
foamy
fo•cal
fo•cal•ize
fo•ci pl.
fo•cus sing.
fo•cused
fo•cus•es
fo•cus•ing

fod•der
fog•bound
fog•gy (weather)
fog•horn
fo•gy (person)
fold•er
fold•ing
fo•liage
fo•li•ate
fo•li•at•ed
fo•li•a•tion
fo•lio
folk•lore
folks•i•ness
folksy
folk•tale
folk•way
fol•low
fol•low•er
fol•low•ing
fol•low up v.
fol•low–up n., adj.
fol•ly
fo•ment
fo•men•ta•tion
fon•dant
fon•dle
fon•dler
fond•ly
fond•ness
food•stuff
fool•ery
fool•har•di•ness
fool•har•dy

fool•ish
fool•proof
fools•cap
foot•ball
foot•bath
foot•board
foot brake
foot•bridge
foot•can•dle
foot•ed
foot•fall
foot fault n.
foot•fault v.
foot•gear
foot•hill
foot•hold
foot•ing
foot•less
foot•lights
foot•lock•er
foot•loose
foot•man
foot•mark
foot•note
foot•pace
foot•pad
foot•path
foot–pound
foot•print
foot•race
foot•rest
foot rule
foot•sore
foot•step

foot•stool
foot–ton
foot•walk
foot•way
foot•wear
foot•work
for•age
for•ay
for•bade
for•bear (be patient;
    cf. forebear)
for•bear•ance
for•bid
for•bid•den
for•bid•der
for•bid•ding
for•bore
forced
force•ful
force ma•jeure
for•ceps
forc•ible
fore•arm
fore•bear (ancestor; cf.
    forbear)
fore•bode
fore•bod•ing
fore•cast
fore•cast•er
fore•cas•tle
fore•close
fore•clo•sure
fore•doom
fore•fa•ther

fore•fin•ger
fore•foot
fore•front
fore•go
fore•go•ing
fore•gone
fore•ground
fore•hand
fore•hand•ed
fore•head
for•eign
for•eign•er
fore•judge
fore•knowl•edge
fore•lock
fore•man
fore•mast
fore•most
fore•name
fore•noon
fo•ren•sic
fore•or•dain
fore•part
fore•quar•ter
fore•run
fore•run•ner
fore•see
fore•see•able
fore•shad•ow
fore•short•en
fore•sight
for•est
fore•stall
for•es•ta•tion

for•est•er
for•est•ry
fore•tell
fore•thought
fore•ev•er
fore•warn
fore•wom•an
fore•word (preface; cf.
    forward)
for•feit
for•fei•ture
for•gave
forg•er
forg•ery
for•get•ful
for•get–me–not
for•get•ta•ble
for•get•ting
for•give•ness
for•giv•ing
for•go
for•got
for•lorn
for•mal
form•al•de•hyde
for•mal•i•ty
for•mal•ize
for•mal•ly
    (ceremonially; cf.
    formerly)
for•mat
for•ma•tion
for•ma•tive
for•mer adj.

form•er n.
for•mer•ly (previously;
    cf. *formally*)
for•mi•da•ble
form•less
for•mu•la
for•mu•la•rize
for•mu•late
for•mu•la•tion
for•sake
for•sooth
for•swear
for•syth•ia
fort (stronghold; cf.
    forte)
forte (talent; cf. *fort*)
forth (forward; cf.
    fourth)
forth•com•ing
forth•right
forth•with
for•ti•eth
for•ti•fi•ca•tion
for•ti•fi•er
for•ti•fy
for•tis•si•mo
for•ti•tude
fort•night
FOR•TRAN
for•tress
for•tu•itous
for•tu•ity
for•tu•nate
for•tune

for•tune–tell•er
for•ty
for•ty–nin•er
fo•rum
for•ward (ahead; cf. *foreword*)
for•ward•er
for•ward•ly
for•ward•ness
for•wards
fos•sil
fos•sil•if•er•ous
fos•ter
foul (bad; cf. *fowl*)
foul•mouthed
foul•ness
foun•da•tion
found•er n.
foun•der v.
found•ling
found•ry
foun•tain
foun•tain•head
four–flush•er
four–in–hand
four•score
four•some
four•teen
four•teenth
fourth (next after third; cf. *forth*)
fowl (poultry; cf. *foul*)
fox•hole
fox•hound

fox•i•ness
fox ter•ri•er
fox–trot
foy•er
fra•cas
frac•tion
frac•tion•al
frac•tious
frac•ture
frag•ile
fra•gil•i•ty
frag•ment
frag•men•tary
fra•grance
fra•grant
frail•ty
fram•er
frame–up
frame•work
fram•ing
franc (money; cf. *frank*)
fran•chise
Fran•cis•can
frank (candid; cf. *franc*)
frank•furt•er
frank•in•cense
frank•ly
frank•ness
fran•tic
fra•ter•nal
fra•ter•ni•ty
frat•er•nize
frat•ri•cide
fraud•u•lence

fraud•u•lent
freak•ish
freck•le
free•board
free•born
freed•man
free•dom
freed•wom•an
free–for–all
free•hand
free•hold
free lance n.
free–lance adj., v.
free•ly
free•man
Free•ma•son
free•ma•son•ry
free•stand•ing
free•stone
free•style
free•think•er
free•way
freeze (from cold; cf. *frieze*)
freeze–dry
freez•er
freight•er
fre•net•ic
fren•zy
Fre•on
fre•quen•cy
fre•quent
fres•co
fresh•en

fresh·ly
fresh·ness
fresh·wa·ter
fret·ful
fret·work
fri·a·ble
fri·ar
fric·as·see
fric·tion
fric·tion·al
Fri·day
friend·less
friend·li·ness
friend·ly
friend·ship
frieze (ornament; cf. *freeze*)
frig·ate
fright
fright·en
fright·ened
fright·ful
frig·id
fri·gid·i·ty
frip·pery
frit·ter
fri·vol·i·ty
friv·o·lous
frog·man
frol·ic
frol·ic·some
frol·icked
frol·ick·ing
front·age

fron·tal
fron·tier
fron·tiers·man
fron·tis·piece
front·less
front man
front mat·ter
frost·bite
frost·i·ness
frost·ing
fro·ward
froze
fro·zen
fru·gal
fru·gal·i·ty
fru·gal·ly
fruit·cake
fruit·er·er
fruit fly
fruit·ful
fru·ition
fruit·less
frus·trate
frus·tra·tion
fud·dy–dud·dy
fu·el
fu·el cell
fu·eled
fu·el·ing
fu·gi·tive
ful·crum
ful·fill
ful·fill·ing
ful·fill·ment

full·back
full–blood·ed
full–blown
full–bod·ied
full dress n.
full–dress adj.
full–fledged
full–length
full·ness
full–scale
full–size
full time n.
full–time adj.
ful·ly
ful·mi·nate
ful·some
fum·ble
fu·mi·gate
fu·mi·ga·tion
fu·mi·ga·tor
func·tion
func·tion·al
func·tion·ary
func·tion keys
fun·da·men·tal·ism
fund–rais·ing
fu·ner·al (burial)
fu·ner·ary
fu·ne·re·al (solemn)
fun·gi (sing.: *fungus*)
fun·gi·ble
fun·gi·cide
fun·gous adj.
fun·gus n. (pl.: *fungi*)

fu·nic·u·lar
fun·nel
fun·neled
fun·nel·ing
fun·ny
fur (hair; cf. *fir*)
fur·be·low
fur·bish
fu·ri·ous
fur·long
fur·lough
fur·nace
fur·nish
fur·ni·ture
fu·ror

fur·ri·er
fur·ring
fur·row
fur·ry (with fur; cf.
  fury)
fur·ther (in addition;
  cf. *farther*)
fur·ther·ance
fur·ther·more
fur·ther·most
fur·thest
fur·tive
fu·ry (rage; cf. *furry*)
furze

fu·se·lage
fus·ibil·i·ty
fus·ible
fu·sion
fuss·bud·get
fuss·i·ly
fuss·i·ness
fussy
fu·tile
fu·til·i·ty
fu·ture
fu·tu·ri·ty
fuzz·i·ness
fuzzy

G

ga·ble
gad·about
gad·fly
gad·get
ga·droon
Gael·ic
gag rule
gai·ety
gain·er
gain·ful
gain·say
gait (manner of walking;
  cf. *gate*)

gai·ter
gal·axy
gal·lant
gal·lant·ry
gal·le·on
gal·lery
gal·ley
gal·leys
gal·li·cism
gal·lon
gal·lop
gal·loped
gal·lop·ing

gal·lows
gall·stone
gal·van·ic
gal·va·ni·za·tion
gal·va·nize
gam·bit
gam·ble (bet; cf.
  gambol)
gam·bler
gam·bling
gam·bol (play; cf.
  gamble)
gam·boled

gam·bol·ing
gam·brel
game·keep·er
game·ness
games·man·ship
game·ster
Gan·dhi·an
gan·gli·on
gang·plank
gan·grene
gang·ster
gang·way
gant·let
ga·rage
gar·bage
gar·den
gar·den·er
gar·de·nia
Gar·di·ner Maine
Gard·ner Mass.
gar·gle
gar·goyle
gar·land
gar·lic
gar·ment
gar·ner
gar·net
gar·nish
gar·nish·ee
gar·nish·ment
gar·ri·son
gar·ru·li·ty
gar·ru·lous
gar·ter

gas·bag
gas cham·ber
gas·eous
gas·es
gas fit·ter
gas·house
gas·ket
gas·light
gas log
gas mask
gas·o·line
gassed
gas·si·ness
gas·sing
gas sta·tion
gas·sy
gas·tight
gas·tric
gas·tri·tis
gas·tro·nom·ic
gas·tron·o·my
gas·works
gate (door; cf. *gait*)
gate·way
gath·er·ing
gauge
gaunt·let
gauze
gav·el
gay·ness
ga·ze·bo
ga·zelle
ga·zette
gear·ing

gel·a·tin
ge·la·ti·nize
ge·lat·i·nous
gen·darme
gen·der
ge·ne·al·o·gy
gen·er·al
gen·er·a·lis·si·mo
gen·er·al·i·ty
gen·er·al·iza·tion
gen·er·al·ize
gen·er·al·ly
gen·er·al·ship
gen·er·ate
gen·er·a·tion
gen·er·a·tive
gen·er·a·tor
ge·ner·ic
gen·er·os·i·ty
gen·er·ous
gen·e·sis
ge·nial
ge·nial·i·ty
ge·nial·ly
gen·i·tal
gen·i·tive
ge·nius (greatly gifted;
    cf. *genus*)
gen·teel
gen·tile
gen·til·i·ty
gen·tle
gen·tle·man
gen·tle·ness

gen·tle·wom·an

gent·ly

gen·try

gen·u·flect

gen·u·flec·tion

gen·u·ine

ge·nus (pl.: *genera;* classification; cf. *genius*)

geo·det·ic

ge·og·ra·pher

geo·graph·ic

geo·graph·i·cal

ge·og·ra·phy

geo·log·ic

geo·log·i·cal

ge·ol·o·gist

ge·ol·o·gy

ge·om·e·ter

geo·met·ric

geo·met·ri·cal

geo·me·tri·cian

ge·om·e·try

Geor·gia

geo·ther·mal

ge·ra·ni·um

ge·ri·at·rics

Ger·man

ger·mane

ger·mi·cide

ger·mi·nate

ger·mi·na·tion

germ·proof

ger·ry·man·der

ger·und

ge·sta·po

ges·tate

ges·ta·tion

ges·tic·u·late

ges·tic·u·la·tion

ges·tic·u·la·to·ry

ges·ture

get·at·able

get·away n.

get–to·geth·er n.

get–up v.

get up n.

gey·ser

ghast·li·ness

ghast·ly

gher·kin

ghet·to

ghost·like

ghost·ly

ghoul (demon; cf. *goal*)

gi·ant

gib·ber·ish

gibe (taunt; cf. *jibe*)

gib·let

Gi·bral·tar

gid·di·ly

gid·di·ness

gid·dy

gi·gan·tic

gig·gle

gig·o·lo

gild (decorate with gold; cf. *guild*)

gilt–edged

gim·crack

gim·let

gim·mick

gin·ger

gin·ger ale

gin·ger·bread

gin·ger·ly

gin·ger·snap

ging·ham

gink·go

gi·raffe

gird·er

gir·dle

gir·dling

girl·hood

girl·ish

girth

gist (essence; cf. *jest*)

give–and–take

giv·en

give up

giv·ing

giz·zard

gla·cial

gla·cial·ly

gla·cier (ice; cf. *glazier*)

glad·den

glad·i·a·tor

glad·i·a·to·ri·al

glad·i·o·lus

glad·ly

glad·ness

glam•or•ize

glam•or•ous

glam•our

glance

glanc•ing

glan•du•lar

glare•proof

glar•ing

glass•blow•er

glass•ful

glass•i•ly

glass•ine

glass•i•ness

glass•ware

glass wool

glassy

glaze

gla•zier (glassworker; cf. *glacier*)

gleamy

glean•ings

glee•ful

glid•er

glim•mer•ing

glimpse

glis•ten

glit•ter

glit•tery

gloam•ing

glob•al•ly

glob•u•lar

glock•en•spiel

gloom•i•ly

gloom•i•ness

gloomy

glo•ri•fi•ca•tion

glo•ri•fi•er

glo•ri•fy

glo•ri•ous

glo•ry

glos•sa•ry

gloss•i•ly

gloss•i•ness

glossy

glow•er

glow•worm

glu•cose

glue

glued

glu•ey

glu•i•er

glu•i•est

glu•ing

glum•ly

glum•mer

glum•mest

glum•ness

glu•ten

glu•ten•ous

glut•ton

glut•ton•ous

glut•tony

glyc•er•in

gnarl

gnarled

gnash

gnat

gnaw

gneiss

gnome

gno•mon

gnu (animal; cf. *knew, new*)

go—ahead

goal (objective; cf. *ghoul*)

goal•post

gob•ble

gob•bler

gob•let

gob•lin

go—cart

god•child

god•daugh•ter

god•dess

god•fa•ther

god•head

god•less

god•like

god•li•ness

god•ly

god•moth•er

god•par•ent

god•send

god•son

God•speed

go—get•ter

gog•gle

go•ing

goi•ter

gold•brick

gold•en

gold·en·rod
gold·field
gold–filled
gold·fish
gold foil
gold leaf
gold·smith
golf
Go·li·ath
gon·do·la
gon·do·lier
goo
good–bye
good–heart·ed
good·hu·mored
good·ly
good–na·tured
good·ness
good–tem·pered
good·will
goo·ey
goof·i·ness
goo·gol
goo·i·er
goo·i·est
goose·ber·ry
goose·flesh
goose·neck
goose step n.
goose–step v.
go·pher
gorge
gor·geous
Gor·gon·zo·la

go·ril·la (animal; cf.
    guerrilla)
gor·man·dize
gos·pel
gos·sa·mer
gos·sip
gos·sip·ing
Goth·ic
gou·lash
gourd
gour·mand (big eater)
gour·met (epicure)
gout
gov·ern
gov·ern·able
gov·er·nance
gov·ern·ess
gov·ern·ment
gov·ern·men·tal
gov·er·nor–
    gen·er·al
gov·er·nor·ship
grab
grabbed
grab·bing
grace·ful
grace·less
gra·cious
gra·da·tion
gra·di·ent
grad·u·al
grad·u·ate
grad·u·a·tion
graf·fi·ti

graft·er
gram·mar
gram·mar·i·an
gram·mat·i·cal
gram·o·phone
gra·na·ry
grand·aunt
grand·child
grand·daugh·ter
gran·deur
grand·fa·ther
gran·dil·o·quence
gran·dil·o·quent
gran·di·ose
gran·di·o·so
grand·moth·er
grand·neph·ew
grand·niece
grand·sire
grand·son
grand·stand
grand·un·cle
grang·er
gran·ite
gran·ite·ware
grant·ee
grant·er
grant–in–aid
gran·u·lar
gran·u·late
gran·u·la·tion
gran·u·la·tor
grape·fruit
grape·shot

grape•vine
graph•ic
graph•i•cal
graph•ite
grap•nel
grap•ple
grasp•ing
grass•hop•per
grassy
grate (fireplace; cf. *great*)
grate•ful
grat•i•fi•ca•tion
grat•i•fy
grat•i•fy•ing
grat•ing
gra•tis
grat•i•tude
gra•tu•itous
gra•tu•ity
gra•va•men
grave•clothes
grav•el
grave•ness
grave•stone
grave•yard
grav•i•tate
grav•i•ta•tion
grav•i•ta•tive
grav•i•ty
gra•vy
gray•beard
gray•ish
gra•zier

greas•er
grease•wood
greasy
great (large; cf. *grate*)
great•coat
great•heart•ed
greed•i•ly
greedy
green•back
green•ery
green–eyed
green•gage
green•gro•cer
green•horn
green•house
green•ing
green•ish
green•room
greet•ing
gre•gar•i•ous
Gre•go•ri•an
grem•lin
gre•nade
gren•a•dier
gren•a•dine
grey•hound
grid•dle cake
grid•iron
griev•ance
griev•ous
grif•fin
grill (broil)
grille (grating)
grill•room

grill•work
gri•mace
grim•ly
grim•ness
grin
grind•stone
grinned
grin•ning
grip (grasp; cf. *gripe,* *grippe*)
gripe (complain; cf. *grip, grippe*)
grippe (sickness; cf. *grip, gripe*)
grip•ping (grasping)
gris•ly (ghastly; cf. *gristly, grizzly*)
gris•tle
gris•tly (full of gristle; cf. *grisly, grizzly*)
grist•mill
grit
grit•ted
grit•ting
grit•ty
griz•zle
griz•zled
griz•zly (bear; cf. *grisly, gristly*)
groan (moan; cf. *grown*)
gro•cer•ies
gro•cery
grog•gy

groove (rut; cf. *grove*)
gross•ly
gro•tesque
ground•hog
ground•less
ground•ling
ground•wa•ter
ground•work
grove (trees; cf.
  groove)
grov•el
grov•eled
grov•el•ing
grow•er
growl•er
grown (matured; cf.
  groan)
grub
grubbed
grub•bing
grub•stake
grudge
grudg•ing•ly
gru•el
gru•el•ing
grue•some
grum•ble
grumpy
guar•an•tee (to
  secure; cf. *guaranty*)
guar•an•tor
guar•an•ty (a pledge;
  cf. *guarantee*)
guard•house

guard•ian
guard•ian•ship
guards•man
gu•ber•na•to•ri•al
guern•sey
guer•ril•la (soldier; cf.
  gorilla)
guess•ti•mate
guess•work
guid•ance
guide•line
guild (association; cf.
  gild)
guild•hall
guile•less•ness
guil•lo•tine
guilt•i•ly
guilt•i•ness
guilt•less
guilty
guimpe
guin•ea
gui•tar
gull•ibil•i•ty
gull•ible
gul•lies
gul•ly
gum•drop
gummed
gum•my
gump•tion
gun•boat
gun•cot•ton
gun•fire

gun•flint
gun•lock
gun•man
gun•met•al
gun•nery
gun•pow•der
gun room
gun•run•ner
gun•shot
gun•wale
gup•py
gur•gle
Gur•kha
gush•er
gus•to
gut•ta–per•cha
Gut•ten•berg N.J.
gut•ter
gut•ter•snipe
gut•tur•al
guz•zle
gym•na•si•um
gym•nast
gym•nas•tic
gym•nas•tics
gy•ne•col•o•gy
gyp•sum
gyp•sy
gy•rate
gy•ra•tion
gy•ro•com•pass
gy•ro•scope
gy•ro•sta•bi•
  liz•er

ha•be•as cor•pus
hab•er•dash•er
hab•er•dash•ery
ha•bil•i•tate
hab•it
hab•it•able
ha•bi•tant
hab•i•tat
hab•i•ta•tion
ha•bit•u•al
ha•bit•u•ate
hab•i•tude
ha•ci•en•da
hack•er
hack•ie
hack•man
hack•ney
hack•neyed
hack•saw
had•dock
hag•gard
hag•gle
ha•gi•og•ra•phy
hail (ice; cf. *hale*)
hail•stone
hail•storm
hair (fur; cf. *hare*)
hair•breadth
hair•brush
hair•cut

hair•do
hair•dress•er
hair•i•ness
hair•line
hair•net
hair•piece
hair•pin
hair–rais•ing
hair shirt
hair•split•ter
hair•split•ting
hair•spring
hairy
Hai•tian
hal•cy•on
hale (healthy; cf. *hail*)
half–and–half
half•back
half–baked
half–breed
half broth•er
half gain•er
half•heart•ed
half hour
half–life n.
half–mast
half–moon
half note
half•pen•ny
half–pint

half sole n.
half–sole v.
half step
half•time
half ti•tle
half•tone
half–track
half–truth
half•way
hal•i•but
hal•i•to•sis
hall (room; cf. *haul*)
hal•le•lu•jah
hall•mark
hal•low
Hal•low•een
hal•lu•ci•nate
hal•lu•ci•na•tion
hal•lu•ci•na•to•ry
hal•lu•ci•no•gen•ic
hall•way
hal•ter
halve (divide in half;
   cf. *have*)
halves
Ham•burg
ham•burg•er
Ham•il•to•ni•an
ham•let
ham•mer

ham•mock
ham•per
ham•ster
ham•string
Ham•tramck Mich.
hand•bag
hand•ball
hand•bill
hand•book
hand•car
hand•cart
hand•clasp
hand•cuff
hand•ed•ness
hand•ful
hand•grip
hand•gun
hand•hold
hand•i•cap
hand•i•capped
hand•i•cap•ping
hand•i•craft
hand•i•ly
hand•i•work
hand•ker•chief
han•dle
han•dle•bar
han•dled
han•dler
hand–let•ter v.
han•dling
hand•list
hand•made adj.
hand•maid•en n.

hand–me–down
hand or•gan
hand•out n.
hand•pick
hand•rail
hand•saw
hands down adv.
hands–down adj.
hand•set
hand•shake
hand•some
hands–on
hand•spike
hand•spring
hand•stamp n., v.
hand•stand
hand truck
hand•work
hand•wo•ven
hand•writ•ing
handy•man
handy•wom•an
han•gar (shed; cf.
    hanger)
hang•dog adj.
hang•er (for clothes;
    cf. hangar)
hang•er–on
hang•ing
hang•man
hang•nail
hang out v.
hang•out n.
hang•over

han•ker
han•ky–pan•ky
han•som
hap•haz•ard
hap•less
hap•ly
hap•pen
hap•pen•ing
hap•pen•stance
hap•pi•ly
hap•pi•ness
hap•py
hap•py–go–lucky
Haps•burg
ha•rangue
ha•rass
ha•rass•ing
har•bin•ger
har•bor
har•bor•age
hard–and–fast
hard•back
hard–bit•ten
hard–boiled
hard copy
hard•cov•er
hard•en
hard•fist•ed
hard•head•ed
hard•heart•ed
har•di•hood
har•di•ly
har•di•ness
hard•ly

hard•ness
hard–nosed
hard–of–hear•ing
hard•pan
hard–pressed
hard sauce
hard sell
hard•ship
hard•tack
hard•top
hard•ware
hard•wood
hard•work•ing
har•dy
hare (rabbit; cf. *hair*)
hare•brained
hare•lip
har•em
har•le•quin
har•le•quin•ade
harm•ful
harm•less
har•mon•ic
har•mon•i•ca
har•mo•ni•ous
har•mo•ni•za•tion
har•mo•nize
har•mo•ny
har•ness
harp•ist
har•poon
harp•si•chord
har•ri•dan
har•ri•er

har•row
har•ry
hart (deer; cf. *heart*)
har•um–scar•um
har•vest
har•vest•er
has–been n.
ha•sen•pfef•fer
hash•ish
hash mark
has•sle
has•ten
hast•i•ly
hast•i•ness
hasty
hat•band
hat•box
hatch•ery
hatch•et
hatch•ing
hatch•way
hate•ful
hat•er
hat•ful
hat•pin
ha•tred
hat•ter
haugh•ty
haul (pull; cf. *hall*)
haul•age
haunt
Ha•vana
have (possess; cf. *halve*)
have•lock

ha•ven
have–not n.
hav•er•sack
hav•oc
Ha•waii
Ha•wai•ian
haw•ser
haw•thorn
hay fe•ver
hay•rack
hay•seed
haz•ard
haz•ard•ous
haze
ha•zel
haz•i•ly
haz•i•ness
haz•ing
hazy
H–bomb
head•ache
head•band
head•board
head•cheese
head cold
head•count
head•dress
head•first
head•gear
head•hunt•er
head•i•ly
head•i•ness
head•ing
head•land

head•less
head•light
head•line
head•lock
head•long
head louse
head•man
head•mas•ter
head•mis•tress
head–on adj.
head•phone
head•piece
head•quar•ters
head•rest
head•room
head•set
head•spring
head•stone
head•strong
head•wait•er
head•wa•ter
head•way
head wind
head•work
heal (cure; cf. *heel*)
health•ful
health•i•ly
health•i•ness
healthy
hear (listen; cf. *here*)
heard (past tense of
    hear; cf. *herd*)
hear•ing

hear•ken
hear•say
heart (in body; cf. *hart*)
heart•ache
heart•beat
heart block
heart•break
heart•break•ing
heart•bro•ken
heart•burn
heart•en
heart•felt
hearth
hearth•stone
heart•i•ly
heart•i•ness
heart•land
heart•less
heart•rend•ing
heart•sick
heart•string
heart•throb
heart•warm•ing
hearty
heat•er
hea•then
heath•er
heat shield
heave
heav•en
heav•en•ly
heav•en•ward
heavi•ly

heavi•ness
heavy
heavy–du•ty
heavy–foot•ed
heavy–hand•ed
heavy•heart•ed
heavy•set
heavy•weight
He•bra•ic
He•brew
hect•are
hec•tic
hec•to•graph
hec•to•me•ter
hedge•hog
hedge•row
hee•bie–jee•bies
heed•ful
heed•less
heel (of foot; cf. *heal*)
he•ge•mo•ny
he•gi•ra
heif•er
height
height•en
hei•nous
heir (inheritor; cf. *air*)
heir•ess fem.
heir•loom
he•li•cop•ter
he•lio•graph
he•lio•trope
he•li•pad

he•li•port
he•li•um
hell–bent
hel•lion
hel•met
helms•man
help•er
help•ful
help•less
help•mate
hel•ter–skel•ter
Hel•ve•tian
hemi•sphere
hemi•spher•ic
hemi•spher•i•cal
hem•line
hem•lock
he•mo•glo•bin
he•mo•phil•ia
hem•or•rhage
hem•or•rhoid
hem•stitch
hence•forth
hence•for•ward
hench•man
hen•nery
hen•peck
he•pat•ic
he•pat•i•ca
hep•a•ti•tis
hep•ta•gon
her•ald
he•ral•dic

her•ald•ry
herb•age
herb•al
her•bi•cide
her•biv•o•rous
Her•cu•le•an
Her•cu•les
herd (of animals; cf. *heard*)
herd•er
here (place; cf. *hear*)
here•abouts
here•af•ter
here•by
he•red•i•tary
he•red•i•ty
here•in
here•in•af•ter
here•in•be•fore
here•on
her•e•sy
her•e•tic
he•ret•i•cal
here•to•fore
here•with
her•i•ta•ble
her•i•tage
Her•mes
her•mit
her•mit•age
her•nia
he•ro
he•roes

he•ro•ic
he•ro•ical
her•o•in (drug; cf. *heroine*)
her•o•ine (woman; cf. *heroin*)
her•o•ism
her•on
her•ring
her•ring•bone
her•self
hes•i•tan•cy
hes•i•tant
hes•i•tate
hes•i•tat•ing•ly
hes•i•ta•tion
het•ero•dox
het•er•o•ge•ne•ity
het•er•o•ge•neous
hew (chop; cf. *hue*)
hexa•gon
hex•ag•o•nal
hey•day
hi•a•tus
Hi•a•wa•tha
hi•ber•nate
hi•ber•na•tion
hi•bis•cus
hic•cup
hick•o•ry
hid•den
hide•away
hide•bound

hid•eous
hide•out
hi•er•arch
hi•er•ar•chi•cal
hi•er•ar•chy
hi•er•at•ic
hi•ero•glyph•ic
high•ball
high•born
high•boy
high•bred
high•brow
high chair
high–class adj.
high•er–up n.
high•fa•lu•tin
high•fi•del•i•ty
high–grade adj.
high–hand•ed
high•land
high•land•er
high–lev•el adj.
high•light
high–mind•ed
high•ness
high–pitched
high–pres•sure
high–rise
high•road
high school
high sea
high–sound•ing
high–spir•it•ed

high–strung
high tech•nol•o•gy
high–ten•sion
high–test
high–toned
high•way
high•way•man
hi•jack
hi•lar•i•ous
hi•lar•i•ty
hill•bil•ly
hill•ock
hill•side
hilly
him (pronoun; cf.
    hymn)
Hi•ma•la•yan
him•self
hin•der v.
hind•er adj.
hin•drance
hind•sight
Hin•du
hinge
hing•ing
hin•ter•land
hip•bone
hip•pie sing.
hip•pies pl.
hip•po•drome
hip•po•pot•a•mus
hire•ling
hir•sute

hiss•ing
his•ta•mine
his•to•ri•an
his•tor•ic
his•tor•i•cal
his•to•ry
his•tri•on•ic
hit–and–miss
hit–and–run
hitch•hike
hith•er
hith•er•to
hoard (amass; cf.
    horde)
hoard•ing
hoar•i•ness
hoarse (voice; cf.
    horse)
hoary
hoax
hob•ble
hob•by•horse
hob•gob•lin
hob•nail
hob•nob
ho•bo
hock•ey
ho•cus–po•cus
hoe
hoe•cake
hoe•down
hoe•ing
hog

hogged

hog•ging

hog•gish

hogs•head

hog•wash

hoi pol•loi

hoist•er

hold•back n.

hold•er

hold•fast

hold•ing

hold over v.

hold•over n.

hold up v.

hold•up n.

hole (cavity; cf. *whole*)

hole•proof

hol•ey (full of holes; cf. *holly, holy, wholly*)

hol•i•day

ho•li•ness

hol•lan•daise

hol•low

hol•ly (shrub; cf. *holey, holy, wholly*)

ho•lo•caust

ho•lo•graph

hol•ster

ho•ly (sacred; cf. *holey, holly, wholly*)

hom•age

hom•burg

home•body

home•bred

home•com•ing

home•grown

home•land

home•less

home•like

home•li•ness

home•ly (plain; cf. *homey*)

home•made

home•mak•er

ho•meo•path

ho•meo•path•ic

ho•me•op•a•thy

home•own•er

home plate

Ho•mer•ic

home•room

home rule

home run

home•sick

home•site

home•spun

home•stead

home•stretch

home•town

home•ward

home•work

hom•ey (homelike; cf. *homely*)

ho•mi•cide

hom•i•lies

hom•i•ly

ho•mo•ge•ne•ity

ho•mo•ge•neous

ho•mog•e•nize

ho•mog•e•nous

ho•mol•o•gous

hom•onym

ho•mo•phone

hon•est

hon•es•ty

hon•ey

hon•ey•bee

hon•ey•comb

hon•ey•dew

hon•eyed

hon•ey•moon

hon•ey•suck•le

hon•ky–tonk

hon•or

hon•or•able

hon•o•rar•i•um

hon•or•ary

hon•or•if•ic

hood•ed

hood•lum

hoo•doo

hood•wink

hoof•er

hoo•kah

hook up v.

hook•up n.

hook•worm

hoop•skirt

hoose•gow

Hoo•sier
hope•ful
hope•less
hop•per
hop•scotch
horde (crowd; cf.
hoard)
hore•hound
ho•ri•zon
hor•i•zon•tal
hor•mone
hor•net
horn•pipe
horny
horo•scope
hor•ri•ble
hor•rid
hor•ri•fy
hor•ror
hors d'oeuvre (pl.:
hors d'oeuvres)
horse (animal; cf.
hoarse)
horse•back
horse•car
horse•flesh
horse•fly
horse•hair
horse•hide
horse•laugh
horse•man
horse op•era
horse•play
horse•pow•er

horse•rad•ish
horse sense
horse•shoe
horse•whip
horse•wom•an
hor•ti•cul•tur•al
hor•ti•cul•ture
ho•siery
hos•pice
hos•pi•ta•ble
hos•pi•tal
hos•pi•tal•i•ty
hos•pi•tal•iza•tion
hos•pi•tal•ize
hos•tage
hos•tel•ry
host•ess
hos•tile
hos•til•i•ty
hos•tler
hot
hot air
hot•bed
hot–blood•ed
hot•box
hotch•potch
hot dog
ho•tel
hot•foot
hot•head
hot•head•ed
hot•house
hot plate
hot rod

hot•shot
hot spring
Hot•ten•tot
hot•ter
hot•test
hot tub
hot–wire
hour (60 minutes; cf.
our)
hour•glass
hour–long adj.
hour•ly
house•boat
house•break•ing
house•bro•ken
house call
house•clean
house•coat
house•dress
house•fa•ther
house•fly
house•ful
house•hold
house•hold•er
house hus•band
house•keep•er
house•less
house•lights
house•maid
house•man
house•moth•er
house par•ty
house•plant
house•room

house sit•ter
house•warm•ing
house•wife
house•wives
house•work
hous•ing
hov•el
hov•er
how•ev•er
how•it•zer
howl•er
how•so•ev•er
how–to
hua•ra•che
hub•bub
huck•le•ber•ry
huck•ster
hud•dle
hue (color; cf. *hew*)
huff•i•ly
huff•i•ness
huffy
huge•ness
Hu•gue•not
hulk•ing
hul•la•ba•loo
hu•man
hu•mane
hu•man•ism
hu•man•ist
hu•man•is•tic
hu•man•i•tar•i•an
hu•man•i•ty
hu•man•ize

hu•man•kind
hu•man•ly
hum•ble
hum•ble•ness
hum•bly
hum•bug
hum•drum
hu•mer•us (bone; cf. *humorous*)
hu•mid
hu•mid•i•fi•er
hu•mid•i•fy
hu•mid•i•ty
hu•mi•dor
hu•mil•i•ate
hu•mil•i•a•tion
hu•mil•i•ty
hummed
hum•ming
hum•ming•bird
hum•mock
hu•mor
hu•mor•ist
hu•mor•ous (funny; cf. *humerus*)
hump•back
hunch•back
hun•dred
hun•dredth
hun•dred•weight
Hun•gar•i•an
hun•ger
hun•gri•er
hun•gri•ly

hun•gry
hunt•er
Hun•ting•don Pa.
Hun•ting•ton Ind., N.Y., W. Va.
hunts•man
hur•dle
hur•dy–gur•dy
hur•ly–bur•ly
Hu•ron
hur•rah
hur•ri•cane
hur•ried
hur•ry
hurt•ful
hus•band
hus•band•man
hus•band•ry
hus•ki•ly
hus•ki•ness
husk•ing
hus•ky
hus•sar
hus•tings
hus•tle
hy•a•cinth
hy•brid
Hy•dra
hy•dran•gea
hy•drant
hy•drate
hy•drau•lic
hy•dro•car•bon
hy•dro•chlo•ric

hy·dro·chlo·ride
hy·dro·dy·nam·ics
hy·dro·elec·tric
hy·dro·gen
hy·dro·ly·sis
hy·drom·e·ter
hy·dro·phane
hy·dro·pho·bia
hy·dro·phone
hy·dro·plane
hy·dro·pon·ics
hy·dro·scope
hy·dro·stat·ic
hy·drous
hy·e·na
hy·giene
hy·gien·ic
hy·grom·e·ter
hy·gro·scope
hy·gro·scop·ic
hymn (song; cf. *him*)
hym·nal

hym·nol·o·gy
hy·per·bo·la (curve)
hy·per·bo·le
    (exaggeration)
hy·per·crit·i·cal
    (overcritical; cf.
    hypocritical)
hy·per·phys·i·cal
hy·per·ten·sion
hy·phen
hy·phen·ate
hy·phen·at·ed
hyp·no·sis
hyp·not·ic
hyp·no·tism
hyp·no·tist
hyp·no·tize
hy·po·chon·dria
hy·po·chon·dri·ac
hy·po·chon·dri·a·
    cal

hy·poc·ri·sy
hyp·o·crite
hyp·o·crit·i·cal
    (deceitful; cf.
    hypercritical)
hy·po·der·mal
hy·po·der·mic
hy·po·der·mis
hy·po·eu·tec·tic
hy·pot·e·nuse
hy·poth·e·cate
hy·poth·e·ses pl.
hy·poth·e·sis sing.
hy·po·thet·i·cal
hy·po·thet·i·cal·ly
hys·sop
hys·ter·e·sis
hys·te·ria
hys·ter·i·cal
hys·ter·ics

iam·bic
iam·bus
Ibe·ri·an
ibex (goat)
ibis (bird)
ice
ice age

ice bag
ice·berg
ice·boat
ice·bound
ice·box
ice·break·er
ice cap

ice–cold
ice cream n.
ice–cream adj.
ice field
ice floe
ice·house
ice·man

ice pack
ice pick
ice plant
ice wa•ter
ici•cle
ic•i•ly
ic•i•ness
ic•ing
icon
icon•ic
icon•o•clast
icy
Ida•ho
ide•al (perfect; cf. *idle, idol, idyll*)
ide•al•ism
ide•al•ist
ide•al•is•tic
ide•al•iza•tion
ide•al•ize
ide•al•ly
iden•ti•cal
iden•ti•fi•ca•tion
iden•ti•fied
iden•ti•fy
ideo•gram
ide•ol•o•gy
id•i•o•cy
id•i•om
id•i•om•at•ic
id•io•syn•cra•sy
id•i•ot
id•i•ot•ic

idle (inactive; cf. *ideal, idol, idyll*)
idle•ness
idly
idol (object of worship; cf. *ideal, idle, idyll*)
idol•a•trous
idol•a•try
idol•ize
idyll (of rustic life; cf. *ideal, idle, idol*)
idyl•lic
if•fy
ig•loo
ig•ne•ous
ig•nes•cent
ig•nis fat•u•us
ig•nit•able
ig•nite
ig•ni•tion
ig•no•ble
ig•no•min•i•ous
ig•no•mi•ny
ig•no•ra•mus
ig•no•rance
ig•no•rant
ig•nore
igua•na
il•e•um (intestine; cf. *ilium*)
il•i•ac
Il•i•ad
il•i•um (pelvic bone; cf. *ileum*)

ilk
ill–ad•vised
ill–bred
il•le•gal
il•le•gal•i•ty
il•leg•i•bil•i•ty
il•leg•i•ble (unreadable; cf. *eligible*)
il•le•git•i•ma•cy
il•le•git•i•mate
ill–fat•ed
ill–fa•vored
il•lib•er•al
il•lic•it (unlawful; cf. *elicit*)
il•lim•it•able
Il•li•nois
il•lit•er•a•cy
il•lit•er•ate
il•lit•er•ate•ness
ill–man•nered
ill–na•tured
ill•ness
il•log•i•cal
ill–starred
ill–treat
il•lu•mi•nate
il•lu•mi•na•tion
il•lu•mi•na•tive
il•lu•mi•na•tor
il•lu•mine
il•lu•sion

il•lu•sive (misleading;
   cf. *elusive*)
il•lu•so•ry
il•lus•trate
il•lus•tra•tion
il•lus•tra•tive
il•lus•tra•tor
il•lus•tri•ous
ill will
im•age
im•ag•ery
imag•in•able
imag•i•nary
imag•i•na•tion
imag•i•na•tive
imag•ine
im•bal•ance
im•be•cile
im•be•cil•i•ty
im•bibe
im•bri•cate
im•bri•cat•ed
im•bri•ca•tion
im•bro•glio
im•bue
im•i•ta•ble
im•i•tate
im•i•ta•tion
im•i•ta•tive
im•i•ta•tor
im•mac•u•late
im•ma•nent
im•ma•te•ri•al
im•ma•te•ri•al•i•ty

im•ma•ture
im•mea•sur•able
im•me•di•a•cy
im•me•di•ate
im•me•di•ate•ly
im•me•mo•ri•al
im•mense
im•men•si•ty
im•merge
im•merse
im•mer•sion
im•mi•grant
   (incoming; cf.
   emigrant)
im•mi•grate
im•mi•gra•tion
im•mi•nence
im•mi•nent
   (impending; cf.
   eminent)
im•mis•ci•ble
im•mo•bile
im•mo•bi•li•za•
   tion
im•mo•bi•lize
im•mod•er•ate
im•mod•er•a•tion
im•mod•est
im•mo•late
im•mo•la•tion
im•mor•al
im•mo•ral•i•ty
im•mor•tal
im•mor•tal•i•ty

im•mor•tal•ize
im•mov•abil•i•ty
im•mov•able
im•mov•ably
im•mune
im•mu•ni•ty
im•mu•nize
im•mu•nol•o•gy
im•mure
im•mu•ta•bil•i•ty
im•mu•ta•ble
im•pact
im•pact print•er
im•pair
im•pair•ment
im•pal•pa•ble
im•pan•el
im•par•i•ty
impark
im•part
im•par•tial
im•par•tial•i•ty
im•par•ti•ble
im•pass•abil•i•ty
im•pass•able
im•passe
im•pas•si•bil•i•ty
im•pas•si•ble
im•pas•sion
im•pas•sioned
im•pas•sive
im•pa•tience
im•pa•tient
im•peach

im•peach•ment
im•pec•ca•bil•i•ty
im•pec•ca•ble
im•pe•cu•ni•os•i•ty
im•pe•cu•nious
im•ped•ance
im•pede
im•ped•i•ment
im•ped•i•men•ta
im•pel
im•pelled
im•pel•lent
im•pel•ling
im•pend
im•pend•ing
im•pen•e•tra•bil•
  i•ty
im•pen•e•tra•ble
im•per•a•tive
im•per•a•tive•ly
im•per•cep•ti•ble
im•per•fect
im•per•fec•tion
im•per•fect•ly
im•per•fect•ness
im•per•fo•rate
im•pe•ri•al
im•pe•ri•al•ism
im•pe•ri•al•ist
im•pe•ri•al•ly
im•per•il
im•pe•ri•ous
im•per•ish•able
im•per•me•able

im•per•son•al
im•per•son•ate
im•per•son•ation
im•per•son•ator
im•per•ti•nence
im•per•ti•nen•cy
im•per•ti•nent
im•per•turb•abil•
  i•ty
im•per•turb•able
im•per•vi•ous
im•pe•ti•go
im•pet•u•os•i•ty
im•pet•u•ous
im•pe•tus
im•pi•ety
im•pinge
im•pinge•ment
im•pi•ous
imp•ish
im•pla•ca•ble
im•plant
im•ple•ment
im•pli•cate
im•pli•ca•tion
im•pli•ca•tive
im•plic•it
im•plied
im•plore
im•plo•sion
im•ply
im•po•lite
im•pol•i•tic
im•pon•der•a•ble

im•port
im•port•able
im•por•tance
im•por•tant
im•por•ta•tion
im•por•tu•nate
im•por•tune
im•por•tu•ni•ty
im•pose
im•pos•ing
im•po•si•tion
im•pos•si•bil•i•ty
im•pos•si•ble
im•post
im•pos•tor (pretender)
im•pos•ture (fraud)
im•po•tence
im•po•ten•cy
im•po•tent
im•pound
im•pov•er•ish
im•prac•ti•ca•bil•
  i•ty
im•prac•ti•ca•ble
im•prac•ti•cal
im•pre•cate
im•pre•ca•tion
im•pre•ca•to•ry
im•preg•na•ble
im•preg•nate
im•pre•sa•rio
im•press
im•press•ible
im•pres•sion

im·pres·sion·able
im·pres·sive
im·pri·mis
im·print
im·pris·on
im·pris·on·ment
im·prob·a·bil·i·ty
im·prob·a·ble
im·promp·tu
im·prop·er
im·pro·pri·ety
im·prov·a·ble
im·prove
im·prove·ment
im·prov·er
im·prov·i·dence
im·prov·i·dent
im·pro·vi·sa·tion
im·pro·vise
im·pru·dence
im·pru·dent
im·pru·dent·ly
im·pu·dence
im·pu·dent
im·pugn
im·pulse
im·pul·sion
im·pul·sive
im·pu·ni·ty
im·pure
im·pu·ri·ty
im·put·able
im·pu·ta·tion
im·pu·ta·tive

im·pute
in·abil·i·ty
in·ac·ces·si·bil·i·ty
in·ac·ces·si·ble
in·ac·cu·ra·cy
in·ac·cu·rate
in·ac·tion
in·ac·tive
in·ac·tiv·i·ty
in·ad·e·qua·cy
in·ad·e·quate
in·ad·mis·si·ble
in·ad·ver·tence
in·ad·ver·tent
in·ad·vis·able
in·alien·able
in·al·ter·able
inane
in·an·i·mate
inan·i·ty
in·ap·peas·able
in·ap·pli·ca·ble
in·ap·po·site
in·ap·pre·cia·ble
in·ap·pre·cia·tive
in·ap·pro·pri·ate
in·apt
in·ar·tic·u·late
in·ar·tis·tic
in·as·much as
in·at·ten·tion
in·at·ten·tive
in·au·di·ble
in·au·gu·ral

in·au·gu·rate
in·au·gu·ra·tion
in·aus·pi·cious
in·born
in·bound
in·bred
in·cal·cu·la·ble
in·ca·les·cent
in·can·desce
in·can·des·cence
in·can·des·cent
in·can·ta·tion
in·ca·pa·bil·i·ty
in·ca·pa·ble
in·ca·pac·i·tate
in·ca·pac·i·ta·tion
in·ca·pac·i·ty
in·car·cer·ate
in·car·cer·a·tion
in·car·na·tion
in·cau·tious
in·cen·di·ary
in·cense
in·cen·tive
in·cep·tion
in·cep·tive
in·ces·sant
in·cest
in·ces·tu·ous
in·cho·ate
in·ci·dence
in·ci·dent
in·ci·den·tal
in·ci·den·tal·ly

in•cin•er•ate
in•cin•er•a•tion
in•cin•er•a•tor
in•cip•i•ent
in•cise
in•ci•sion
in•ci•sive
in•ci•sor
in•ci•ta•tion
in•cite (stir up; cf. *insight*)
in•cite•ment
in•cit•er
in•ci•vil•i•ty
in•clem•en•cy
in•clem•ent
in•cli•na•tion
in•cline
in•clined
in•clin•ing
in•clude
in•clud•ed
in•clu•sion
in•clu•sive
in•co•erc•ible
in•cog•ni•to
in•co•her•ence
in•co•her•ent
in•com•bus•ti•ble
in•come
in•com•ing
in•com•men•su•ra•ble
in•com•men•su•rate

in•com•mu•ni•ca•ble
in•com•pa•ra•ble
in•com•pat•i•bil•i•ty
in•com•pat•i•ble
in•com•pe•tence
in•com•pe•tent
in•com•plete
in•com•pre•hen•si•ble
in•com•press•ible
in•com•put•able
in•con•ceiv•able
in•con•clu•sive
in•con•gru•ity
in•con•gru•ous
in•con•se•quent
in•con•se•quen•tial
in•con•sid•er•able
in•con•sid•er•ate
in•con•sis•ten•cy
in•con•sis•tent
in•con•sol•able
in•con•spic•u•ous
in•con•stant
in•con•test•able
in•con•tro•vert•ible
in•con•ve•nience
in•con•ve•nient
in•con•vert•ible
in•cor•po•rate
in•cor•po•ra•tion
in•cor•po•ra•tor
in•cor•po•re•al

in•cor•rect
in•cor•ri•gi•bil•i•ty
in•cor•ri•gi•ble
in•cor•rupt
in•cor•rupt•ible
in•creas•able
in•crease
in•creas•ing•ly
in•cred•ibil•i•ty
in•cred•i•ble (unbelievable; cf. *incredulous*)
in•cre•du•li•ty
in•cred•u•lous (unbelieving; cf. *incredible*)
in•cre•ment
in•cre•men•tal
in•crim•i•nate
in•crim•i•na•to•ry
in•crus•ta•tion
in•cu•bate
in•cu•ba•tion
in•cu•ba•tor
in•cu•bus
in•cul•cate
in•cul•ca•tion
in•cul•pate
in•cul•pa•tion
in•cul•pa•to•ry
in•cum•ben•cy
in•cum•bent
in•cur
in•cur•able

in·cu·ri·ous
in·curred
in·cur·ring
in·cur·sion
in·cur·vate
in·cur·va·tion
in·debt·ed·ness
in·de·cen·cy
in·de·cent
in·de·ci·pher·able
in·de·ci·sion
in·de·ci·sive
in·de·clin·able
in·de·co·rous
in·de·co·rum
in·deed
in·de·fat·i·ga·ble
in·de·fen·si·ble
in·de·fin·able
in·def·i·nite
in·del·i·ble
in·del·i·ca·cy
in·del·i·cate
in·dem·ni·fi·ca·tion
in·dem·ni·fied
in·dem·ni·fy
in·dem·ni·ty
in·dent
in·den·ta·tion
in·den·tion
in·den·ture
in·de·pen·dence
in·de·pen·dent
in·de·scrib·able

in·de·struc·ti·ble
in·de·ter·min·able
in·de·ter·mi·nate
in·de·ter·mi·na·tion
in·dex (pl.: *indexes* or
    indices)
in·dex·er
in·dex·es pl.
In·dia
In·di·an
In·di·ana
in·di·cate
in·di·ca·tion
in·dic·a·tive
in·di·ca·tor
in·dic·a·to·ry
in·di·ces pl.
in·dict (charge with a
    crime; cf. *indite*)
in·dict·able
in·dic·tion
in·dict·ment
In·dies
in·dif·fer·ence
in·dif·fer·ent
in·dif·fer·ent·ly
in·di·gence
in·dig·e·nous (native
    to)
in·di·gent (poor)
in·di·gest·ibil·i·ty
in·di·gest·ible
in·di·ges·tion
in·dig·nant

in·dig·na·tion
in·dig·ni·ty
in·di·go
in·di·rect
in·di·rec·tion
in·di·rect·ly
in·di·rect·ness
in·dis·cern·ible
in·dis·creet
in·dis·crete
in·dis·cre·tion
in·dis·crim·i·nate
in·dis·crim·i·na·
    tion
in·dis·pens·able
in·dis·posed
in·dis·po·si·tion
in·dis·put·able
in·dis·sol·u·ble
in·dis·tinct
in·dis·tinct·ly
in·dis·tin·guish·
    able
in·dite (write; cf.
    indict)
in·di·vert·ible
in·di·vid·u·al
in·di·vid·u·al·ism
in·di·vid·u·al·ist
in·di·vid·u·al·i·ty
in·di·vid·u·al·ize
in·di·vid·u·al·ly
in·di·vis·i·ble
In·do·chi·na

In·do–Chi·nese
in·doc·ile
in·doc·tri·nate
in·do·lence
in·do·lent
in·dom·i·ta·ble
in·door
in·doors
in·drawn
in·du·bi·ta·ble
in·duce
in·duce·ment
in·duct
in·duc·tile
in·duc·tion
in·duc·tive
in·duc·tor
in·dulge
in·dul·gence
in·dul·gent
in·du·rate
in·du·ra·tion
in·dus·tri·al
in·dus·tri·al·ism
in·dus·tri·al·ist
in·dus·tri·al·ize
in·dus·tri·ous
in·dus·try
ine·bri·ant
ine·bri·ate
ine·bri·a·tion
in·ebri·ety
in·ed·i·ble
in·ef·fa·ble

in·ef·face·able
in·ef·fec·tive
in·ef·fec·tu·al
in·ef·fi·ca·cious
in·ef·fi·ca·cy
in·ef·fi·cien·cy
in·ef·fi·cient
in·el·e·gance
in·el·e·gant
in·el·i·gi·bil·i·ty
in·el·i·gi·ble
in·el·o·quent
in·eluc·ta·ble
in·ept
in·ep·ti·tude
in·equal·i·ty
in·eq·ui·ta·ble
in·eq·ui·ty
(unfairness; cf.
iniquity)
in·erad·i·ca·ble
in·er·rant
in·ert
in·er·tia
in·es·cap·ably
in·es·sen·tial
in·es·ti·ma·ble
in·ev·i·ta·bil·i·ty
in·ev·i·ta·ble
in·ex·act
in·ex·ac·ti·tude
in·ex·cus·able
in·ex·haust·ibil·i·ty
in·ex·haust·ible

in·ex·o·ra·ble
in·ex·pe·di·ent
in·ex·pen·sive
in·ex·pe·ri·ence
in·ex·pert
in·ex·pi·a·ble
in·ex·plain·able
in·ex·pli·ca·ble
in·ex·plic·it
in·ex·press·ible
in·ex·pres·sive
in·ex·pug·na·ble
in·ex·ten·si·ble
in·ex·tin·guish·able
in·ex·tri·ca·ble
in·fal·li·bil·i·ty
in·fal·li·ble
in·fa·mous
in·fa·my
in·fan·cy
in·fant
in·fan·ta fem.
in·fan·te mas.
in·fan·tile
in·fan·try
in·fat·u·ate
in·fat·u·a·tion
in·fect
in·fec·tion
in·fec·tious
in·fec·tive
in·fec·tor
in·fe·lic·i·tous
in·fe·lic·i·ty

in•fer
in•fer•ence
in•fer•en•tial
in•fe•ri•or
in•fe•ri•or•i•ty
in•fer•nal
in•fer•no
in•ferred
in•fer•ring
in•fest
in•fes•ta•tion
in•fi•del
in•fi•del•i•ty
in•field
in•fil•trate
in•fi•nite
in•fin•i•tes•i•mal
in•fin•i•tive
in•fin•i•ty
in•firm
in•fir•ma•ry
in•fir•mi•ty
in•flame
in•flam•ma•ble
in•flam•ma•tion
in•flam•ma•to•ry
in•flate
in•flat•ed
in•fla•tion
in•fla•tion•ary
in•flect
in•flec•tion
in•flex•i•ble
in•flict

in•flic•tion
in•flow
in•flu•ence
in•flu•en•tial
in•flu•en•za
in•flux
in•form
in•for•mal
in•for•mal•i•ty
in•for•mant
in•for•ma•tion
in•for•ma•tion
    pro•cess•ing
in•for•ma•tive
in•form•er
in•frac•tion
in•fra•red
in•fra•struc•ture
in•fre•quent
in•fringe
in•fringe•ment
in•fu•ri•ate
in•fuse
in•fu•sion
in•ge•nious
    (inventive; cf.
    ingenuous)
in•ge•nue
in•ge•nu•ity
in•gen•u•ous (candid;
    cf. *ingenious*)
in•ges•tion
in•glo•ri•ous
in•got

in•grained
in•grate
in•gra•ti•ate
in•grat•i•tude
in•gre•di•ent
in•gress
in•grown
in•hab•it
in•hab•it•ant
in•hale
in•har•mo•ni•ous
in•here
in•her•ence
in•her•ent
in•her•it
in•her•i•tance
in•hib•it
in•hi•bi•tion
in•hib•i•tor
in•hos•pi•ta•ble
in–house
in•hu•man
in•hu•man•i•ty
in•hu•ma•tion
in•im•i•cal
in•im•i•ta•ble
in•iq•ui•tous
in•iq•ui•ty
    (wickedness; cf.
    inequity)
ini•tial
ini•ti•ate v.
ini•tiate n.
ini•tia•tive

ini•ti•a•tor
in•ject
in•jec•tion
in•jec•tor
in•ju•di•cious
in•junc•tion
in•jure
in•ju•ries
in•ju•ri•ous
in•ju•ry
in•jus•tice
ink–jet print•er
in•kling
ink•stand
ink•well
in•laid
in•land
in•lay
in•let
in•mate
in•most
in•nate
in•ning
inn•keep•er
in•no•cence
in•no•cent
in•noc•u•ous
in•no•vate
in•no•va•tion
in•nu•en•do
in•nu•mer•a•ble
in•oc•u•late
in•oc•u•la•tion
in•of•fen•sive

in•op•er•a•ble
in•op•por•tune
in•or•di•nate
in•or•gan•ic
in•put
in•quest
in•qui•etude
in•quire
in•qui•ries
in•qui•ry
in•qui•si•tion
in•quis•i•tive
in•quis•i•tor
in•road
in•rush
in•sane
in•san•i•tary
in•san•i•ty
in•sa•tia•ble
in•scribe
in•scrip•tion
in•scru•ta•ble
in•sect
in•sec•ti•cide
in•se•cure
in•se•cu•ri•ty
in•sen•sate
in•sen•si•ble
in•sen•si•tive
in•sep•a•ra•ble
in•sert
in•ser•tion
in•side
in•sid•i•ous

in•sight
(understanding; cf.
  incite)
in•sig•nia
in•sig•nif•i•cance
in•sig•nif•i•cant
in•sin•cere
in•sin•u•ate
in•sin•u•a•tion
in•sip•id
in•sist
in•sis•tence
in•sis•tent
in•so•far
in•sole
in•so•lence
in•so•lent
in•sol•u•ble
in•sol•ven•cy
in•sol•vent
in•som•nia
in•sou•ci•ance
in•sou•ci•ant
in•spect
in•spec•tion
in•spec•tor
in•spi•ra•tion
in•spire
in•sta•bil•i•ty
in•stall
in•stal•la•tion
in•stalled
in•stall•ing
in•stall•ment

in•stance
in•stan•ta•neous
in•stan•ter
in•stant•ly
in•stead
in•step
in•sti•gate
in•sti•ga•tion
in•sti•ga•tor
in•still
in•stilled
in•still•ing
in•stinct
in•stinc•tive
in•sti•tute
in•sti•tu•tion
in•sti•tu•tion•al
in•sti•tu•tion•al•iza•
  tion
in•struct
in•struct•ed
in•struc•tion
in•struc•tion•al
in•struc•tive
in•struc•tor
in•stru•ment
in•stru•men•tal
in•stru•men•tal•i•ty
in•stru•men•ta•tion
in•sub•or•di•nate
in•sub•or•di•na•tion
in•suf•fer•able
in•suf•fi•cient

in•su•lar
in•su•late
in•su•la•tion
in•su•la•tor
in•su•lin
in•sult
in•su•per•a•ble
in•sup•port•able
in•sup•press•ible
in•sur•abil•i•ty
in•sur•able
in•sur•ance
in•sure
in•sur•er
in•sur•gent
in•sur•rec•tion
in•tact
in•ta•glio
in•take
in•tan•gi•ble
in•te•ger
in•te•gral
in•te•grate
in•te•gra•tion
in•teg•ri•ty
in•teg•u•ment
in•tel•lect
in•tel•lec•tu•al
in•tel•li•gence
in•tel•li•gent
in•tel•li•gent
  copi•er/print•er
in•tel•li•gi•ble

in•tem•per•ance
in•tem•per•ate
in•tend
in•ten•dant
in•tense
in•ten•si•fied
in•ten•si•fy
in•ten•si•ty
in•ten•sive
in•tent
in•ten•tion
in•ter
in•ter•ac•tion
in•ter•ac•tive
in•ter•agen•cy
in•ter•cede
in•ter•cept
in•ter•cep•tor
in•ter•ces•sion
in•ter•change•abil•
  i•ty
in•ter•change•able
in•ter•col•le•giate
in•ter•com
in•ter•com•mu•ni•
  ca•tion
in•ter•com•pa•ny
in•ter•con•nect
in•ter•course
in•ter•de•nom•i•na•
  tion•al
in•ter•de•part•men•
  tal

in·ter·de·pen·dent
in·ter·dict
in·ter·dig·i·ta·tion
in·ter·dis·ci·plin·
ary
in·ter·est
in·ter·face
in·ter·fere
in·ter·fered
in·ter·fer·ence
in·ter·fer·ing
in·ter·im
in·te·ri·or
in·ter·ject
in·ter·jec·tion
in·ter·leave
in·ter·line
in·ter·lin·ear
in·ter·lock
in·ter·loc·u·tor
in·ter·loc·u·to·ry
in·ter·lope
in·ter·lude
in·ter·mar·riage
in·ter·mar·ry
in·ter·me·di·ary
in·ter·me·di·ate
in·ter·ment
in·ter·mez·zo
in·ter·mi·na·ble
in·ter·min·gle
in·ter·mis·sion
in·ter·mit·tent

in·ter·mod·al
in·ter·nal
in·ter·nal pro·ces·
sor
in·ter·nal stor·age
in·ter·na·tion·al
in·ter·ne·cine
in·ter·nist
in·tern·ment
in·ter·of·fice
in·ter·pel·late
(question)
in·ter·per·son·al
in·ter·po·late (insert)
in·ter·pose
in·ter·pret (translate;
cf. *interrupt*)
in·ter·pre·ta·tion
in·ter·pret·er
in·ter·pre·tive
in·ter·ra·cial
in·terred
in·ter·reg·num
in·ter·re·late
in·ter·re·la·tion·
ship
in·ter·ring
in·ter·ro·gate
in·ter·ro·ga·tion
in·ter·rog·a·tive
in·ter·rog·a·to·ry
in·ter·rupt (break
into; cf. *interpret*)

in·ter·rupt·ible
in·ter·rup·tion
in·ter·sect
in·ter·sec·tion
in·ter·sperse
in·ter·state (between
states; cf. *intrastate*)
in·ter·stice
in·ter·sti·tial
in·ter·twined
in·ter·ur·ban
in·ter·val
in·ter·vene
in·ter·ven·tion
in·ter·view
in·ter·view·er
in·tes·tate
in·tes·ti·nal
in·tes·tine
in·ti·ma·cy
in·ti·mate
in·ti·ma·tion
in·tim·i·date
in·tim·i·da·tion
in·tol·er·a·ble
in·tol·er·ance
in·tol·er·ant
in·to·na·tion
in·tone
in·tox·i·cant
in·tox·i·cate
in·tra·bank
in·trac·ta·ble

in•tra•li•brary
in•tra•mu•ral
in•tran•si•gent
in•tran•si•tive
in•tra•of•fice
in•tra•state (within the state; cf. *interstate*)
in•trep•id
in•tre•pid•i•ty
in•tri•ca•cy
in•tri•cate
in•trigue
in•trigued
in•trigu•ing
in•trin•sic
in•tro•duce
in•tro•duc•tion
in•tro•duc•to•ry
in•troit
in•tro•spec•tion
in•tro•vert
in•trude
in•tru•sion
in•tu•ition
in•tu•itive
in•unc•tion
in•un•date
in•un•da•tion
in•ure
in•vade
in•val•id adj.
in•va•lid n.
in•val•i•date

in•val•id•i•ty
in•valu•able
in•vari•able
in•va•sion
in•vec•tive
in•veigh
in•vei•gle
in•vent
in•ven•tion
in•ven•tive
in•ven•tor
in•ven•to•ries
in•ven•to•ry
in•verse
in•ver•sion
in•vert
in•vest
in•ves•ti•gate
in•ves•ti•ga•tion
in•ves•ti•ga•tive
in•ves•ti•ga•tor
in•ves•ti•ture
in•vest•ment
in•ves•tor
in•vet•er•ate
in•vid•i•ous
in•vig•o•rate
in•vin•ci•ble
in•vi•o•la•ble
in•vi•o•late
in•vis•i•ble
in•vi•ta•tion
in•vite
in•vit•ing

in•vo•ca•tion
in•voice
in•voke
in•vol•un•tari•ly
in•vol•un•tary
in•vo•lute
in•volve
in•vul•ner•a•ble
in•ward
io•dine
ion•iza•tion
ion•ize
ion•o•sphere
io•ta
IOU
Io•wa
ip•e•cac
ip•so fac•to
iras•ci•ble (quick to anger; cf. *erasable*)
irate
ir•i•des•cence
ir•i•des•cent
irid•i•um
irk•some
iron•clad
iron gray
iron•i•cal
iron lung
iron•mas•ter
iron•ware
iron•wood
iron•work
iro•ny

ir·ra·di·ate
ir·ra·tio·nal
ir·rec·on·cil·able
ir·re·deem·able
ir·re·duc·ible
ir·re·fra·ga·ble
ir·re·fut·able
ir·reg·u·lar
ir·rel·e·vance
ir·rel·e·vant
ir·re·li·gious
ir·rep·a·ra·ble
ir·re·press·ible
ir·re·proach·able
ir·re·sist·ible
ir·re·sol·u·ble
ir·res·o·lute
ir·res·o·lu·tion
ir·re·spec·tive
ir·re·spon·si·ble
ir·re·triev·able
ir·rev·er·ent
ir·re·vers·ible

ir·re·vo·ca·ble
ir·ri·gate
ir·ri·ga·tion
ir·ri·ta·ble
ir·ri·tant
ir·ri·tate
ir·ri·ta·tion
ir·rupt (break in; cf. *erupt*)
ir·rup·tion
is·chi·um
isin·glass
is·land
isle (small island; cf. *aisle*)
is·let (small island; cf. *eyelet*)
iso·bar
iso·late
iso·la·tion·ism
iso·la·tion·ist
iso·met·rics
isos·ce·les

iso·therm
iso·ther·mal
iso·tope
Is·ra·el
Is·rae·li
Is·ra·el·ite
is·su·able
is·su·ance
is·sue
isth·mus
ital·ic
ital·i·cize
item
item·iza·tion
item·ize
itin·er·ant
itin·er·ary
itin·er·ate
its (possessive)
it's (it is)
it·self
ivo·ry

J

ja·bot
jack·al
jack·a·napes
jack·ass
jack·boot

jack·et
jack·ham·mer
jack–in–the–box
jack–in–the–pul·pit
jack·knife

jack–of–all–trades
jack–o'–lan·tern
jack·pot
jack·rab·bit
jack·screw

jack•straw
jack–tar
Jac•o•bin
jag•uar
jail•bird
jail•break
ja•lopy
jam (food)
jamb (of a door)
jam•bo•ree
jan•i•tor
jan•i•to•ri•al
Jan•u•ary
ja•pan (varnish)
Jap•a•nese
ja•panned
ja•pan•ning
jar
jar•gon
jarred
jar•ring
jas•mine
jas•per
jaun•dice
jaun•ti•ly
jaun•ty
jav•e•lin
jaw•bone
jaw•break•er
jay•walk
jeal•ous
jeal•ou•sy
Je•ho•vah
je•june

je•ju•num
jel•lied
jel•li•fy
jel•ly•fish
jeop•ar•dize
jeop•ar•dy
jer•e•mi•ad
jerk•i•ly
jer•ky
jest (joke; cf. *gist*)
Je•su•it
jet–pro•pelled
jet•sam
jet stream
jet•ti•son
jet•ty
jeu d'es•prit
jew•el
jew•eled
jew•el•er
jew•el•ry
jibe (agree; cf. *gibe*)
jig•gle
jig•saw
jin•go
jin•rik•i•sha
jit•ney
jit•ter•bug
job
job•ber
job•bing
job•less
job lot
job work

jock•ey
jo•cose
joc•u•lar
joc•u•lar•i•ty
jo•cund
jodh•pur
jog
jogged
jog•ging
John•ston R.I.
Johns•town N.Y., Pa.
joie de vi•vre
join•der
join•er
joint•ly
join•ture
jok•er
jol•li•ty
jol•ly
jon•quil
josh
jos•tle
jour•nal
jour•nal•ism
jour•nal•ist
jour•nal•is•tic
jour•nal•ize
jour•ney
jour•ney•man
jo•vial
jowl
joy•ful
joy•ous
joy•ride

ju•bi•lant
ju•bi•la•tion
ju•bi•lee
judge•ship
judg•ment
ju•di•ca•to•ry
ju•di•ca•ture
ju•di•cial (of a judge; cf. *judicious*)
ju•di•cia•ry
ju•di•cious (of a judgment; cf. *judicial*)
ju•do
jug•ger•naut
jug•gle
jug•u•lar
juic•i•ly
juic•i•ness
ju•jit•su

juke•box
ju•lep
ju•li•enne
Ju•ly
jum•ble
jum•bo
jump•er
jump•i•ness
jump•ing jack
jump seat
junc•tion (joining)
junc•ture (crisis)
June
jun•gle
ju•nior
ju•ni•per
jun•ket
junk•ie
jun•ta

ju•rid•i•cal
juries
ju•ris•dic•tion
ju•ris•pru•dence
ju•rist
ju•ror
ju•ry
ju•ry•man
ju•ry•wom•an
jus•tice
jus•ti•fi•able
jus•ti•fi•ca•tion
jus•ti•fied
jus•ti•fied text
jus•ti•fi•er
jus•ti•fy
ju•ve•nile
jux•ta•po•si•tion

K

kaf•fee•klatsch
kai•ser
ka•lei•do•scope
ka•mi•ka•ze
kan•ga•roo
Kan•sas
ka•olin
ka•pok
kar•a•kul

kar•at *or* car•at (weight; cf. *caret*, *carrot*)
ka•ra•te
kar•ma
ka•ty•did
kay•ak
Kear•ney Nebr.
Kear•ny N.J.

keel•haul
keel•son
keen•ness
keep•sake
ken•nel
Ken•tucky
ker•nel (seed; cf. *colonel*)
ker•o•sene

ket•tle•drum
key (to a door; cf. *quay*)
key•board
key•board•ing
key•hole
Keynes•ian
key•note
key•punch
key•stone
key word
kha•ki
khe•dive
kick•back
kick off v.
kick•off n.
kid•nap
kid•napped
kid•nap•ping
kid•ney
kill (slay; cf. *kiln*)
kill•er
kill•ing
kill•joy
kiln (oven; cf. *kill*)
kilo•cy•cle
ki•lo•gram
ki•lo•hertz
ki•lo•me•ter
ki•lo•volt
kilo•watt
kilo•watt–hour
ki•mo•no
kin•der•gar•ten
kind•heart•ed

kind•li•ness
kin•dling
kind•ness
kin•dred
ki•net•ic
king•bird
king•bolt
king crab
king•dom
king•fish
king•li•ness
king•ly
king•mak•er
king•pin
king•ship
king–size
kins•folk
kin•ship
kins•man
kins•wom•an
ki•osk
kis•met
kitch•en
kitch•en•ette
kitch•en•ware
kit•ten
knap•sack
knave (rogue; cf. *nave*)
knav•ery
knead (dough; cf. *need*)
knee•cap
knee–deep
knee–high

knew (did know; cf. *gnu, new*)
knick•knack
knife
knight (title; cf. *night*)
knight•hood
knit
knit•ted
knit•ting
knives
knock•about
knock down v.
knock•down n., adj.
knock out v.
knock•out n.
knot (tied; cf. *not*)
knot•hole
knot•ted
knot•ting
knot•ty
know•able
know–how n.
know–it–all
knowl•edge
knowl•edge•able
knuck•le
knuck•le•bone
Ko•dak
koh–i–noor
kohl•ra•bi
kow•tow
ku•dos
küm•mel
kum•quat

L

la•bel
la•beled
la•bel•ing
la•bor
lab•o•ra•to•ry
   (science; cf. *lavatory*)
la•bor•er
la•bor–in•ten•sive
la•bo•ri•ous
la•bor•sav•ing
la•bur•num
lab•y•rinth
lab•y•rin•thine
lac•er•ate
lac•er•a•tion
lach•ry•mal
lach•ry•mose
lack•a•dai•si•cal
la•con•ic
lac•quer
la•crosse
lac•ta•tion
la•cu•na
lad•der
lad•der–back
la•dy•bird
la•dy•bug
la•dy•fin•ger
la•dy•like
la•dy•ship

la•dy's slip•per
lag•gard
lag•ging
la•goon
laid–back adj.
lain (rested; cf. *lane*)
la•ity
lake•shore
lam•ben•cy
lam•bent
lam•bre•quin
lamb•skin
lame
la•mé
la•ment
la•men•ta•ble
lam•en•ta•tion
lam•i•nate
lam•i•nat•ed
lamp•black
lam•poon
lamp•post
lam•prey
lan•cet
lan•dau
land•fall
land•fill
land•grave
land•hold•er
land•ing craft

land•ing field
land•ing gear
land•ing strip
land•la•dy
land•locked
land•lord
land•lub•ber
land•mark
land•own•er
land–poor
land•scape
land•slide
land•slip
lands•man
land•ward
lane (path; cf. *lain*)
lan•guage
lan•guid
lan•guish
lan•guor•ous
lank•i•ness
lanky
lan•o•lin
lan•tern
lan•yard
lap•dog
la•pel
lap•i•dary
la•pis la•zu•li
lap•ping

lapse (terminate; cf. *elapse*)
lar·board
lar·ce·nous
lar·ce·ny
large–scale
lar·ghet·to
lar·i·at
lark·spur
lar·va sing.
lar·vae pl.
lar·yn·gi·tis
lar·ynx
las·civ·i·ous
la·ser
la·ser print·er
las·si·tude
last–ditch adj.
last min·ute
latch·key
latch·string
late·ness
la·tent
lat·er (afterward; cf. *latter*)
lat·er·al
lat·ish
lat·i·tude
lat·ter (subsequent; cf. *later*)
lat·tice
lat·tice·work
laud·able
lau·da·num

lau·da·to·ry
laugh·able
laugh·ing·stock
laugh·ter
launch
laun·der
laun·der·er
laun·der·ette
laun·dress
Laun·dro·mat
laun·dry
lau·re·ate
lau·rel
lav·a·to·ry (for washing; cf. *laboratory*)
lav·en·der
lav·ish
law–abid·ing
law·ful
law·giv·er
law·less
law·mak·er
law·mak·ing
lawn mow·er
law·suit
law·yer
lax·a·tive
lax·ity
lay·away n.
lay·er
lay·man
lay off v.
lay·off n.

lay out v.
lay·out n.
lay over v.
lay·over n.
lay·per·son
lay up v.
lay–up n.
lay·wom·an
la·zi·ly
la·zi·ness
la·zy
la·zy·bones
la·zy Su·san
la·zy tongs
lead (to guide)
lead (a metal; cf. *led*)
lead·en
lead·er
lead·er·ship
lead–in n., adj.
lead off v.
lead·off n., adj.
leads·man
lead time
lead up v.
lead–up n.
lead·work
leaf·let
leaf mold
league
leak·age
leak·proof
lean (thin; cf. *lien*)
lean–to

leap·frog

leap year

lease·back

lease·hold

leath·er

Leath·er·ette

leath·er·neck

leav·en

lec·tern

lec·ture

led (guided; cf. *lead*)

led·ger

lee·ward

lee·way

left–hand·ed

left·over

leg·a·cy

le·gal

le·gal·ism

le·gal·i·ty

le·gal·ize

le·gal·ly

leg·ate

leg·a·tee

le·ga·tion

le·ga·to

leg·end

leg·end·ary

leg·er·de·main

leg·ging

leg·horn

leg·i·bil·i·ty

leg·i·ble

le·gion

leg·is·late

leg·is·la·tion

leg·is·la·tive

leg·is·la·tor

leg·is·la·ture

le·git·i·ma·cy

le·git·i·mate

le·git·i·ma·tize

leg·man

leg·room

le·gu·mi·nous

leg·work

lei·sure

lei·sure·li·ness

lei·sure·ly

lem·ming

lem·on·ade

le·mur

length

length·en

length·i·ness

length·wise

lengthy

le·nien·cy

le·nient

Le·nin·ism

len·i·ty

len·tic·u·lar

len·til

leop·ard

le·o·tard

lep·re·chaun

lep·ro·sy

lep·rous

le·sion

les·see

less·en (decrease; cf. *lesson*)

less·er

les·son (study; cf. *lessen*)

les·sor

let alone

let·down n.

le·thal

le·thar·gic

leth·ar·gy

let out

lets (permits)

let's (let us)

let·ter car·ri·er

let·tered

let·ter·head

let·ter–per·fect

let·ter·press

let·tuce

let up v.

let·up n.

leu·ke·mia

lev·ee (embankment; cf. *levy*)

lev·el

lev·eled

le·ver·age

le·vi·a·than

lev·i·ta·tion

lev·i·ty

levy (tax; cf. *levee*)

Lew·is·ton Idaho,
  Maine
Lew·is·town Mont.,
  Pa.
lex·i·cog·ra·pher
li·a·bil·i·ty
li·a·ble (obligated; cf.
  libel)
li·ai·son
li·ar (tells untruths; cf.
  lyre)
li·ba·tion
li·bel (defamation; cf.
  liable)
li·bel·ant
li·bel·ee
li·bel·ing
li·bel·ous
lib·er·al
lib·er·al·i·ty
lib·er·al·iza·tion
lib·er·al·ize
lib·er·al·ly
lib·er·ate
lib·er·a·tion
lib·er·a·tor
lib·er·tine
lib·er·ty
li·bid·i·nous
li·brar·i·an
li·brary
li·bret·tist
li·bret·to

li·cense
li·cen·tious
li·chen
lic·o·rice
lie (untruth; cf. *lye*)
lien (claim; cf. *lean*)
lieu·ten·an·cy
lieu·ten·ant
life belt
life·blood
life·boat
life buoy
life·guard
life jack·et
life·less
life·like
life·line
life·long
life net
life raft
life·sav·er
life·sav·ing
life–size
life span
life–style
life–sup·port
  sys·tem
life·time
lift–off n.
lig·a·ment
li·ga·tion
lig·a·ture
light·en

light·en·ing
  (becoming light; cf.
  lightning)
ligh·ter·age
light·fast
light–fin·gered
light–head·ed
light·heart·ed
light·house
light–mind·ed
light·ning (electrical
  discharge; cf.
  lightening)
light·proof
light·ship
light·some
light–struck
light·tight
light·weight
light–year
lig·ne·ous
lig·nite
lik·able
like·li·hood
like·ly
like–mind·ed
like·ness
like·wise
li·lac
lil·li·pu·tian
lily–liv·ered
lily–white
limb (branch; cf. *limn*)

lim·ber
lim·bo
lime·ade
lime·kiln
lime·light
lim·er·ick
lime·stone
lime·wa·ter
lim·i·nal
lim·it
lim·i·ta·tion
lim·it·less
limn (draw; cf. *limb*)
lim·ou·sine
lim·pet
lim·pid
lin·age (number of lines; cf. *lineage*)
linch·pin
lin·eage (family; cf. *linage*)
lin·eal (ancestral line; cf. *linear*)
lin·ea·ment
lin·ear (of lines; cf. *lineal*)
line·cut
line·man
lin·en
line print·er
line up v.
line·up n.
lin·ger

lin·ge·rie
lin·go
lin·guist
lin·i·ment
lin·ing
link·age
links (of chain; cf. *lynx*)
li·no·leum
Li·no·type
lin·seed
lin·tel
li·on·ess
li·on·heart·ed
li·po·ma
lip–read v.
lip–read·er n.
lip·read·ing n.
lip·stick
liq·ue·fac·tion
liq·ue·fi·able
liq·ue·fy
li·ques·cence
li·ques·cent
li·queur
liq·uid
liq·ui·date
liq·ui·da·tion
li·quid·i·ty
li·quor
lis·ten
list·less
list price
li·ter

lit·er·a·cy
lit·er·al (exact; cf. *littoral*)
lit·er·al·ly
lit·er·ary
lit·er·ate
lit·er·a·tim
lit·er·a·ture
lith·ia
lith·i·um
litho·graph
li·tho·gra·pher
li·thog·ra·phy
lit·i·gant
lit·i·gate
lit·i·ga·tion
li·ti·gious
lit·mus
lit·ter
lit·ter·bug
lit·tle
lit·tle·neck clam
lit·to·ral (shore; cf. *literal*)
li·tur·gi·cal
lit·ur·gy
liv·able
live–in adj.
live·li·hood
live·long
liv·ery
liv·ery·man
live·stock

liv•ing room
liz•ard
lla•ma
load (burden; cf. *lode*)
loan (borrow; cf. *lone*)
loan shark
loath•some
lob•by•ing
lob•ster
lo•cal (nearby)
lo•cale (locality)
lo•cal•i•ty
lo•cal•ize
lo•cate
lo•ca•tion
lock•jaw
lock•nut
lock•out n.
lock•smith
lock•step
lock•stitch
lock•up n.
lo•co•mo•tion
lo•co•mo•tive
lo•co•mo•tor
lo•cust
lo•cu•tion
lode (ore; cf. *load*)
lode•stone
lodg•ing
lodg•ment
log•a•rithm
log•gia
log•ging

log•ic
log•i•cal
lo•gi•cian
lo•gis•tics
logo•type
log•roll•ing
loll•ing
lol•li•pop
lone (solitary; cf. *loan*)
lone•li•ness
lone•some
long•boat
long•bow
lon•gev•i•ty
long•hand
long•head•ed
long•horn
lon•gi•tude
lon•gi•tu•di•nal
long–range adj.
long run
long•shore•man
long shot
long–suf•fer•ing
long suit
long–term
long–wind•ed
look•ing glass
look•out
loop•hole
loose (unattached; cf. *lose, loss*)
loose–joint•ed
loose–leaf

loose•ly
loos•en
lop
lopped
lop•ping
lop•sid•ed
lo•qua•cious
lo•ran
lord•li•ness
lor•gnette
lose (misplace; cf. *loose, loss*)
loss (something lost; cf. *loose, lose*)
lo•tion
lot•tery
loud–mouthed
loud•speak•er
Lou•i•si•ana
lou•ver
lov•able
love•less
love•li•ness
love•lorn
love•ly
love•mak•ing
love seat
love•sick
low–born
low•boy
low–bred
low–brow
low–down adj.
low•down n.

low·er·case
low·er·class·man
low–grade
low–key
low·land
low–lev·el adj.
low·li·ness
low–mind·ed
low–necked
low–pres·sure
low–pro·file
low–spir·it·ed
low–ten·sion
lox
loy·al·ty
loz·enge
LSD
lu·bri·cant
lu·bri·cate
lu·bri·ca·tion
lu·cid
lu·cid·i·ty
luck·i·er
luck·i·est
luck·i·ly
lucky

lu·cra·tive
lu·cu·bra·tion
lu·di·crous
lug·gage
lu·gu·bri·ous
luke·warm
lul·la·by
lum·ba·go
lum·bar (nerve)
lum·ber (wood)
lum·ber·yard
lu·mi·nance
lu·mi·nary
lu·mi·nous
lu·na·cy
lu·nar
lu·na·tic
lun·cheon
lun·cheon·ette
lunch·room
lu·nette
lurch
lu·rid
lus·cious
lus·ter

lus·ter·ware
lust·ful
lust·i·ly
lus·trous
lusty
Lu·ther·an
lux·u·ri·ant
  (abundant; cf.
  luxurious)
lux·u·ri·ate
lux·u·ri·ous (with
  luxury; cf. *luxuriant*)
lux·u·ry
ly·ce·um
lych–gate
lye (chemical; cf. *lie*)
ly·ing
lym·phat·ic
lynch
lynx (animal; cf. *links*)
ly·on·naise
lyre (harp; cf. *liar*)
lyr·ic
lyr·i·cal
lyr·i·cism

M

ma·ca·bre
mac·ad·am
mac·ad·am·ize

mac·a·ro·ni
mac·a·roon
ma·cé·doine

mac·er·ate
mac·er·a·tion
Ma·chi·a·vel·lian

ma•chic•o•la•tion
ma•chin•able
mach•i•na•tion
ma•chine gun n.
ma•chine–gun v.
ma•chine•like
ma•chine–made
ma•chine–read•able
ma•chin•ery
ma•chine–tooled
ma•chin•ist
ma•chree
mack•er•el
mack•in•tosh
  (raincoat; cf.
  McIntosh)
mac•ro•cosm
mac•ro•eco•nom•ics
ma•cron
mad•cap
mad•den•ing
  (enraging)
made (did make; cf.
  maid)
made–up adj.
mad•house
mad•ness
mad•ri•gal
mael•strom
mag•a•zine
ma•gen•ta
mag•got
mag•ic
ma•gi•cian

mag•is•te•ri•al
mag•is•tra•cy
mag•is•trate
mag•is•tra•ture
Mag•na Char•ta
mag•na•nim•i•ty
mag•nan•i•mous
mag•nate (rich person;
  cf. *magnet*)
mag•ne•sia
mag•ne•sium
mag•net (attracts iron;
  cf. *magnate*)
mag•net•ic
mag•net•ic me•dia
mag•ne•tism
mag•ne•tite
mag•ne•tize
mag•ne•to
mag•ne•tos
mag•ni•fi•ca•tion
mag•nif•i•cence
mag•nif•i•cent
  (splendid; cf.
  munificent)
mag•nif•i•co
mag•ni•fi•er
mag•ni•fy
mag•nil•o•quent
mag•ni•tude
mag•no•lia
mag•num
mag•pie
ma•guey

Mag•yar
ma•ha•ra•ja
ma•hat•ma
ma•hog•a•ny
maid (girl; cf. *made*)
maid•en
maid•en•hair
maid•en•li•ness
maid•en•ly
maid•en name
maid•ser•vant
mail (letters; cf. *male*)
mail•abil•i•ty
mail•able
mail•bag
mail•box
mail car•ri•er
mail clerk
mail•er
mail•man
mail or•der n.
mail–or•der adj.
mail•room
main (chief; cf. *mane*)
Maine
main•frame
main•frame
  com•put•er
main•land
main line n.
main•line v.
main•ly
main•mast
main•sail

main•spring
main•stay
main stem
main•stream
main•tain
main•te•nance
maize (corn; cf. *maze*)
ma•jes•tic
maj•es•ty
ma•jol•i•ca
ma•jor
ma•jor•do•mo
ma•jor•i•ty
ma•jus•cule
make–be•lieve
make•shift
make up v.
make•up n.
make•weight
mak•ing
mal•a•chite
mal•ad•just•ment
mal•ad•min•is•ter
mal•ad•min•is•tra•tion
mal•adroit
mal•a•dy
mal•aise
mal•apert
mal•a•prop•ism
mal•ap•ro•pos
ma•lar•ia
ma•lar•i•al
Ma•lay

mal•con•tent
male (masculine; cf. *mail*)
male•dic•tion
male•fac•tion
male•fac•tor
ma•lef•ic
ma•lef•i•cence
ma•lef•i•cent
ma•lev•o•lence
ma•lev•o•lent
mal•fea•sance
mal•for•ma•tion
mal•formed
mal•func•tion
mal•ice
ma•li•cious (harmful)
ma•lign
ma•lig•nan•cy
ma•lig•nant
ma•lig•ni•ty
ma•lin•ger
ma•lin•ger•er
mal•lard
mal•lea•bil•i•ty
mal•lea•ble
mal•let
mal•nu•tri•tion
mal•odor
mal•odor•ous
mal•po•si•tion
mal•prac•tice
Mal•tese
Mal•thu•sian

malt•ose
mal•treat
malt•ster
mal•ver•sa•tion
mam•mal
mam•mon
mam•moth
man–about–town
man•a•cle
man•age
man•age•able
man•age•ment
man•ag•er
man•a•ge•ri•al
man•a•tee
Man•chu
man•ci•ple
man•da•mus
man•da•rin
man•da•tary (agent; cf. *mandatory*)
man•date
man•da•to•ry (compelling; cf. *mandatary*)
man•di•ble
man•do•lin
man•drel (metal)
man•drill (baboon)
mane (hair; cf. *main*)
man–eat•er
man–eat•ing
ma•nège
ma•neu•ver

man•ful
man•ga•nese
man•ger
man•gi•ly
man•gle
man•go
man•grove
mangy
man•han•dle
man•hat•tan
man•hole
man•hood
man–hour
man•hunt
ma•nia
ma•ni•ac
ma•ni•a•cal
man•i•cure
man•i•cur•ist
man•i•fest
man•i•fes•ta•tion
man•i•fest•ly
man•i•fes•to
man•i•fold
man•i•kin
ma•nila
ma•nip•u•late
ma•nip•u•la•tion
ma•nip•u•la•tive
ma•nip•u•la•tor
ma•nip•u•la•to•ry
Man•i•to•ba
man•i•tou
man•kind

man•like
man•li•ness
man•ly
man–made
man•na
manned
man•ne•quin
man•ner (mode; cf. *manor*)
man•ner•ism
man•nish
man•ni•tol
man–of–war
ma•nom•e•ter
man•or (estate; cf. *manner*)
ma•no•ri•al
man pow•er (1/10 horsepower)
man•pow•er (personnel available)
man•rope
man•sard
man•ser•vant
man•sion
man•slaugh•ter
man•slay•er
man•sue•tude
man•teau
man•tel (shelf; cf. *mantle*)
man•telet
man•tel•piece
man•til•la

man•tle (cloak; cf. *mantel*)
man•trap
man•u•al
man•u•fac•ture
man•u•fac•tur•er
man•u•mis•sion
ma•nure
manu•script
many
many•fold
many–sid•ed
ma•ple
mapped
map•ping
mar•a•schi•no
mar•a•thon
ma•raud
mar•ble
mar•ble•ize
mar•bling
marc
mar•ca•site
March
mar•che•sa fem.
mar•che•se mas.
mar•chio•ness fem.
Mar•co•ni
mar•co•ni•gram
Mar•di Gras
mare's nest
mare's tail
mar•ga•rine
mar•ga•ri•ta

mar•gin
mar•gin•al
mar•gi•na•lia
mar•grave
mari•gold
mar•i•jua•na
mar•i•nade
ma•rine
mar•i•ner
mar•i•o•nette
mar•i•tal (marriage; cf.
   martial)
mar•i•time
mark down v.
mark•down n.
mar•ket
mar•ket•able
mar•ket•ing
mar•ket•place
marks•man
marks•wom•an
mark up v.
mark•up n.
mar•line•spike
mar•ma•lade
mar•mo•set
mar•mot
ma•roon
mar•quee (canopy)
mar•que•try
mar•quis mas.
   (nobleman)
mar•quise fem.
mar•riage

mar•riage•able
mar•row
mar•row•bone
mar•ry
Mar•seilles
mar•shal (officer; cf.
   martial)
mar•shaled
mar•shal•ing
marsh gas
marsh•i•ness
marsh•mal•low
marshy
mar•su•pi•al
mar•ten (furbearing
   animal; cf. *martin*)
mar•tial (warlike; cf.
   marital, marshal)
mar•tial•ly
mar•tian
mar•tin (bird; cf.
   marten)
mar•ti•net
Mar•tin•mas
mar•tyr
mar•tyr•dom
mar•tyr•ol•o•gy
mar•vel
mar•veled
mar•vel•ing
mar•vel•ous
Marx•ian
Mary•land
mas•cot

mas•cu•line
mas•cu•lin•i•ty
mash•er
mash•ie
mask•er
ma•son
Ma•son•ic
Ma•son•ite
ma•son•ry
mas•quer•ade
Mas•sa•chu•setts
mas•sa•cre
mas•sage
mas•seur mas.
mas•seuse fem.
mas•si•cot
mas•sif
mas•sive
mass me•dia
mass–pro•duce
massy
mas•ter
mas•ter-at–arms
mas•ter•ful
mas•ter key
mas•ter•mind
mas•ter of cer•e•
   mo•nies
mas•ter•piece
mas•ter plan
mas•ter's de•gree
mas•ter ser•geant
mas•ter•ship
mas•ter•stroke

mas•ter•work
mas•tery
mast•head
mas•ti•cate
mas•ti•ca•tion
mas•tiff
mast•odon
mas•toid
mat•a•dor
match•board
match•book
match•less
match•lock
match•mak•er
match play
match•stick
match•wood
ma•te•ri•al (substance;
   cf. *matériel*)
ma•te•ri•al•ism
ma•te•ri•al•ist
ma•te•ri•al•is•tic
ma•te•ri•al•i•ty
ma•te•ri•al•iza•tion
ma•te•ri•al•ize
ma•te•ri•al•ly
ma•te•ria med•i•ca
ma•té•ri•el
   (equipment; cf.
   material)
ma•ter•nal
ma•ter•ni•ty
math•e•mat•i•cal

math•e•ma•ti•cian
math•e•mat•ics
mat•i•nee
ma•tri•arch
ma•tri•ar•chate
ma•tri•ar•chy
ma•tri•cide
ma•tric•u•lant
ma•tric•u•late
ma•tric•u•la•tion
mat•ri•mo•nial
mat•ri•mo•ny
ma•trix
ma•tron
ma•tron•ize
ma•tron•ly
mat•ter
mat•ter–of–fact
mat•ting
mat•tock
mat•tress
mat•u•rate
mat•u•ra•tion
ma•ture
ma•ture•ly
ma•ture•ness
ma•tu•ri•ty
ma•tu•ti•nal
mat•zo
maud•lin
maul•stick
mau•so•le•um
mauve

mav•er•ick
mawk•ish
max•il•la
max•il•lary
max•im
max•i•mal
max•i•mize
max•i•mum
may•be
May Day (May 1)
May•day (a signal)
may•flow•er
may•hem
may•on•naise
may•or
may•or•al•ty
may•pole
maze (puzzle; cf.
   maize)
ma•zur•ka
mazy
Mc•In•tosh (apple; cf.
   mackintosh)
mead•ow
mead•ow•lark
mea•ger
meal•time
meal•worm
mealy•mouthed
mean (stingy; cf. *mien*)
me•an•der
mean•ing•less
mean•ly

mean•ness
mean•time
mean•while
mea•sles
mea•sly
mea•sur•able
mea•sure
mea•sured
mea•sure•less
mea•sure•ment
mea•sur•er
meat (food; cf. *meet,*
    mete)
me•atus
me•chan•ic
me•chan•i•cal
mech•a•ni•cian
me•chan•ics
mech•a•nism
mech•a•nist
med•al (award; cf.
    meddle)
med•al•ist
me•dal•lion
med•dle (interfere; cf.
    medal)
med•dle•some
me•dia (sing.: *medium*)
me•di•al
me•di•an
me•di•ate
me•di•a•tion
me•di•a•tive

me•di•a•tor
me•di•a•to•ry
med•i•ca•ble
med•ic•aid
med•i•cal
me•di•ca•ment
medi•care
med•i•cate
med•i•ca•tion
me•dic•i•na•ble
me•dic•i•nal
med•i•cine
med•i•cine ball
med•i•cine man
me•di•eval
me•di•eval•ism
me•di•eval•ist
me•di•o•cre
me•di•oc•ri•ty
med•i•tate
med•i•ta•tion
med•i•ta•tive
Med•i•ter•ra•nean
me•di•um (pl.: *media*)
me•di•um•is•tic
med•lar
med•ley
meer•schaum
meet (encounter; cf.
    meat, mete)
meet•ing
meet•ing•house
mega•byte

mega•cy•cle
meg•a•lo•ma•nia
mega•phone
Mei•ster•sing•er
mel•an•cho•lia
mel•an•chol•ic
mel•an•choly
Mel•a•ne•sian
mé•lange
mel•a•nin
mel•a•nism
me•lee
me•lio•rate
me•lio•ra•tion
me•lio•ra•tive
me•lio•ra•tor
me•lio•rism
mel•lif•lu•ous
mel•low
me•lo•de•on
me•lod•ic
me•lo•di•ous
mel•o•dist
mel•o•dize
melo•dra•ma
melo•dra•mat•ic
melo•dra•ma•tist
mel•o•dy
mel•on
melt•able
mem•ber
mem•ber•ship
mem•brane

mem•bra•nous

me•men•to

mem•oir

mem•o•ra•ble

mem•o•ran•dum

   (pl.: *memoranda* or

   memorandums)

me•mo•ri•al

me•mo•ri•al•ist

me•mo•ri•al•ize

mem•o•rize

mem•o•ry

men•ace

mé•nage

me•nag•er•ie

men•da•cious

men•dac•i•ty

Men•de•lian

men•di•can•cy

men•di•cant

me•nial

men•in•gi•tis

me•nis•cus

Men•no•nite

meno•pause

men•ses

men•stru•ate

men•tal

men•tal•i•ty

men•tal•ly

men•thol

men•tion

men•tion•er

men•tor

menu

Meph•is•toph•e•les

me•phi•tis

mer•can•tile

mer•can•til•ism

mer•ce•nary

mer•cer

mer•cer•ize

mer•chan•dise

mer•chant

mer•chant•able

mer•chant•man

mer•ci•ful

mer•ci•less

mer•cu•ri•al

mer•cu•ric

mer•cu•rous

mer•cu•ry

mer•cy

mere•ly

mer•e•tri•cious

mer•gan•ser

merge

mer•gence

merg•er

me•rid•i•an

me•rid•i•o•nal

me•ringue

me•ri•no

mer•it

mer•i•to•ri•ous

mer•lin

mer•maid

mer•ri•ly

mer•ri•ment

mer•ry

mer•ry–an•drew

mer•ry–go–round

mer•ry•mak•ing

me•sa

mesh•work

me•si•al

mes•mer•ic

mes•mer•ism

mes•mer•ize

me•son

mes•quite

mes•sage

mes•sen•ger

mes•si•ah

mes•si•an•ic

Messrs. (sing.: *Mr.*)

messy

me•tab•o•lism

meta•car•pal

meta•car•pus

met•al (iron; cf. *mettle*)

me•tal•lic

met•al•lif•er•ous

met•al•log•ra•phy

met•al•loid

met•al•lur•gi•cal

met•al•lur•gy

met•al•work

meta•mor•phic

meta·mor·phism

meta·mor·phose

meta·mor·pho·ses pl.

meta·mor·pho·sis sing.

met·a·phor

met·a·phor·i·cal

meta·phys·ic

meta·phy·si·cian

meta·phys·ics

me·tas·ta·sis

meta·tar·sal

meta·tar·sus

mete (measure; cf. *meat, meet*)

me·te·or

me·te·or·ic

me·te·or·ite

me·te·or·o·graph

me·te·or·oid

me·te·o·ro·log·i·cal

me·te·o·rol·o·gist

me·te·o·rol·o·gy

me·ter

me·ter maid

meth·a·done

meth·ane

me·theg·lin

meth·od

me·thod·i·cal

meth·od·ist

meth·od·ize

meth·od·ol·o·gy

me·tic·u·los·i·ty

me·tic·u·lous

mé·tier

me·ton·y·my

met·ric

met·ri·cal

met·ri·ca·tion

met·ri·fi·ca·tion

me·trol·o·gy

met·ro·nome

me·trop·o·lis

met·ro·pol·i·tan

met·tle (spirit; cf. *metal*)

met·tle·some

mews (stables; cf. *muse*)

Mex·i·can

mez·za·nine

mez·zo–so·pra·no

mez·zo·tint

mi·as·ma

Mich·ael·mas

Mich·i·gan

mi·crobe

mi·cro·bi·al

mi·cro·bic

mi·cro·bi·ol·o·gy

mi·cro·com·put·er

mi·cro·cosm

mi·cro·fiche

mi·cro·film

mi·cro·form

mi·cro·graph

mi·cro·groove

mi·crom·e·ter

mi·cron

mi·cro·or·gan·ism

mi·cro·phone

mi·cro·pro·ces·sor

mi·cro·scope

mi·cro·scop·ic

mi·cro·scop·i·cal·ly

mi·cro·sec·ond

mi·cro·wave

mid·air

mid·brain

mid·day

mid·dle

mid·dle–aged

mid·dle·brow

mid·dle class n.

mid·dle–class adj.

mid·dle·man

mid·dle·weight

mid·dling

midg·et

mid·iron

mid·land

mid–life

mid·most

mid·night

mid·range

mid·riff

mid·ship·man

mid•size

mid•sum•mer

mid•term

mid•way

mid•week

mid•west

mid•west•ern•er

mid•wife

mid•win•ter

mid•year

mien (bearing; cf. *mean*)

miff

might (strength; cf. *mite*)

might•i•ly

might•i•ness

mighty

mi•gnon•ette

mi•graine

mi•grate

mi•gra•tion

mi•gra•to•ry

mi•ka•do

mi•la•dy

milch

mil•dew

mild•ly

mile•age

mile•post

mile•stone

mil•i•tance

mil•i•tan•cy

mil•i•tant

mil•i•ta•rism

mil•i•ta•rist

mil•i•ta•ris•tic

mil•i•ta•rize

mil•i•tary

mil•i•tate

mi•li•tia

mi•li•tia•man

milk choc•o•late

milk•er

milk glass

milk•i•ness

milk leg

milk–liv•ered

milk•maid

milk•man

milk punch

milk shake

milk snake

milk•sop

milk sug•ar

milk toast n.

milk–toast adj.

milk tooth

milk•weed

milky

mill•board

mill•dam

mil•le•nar•i•an

mil•le•na•ry (1000th anniversary; cf. *millinery*)

mil•len•ni•al

mil•len•ni•um

mill•er

mil•let

mil•li•am•pere

mil•li•gram

mil•li•me•ter

mil•li•ner

mil•li•nery (hats; cf. *millenary*)

mill•ing

mil•lion

mil•lion•aire

mil•lionth

mil•li•sec•ond

mil•li•volt

mil•li•watt

mill•pond

mill•race

mill•stone

mill•stream

mill wheel

mill•wright

Mil•ton•ic

mim•eo•graph

mi•me•sis

mi•met•ic

mim•ic

mim•icked

mim•ick•ing

mim•ic•ry

mi•mo•sa

min•a•ret

mi•na•to•ry

mince•meat

mince pie

minc•er

minc•ing•ly

mind (brain; cf. *mined*)

mind–bog•gling

mind•er

mind•ful

mind read•er

mined (dug out; cf. *mind*)

min•er (a mine worker; cf. *minor*)

min•er•al

min•er•al•ize

min•er•al•og•i•cal

min•er•al•o•gist

min•er•al•o•gy

Mi•ner•va

min•gle

min•gling

min•ia•ture

mini•com•put•er

mini•course

min•i•mal

min•i•mi•za•tion

min•i•mize

min•i•mum

min•ing

min•ion

mini•state

min•is•ter (clergyman; cf. *minster*)

min•is•te•ri•al

min•is•trant

min•is•tra•tion

min•is•try

min•i•um

min•i•ver

min•ne•sing•er

Min•ne•so•ta

min•now

mi•nor (underage; cf. *miner*)

mi•nor•i•ty

Mi•no•taur

min•ster (church; cf. *minister*)

min•strel•sy

mint•age

min•u•end

min•u•et

mi•nus

min•ute n. (60 seconds)

mi•nute adj. (small)

min•ute hand

mi•nute•ly (in detail)

min•ute•man

mi•o•sis (pl.: *mioses*)

mir•a•cle

mi•rac•u•lous

mi•rage

mir•ror

mirth•ful

mirth•less

mis•ad•ven•ture

mis•aligned

mis•al•li•ance

mis•an•thrope

mis•an•throp•ic

mis•an•thro•py

mis•ap•pli•ca•tion

mis•ap•pre•hen•sion

mis•ap•pro•pri•ate

mis•be•got•ten

mis•be•have

mis•be•lief

mis•cal•cu•late

mis•car•riage

mis•car•ry

mis•ce•ge•na•tion

mis•cel•la•nea

mis•cel•la•neous

mis•cel•la•ny

mis•chance

mis•chief

mis•chie•vous

mis•com•mu•ni•ca•tion

mis•con•cep•tion

mis•con•duct

mis•con•struc•tion

mis•con•strue

mis•cre•ant

mis•cue

mis•deal

mis•de•mean•or

mis•di•rect

mi•ser

mis•er•a•ble

mi•se•re•re

mi•ser•li•ness

mi•ser•ly

mis•ery

mis•fea•sance

mis•file

mis•fire

mis•fit

mis•for•tune

mis•giv•ing

mis•gov•ern

mis•guide

mis•hap

mis•in•form

mis•in•ter•pret

mis•in•ter•pre•ta•tion

mis•join•der

mis•judge

mis•lay

mis•lead

mis•man•age

mis•no•mer

mi•sog•a•my

mi•sog•y•nist

mi•sol•o•gy

mis•place

mis•print

mis•pri•sion

mis•pro•nounce

mis•quo•ta•tion

mis•read

mis•reck•on

mis•rep•re•sent

mis•rep•re•sen•ta•tion

mis•rule

mis•sal (book; cf. *missile, missive*)

mis•sile (weapon; cf. *missal, missive*)

miss•ing

mis•sion

mis•sion•ary

Mis•sis•sip•pi

mis•sive (letter; cf. *missal, missile*)

Mis•sou•ri

mis•spell

mis•state

mis•tak•able

mis•take

mis•tak•en

mist•i•ness

mis•tle•toe

mis•took

mis•tral

mis•treat

mis•treat•ment

mis•tress

mis•tri•al

mis•trust

misty

mis•un•der•stand

mis•un•der•stand•ing

mis•us•age

mis•use

mite (something tiny; cf. *might*)

mi•ter

mit•i•ga•ble

mit•i•gate

mit•i•ga•tion

mit•i•ga•tive

mit•i•ga•tor

mi•tral

mit•ten

mit•ti•mus

mix•er

mix•ture

mix–up

miz•zen•mast

mne•mon•ic adj.

mne•mon•ics n.

Mo•ab•ite

moan (groan; cf. *mown*)

moat (ditch; cf. *mote*)

mob•cap

mo•bile

mo•bil•i•ty

mo•bi•li•za•tion

mo•bi•lize

mob•oc•ra•cy

mob•ocrat•ic

moc•ca•sin

mo•cha

mock•er

mock•ery

mock•ing•bird

mock•ing•ly

mock–up

mod•al (of a mode; cf. *model*)

mo•dal•i•ties

mode (fashion; cf. *mood*)

mod•el (pattern; cf. *modal*)

mod•eled

mod•el•ing

mo•dem

mod•er•ate

mod•er•a•tion

mod•er•a•tor

mod•ern

mod•ern•ism

mod•ern•ist

mo•der•ni•ty

mod•ern•iza•tion

mod•ern•ize

mod•est

mod•es•ty

mo•di•cum

mod•i•fi•able

mod•i•fi•ca•tion

mod•i•fi•er

mod•i•fy

mod•ish

mo•diste

mod•u•lar

mod•u•late

mod•u•la•tion

mod•u•la•tor

mod•ule

mod•u•lus

mo•dus vi•ven•di

mo•hair

Mo•ham•med•an

Mo•hawk

moi•ety

moist

moist•en

moist•en•er

mois•ture

mo•lar

mo•las•ses

mold

mold•able

mold•er

mold•i•ness

mold•ing

moldy

mo•lec•u•lar

mol•e•cule

mole•hill

mole•skin

mo•lest

mo•les•ta•tion

mol•li•fi•ca•tion

mol•li•fy

mol•lusk

mol•ly•cod•dle

mol•ten

mo•lyb•de•num

mo•ment

mo•men•tari•ly

mo•men•tary

mo•ment•ly

mo•men•tous

mo•men•tum

mon•arch

mon•ar•chism

mon•ar•chy

mon•as•te•ri•al

mon•as•tery

mo•nas•tic

mo•nas•ti•cism

mon•au•ral

Mon•day

mon•e•tary

mon•e•tize

mon•ey

mon•ey•bags

mon•eyed

mon•ey•lend•er

mon•ey–mak•er

mon•eys

mon•ey•wise

mon•ger

Mon•gol

Mon•go•lian

mon•grel

mon•ies

mo•ni•tion

mon•i•tor

mon•i•tor•ship

mon•i•to•ry

mon•i•tress

monk•ery

mon•key

mon•keys

mon•key•shine

mon•key wrench

monk•ish

mono•chro•mat•ic

mono•chrome

mon•o•cle
mo•noc•ra•cy
mon•oc•u•lar
mon•o•dy
mo•nog•a•mist
mo•nog•a•mous
mo•nog•a•my
mono•gram
mono•graph
mono•lith
mono•logue
mono•logu•ist
mono•ma•nia
mono•me•tal•lic
mono•met•al•lism
Mo•non•ga•he•la
mono•plane
mo•nop•o•list
mo•nop•o•lis•tic
mo•nop•o•li•za•tion
mo•nop•o•lize
mo•nop•o•ly
mono•rail
mono•syl•lab•ic
mono•syl•la•ble
mono•tone
mo•not•o•nous
mo•not•o•ny
Mono•type
mon•ox•ide
mon•sei•gneur
mon•sieur
mon•si•gnor
mon•soon

mon•ster
mon•strance
mon•stros•i•ty
mon•strous
mon•tage
Mon•tana
month•ly
mon•u•ment
mon•u•men•tal
mood (feeling; cf. *mode*)
mood•i•ly
mood•i•ness
moody
moon•beam
moon–blind
moon•fish
moon•light
moon•light•er
moon•lit
moon•rise
moon•shine
moon•shin•er
moon•stone
moon•struck
moor•age
moor•ing
Moor•ish
moose (animal; cf. *mouse, mousse*)
mop•board
mop•ping
mop up v.
mop–up n.

mo•raine
mor•al (ethical)
mo•rale (attitude)
mor•al•ism
mor•al•ist
mo•ral•i•ty (virtue; cf. *mortality*)
mor•al•iza•tion
mor•al•ize
mo•rass
mor•a•to•ri•um
Mo•ra•vi•an
mor•bid
mor•bid•i•ty
mor•dant (dyeing term)
mor•dent (musical term)
more or less
more•over
mo•res
mor•ga•nat•ic
Mor•gan•ton N.C.
Mor•gan•town W.Va.
mor•i•bund
Mor•mon
morn•ing (forenoon; cf. *mourning*)
morn•ing glo•ry
Mo•roc•co (country)
mo•roc•co (leather)
mo•ron
mo•rose
mo•rose•ness

Mor•pheus
mor•phine
mor•ris chair
mor•row
mor•sel
mor•tal
mor•tal•i•ty (death
　rate; cf. *morality*)
mor•tar
mor•tar•board
mort•gage
mort•gag•ee
mort•gag•or
mor•ti•cian
mor•ti•fi•ca•tion
mor•ti•fy
mor•tise
mor•tu•ary
mo•sa•ic
Mo•ses
mo•sey
Mos•lem
mos•qui•to
moss•back
moss–grown
most•ly
mote (speak; cf. *moat*)
mo•tel
moth•ball
moth–eat•en
moth•er
moth•er•hood
moth•er–in–law
moth•er•land

moth•er•less
moth•er•li•ness
moth•er•ly
moth•er–of–pearl
moth•proof
mo•tif
mo•tion
mo•tion•less
mo•ti•vate
mo•ti•va•tion
mo•tive
mot•ley
mo•tor
mo•tor•bike
mo•tor•boat
mo•tor bus
mo•tor•cade
mo•tor•car
mo•tor•cy•cle
mo•tor•drome
mo•tor home
mo•tor•ist
mo•tor•ize
mo•tor•man
mo•tor•truck
mot•tle
mot•to
mount•able
moun•tain
moun•tain•eer
moun•tain•ous
moun•tain•side
moun•te•bank
Mount•ie

mount•ing
mourn•ful
mourn•ing (grieving;
　cf. *morning*)
mouse (animal; cf.
　moose, mousse)
mouse—ear
mous•er
mouse•trap
mousse (food; cf.
　moose, mouse)
mous•tache
mouth•ful
mouth•piece
mouth–to–mouth
mov•abil•i•ty
mov•able
mov•able•ness
move•ment
mov•ie
mov•ies
mov•ing
mow•er
mown (cut down; cf.
　moan)
moz•zet•ta
Mr. (pl.: *Messrs.*)
Mrs. (pl.: *Mesdames*)
Ms. (pl.: *Mses.* or *Mss.*)
mu•ci•lage
mu•ci•lag•i•nous
muck•rake
muck•rak•er
mu•cous adj.

mu•cus n.

mud•di•ly

mud•di•ness

mud•dle

mud•dy

mud•guard

mud•sling•er

mu•ez•zin

muf•fin

muf•fle

muf•fler

muf•ti

mugged

mug•ger

mug•gi•ness

mug•ging

mug•wump

mu•lat•to

mul•ber•ry

mulct

mu•le•teer

mul•ish

mull•er

mul•lion

mul•ti•dis•ci•plin•ary

mul•ti•far•i•ous

mul•ti•form

Mul•ti•graph

mul•ti•lat•er•al

Mul•ti•lith

mul•ti•me•dia

mul•ti•mil•lion•aire

mul•ti•na•tion•al

mul•ti•ped

mul•ti•ple

mul•ti•ple scle•ro•sis

mul•ti•plex

mul•ti•pli•able

mul•ti•pli•cand

mul•ti•pli•ca•tion

mul•ti•pli•ca•tive

mul•ti•plic•i•ty

mul•ti•pli•er

mul•ti•ply

mul•ti•pro•cess•ing

mul•ti•ra•cial

mul•ti•sea•son

mul•ti•tude

mul•ti•tu•di•nous

mum•bo jum•bo

mum•mery

mum•mi•fy

mum•my

mun•dane

mu•nic•i•pal

mu•nic•i•pal•i•ty

mu•nic•i•pal•ize

mu•nif•i•cence

mu•nif•i•cent

(generous; cf.
magnificent)

mu•ni•ment

mu•ni•tion

mu•ral

mur•der

mur•der•er

mur•der•ous

murk•i•ly

murk•i•ness

murky

mur•mur

mur•mur•ing

mur•mur•ous

mus•ca•dine

mus•ca•tel

mus•cle (of body; cf.
mussel, muzzle)

mus•cle–bound

mus•cu•lar

mus•cu•la•ture

muse (meditate; cf.
mews)

mu•se•um

mush•room

mushy

mu•sic

mu•si•cal

mu•si•cale

mu•si•cian

mu•si•col•o•gist

mus•ing

musk deer

mus•ket

mus•ke•teer

mus•ket•ry

musk•mel•on

musk–ox

musk•rat

musky

Mus•lim (religion)

mus•lin (cloth)

mus•sel (shellfish; cf. *muscle, muzzle*)

mus•tang

mus•tard (plant; cf. *mustered*)

mus•ter

mus•tered (assembled; cf. *mustard*)

must•i•ness

musty

mu•ta•bil•i•ty

mu•ta•ble

mu•tant

mu•tate

mu•ta•tion

mu•ta•tive

mute•ness

mu•ti•late

mu•ti•la•tion

mu•ti•neer

mu•ti•nous

mu•ti•ny

mut•ism

mut•ter

mut•ton

mut•ton•chops n.

mu•tu•al

mu•tu•al•i•ty

mu•tu•al•ly

muz•zle (mouth; cf. *muscle, mussel*)

my•al•gia

my•col•o•gy

my•o•pia

my•o•pic

myr•i•ad

myr•mi•don

myrrh

my•self

mys•te•ri•ous

mys•tery

mys•tic

mys•ti•cal

mys•ti•cism

mys•ti•fi•ca•tion

mys•ti•fy

mys•tique

myth•i•cal

myth•o•log•i•cal

my•thol•o•gy

na•cre

na•cre•ous

na•dir

nain•sook

na•ive

na•ive•té

na•ked

nam•by–pam•by

name•able

name•less

name•ly

name•plate

name•sake

nan•keen

nano•sec•ond

na•palm

na•pery

naph•tha

nap•kin

Na•po•le•on•ic

nap•per

nap•ping

nar•cis•sism

nar•cis•sus

nar•co•sis

nar•cot•ic

nar•co•tize

nar•rate

nar•ra•tion

nar•ra•tive

nar•ra•tor
nar•row
nar•row•ly
nar•row–mind•ed
nar•row•ness
na•sal
na•sal•i•ty
na•sal•ize
na•sal•ly
na•scent
nas•ti•ly
nas•ti•ness
nas•tur•tium
nas•ty
na•tal
na•tant
na•ta•tion
na•ta•to•ri•al
na•ta•to•ri•um
na•ta•to•ry
na•tion
na•tion•al
na•tion•al•ism
na•tion•al•i•ty
na•tion•al•ize
na•tion•al•iz•er
na•tion•al•ly
na•tion•wide
na•tive
na•tive•ly
na•tive•ness
na•tiv•ism
na•tiv•i•ty
nat•ty

nat•u•ral
nat•u•ral•ism
nat•u•ral•ist
nat•u•ral•is•tic
nat•u•ral•iza•tion
nat•u•ral•ize
nat•u•ral•ly
nat•u•ral•ness
na•ture
naugh•ti•ly
naugh•ti•ness
naugh•ty
nau•sea
nau•se•ate
nau•seous
nau•ti•cal
nau•ti•lus
na•val (of navy)
nave (of church; cf. *knave*)
na•vel (of abdomen)
nav•i•ga•ble
nav•i•gate
nav•i•ga•tion
nav•i•ga•tor
na•vy
na•vy yard
nay (no; cf. *née, neigh*)
Naz•a•rene
Ne•an•der•thal
Ne•a•pol•i•tan
near•by
near•ly
near•ness

near•sight•ed
neat•ly
neat•ness
Ne•bras•ka
neb•u•la sing.
neb•u•lar
neb•u•las pl.
neb•u•lize
neb•u•los•i•ty
neb•u•lous
nec•es•sar•i•ly
nec•es•sary
ne•ces•si•tate
ne•ces•si•tous
ne•ces•si•ty
neck•er•chief
neck•ing
neck•lace
neck•line
neck•piece
neck•tie
neck•wear
nec•ro•log•i•cal
ne•crol•o•gist
ne•crol•o•gy
nec•ro•man•cy
ne•crop•o•lis
ne•cro•sis
nec•tar
nec•tar•ine
née (born; cf. *nay, neigh*)
need (require; cf. *knead*)

need•ful
need•i•est
need•i•ness
nee•dle
nee•dle•fish
nee•dle•point
need•less
nee•dle•wom•an
nee•dle•work
needy
ne'er–do–well
ne•far•i•ous
ne•gate
ne•ga•tion
neg•a•tive
ne•glect
ne•glect•ful
neg•li•gee
neg•li•gence
neg•li•gent
neg•li•gi•ble
ne•go•tia•bil•i•ty
ne•go•tia•ble
ne•go•ti•ate
ne•go•ti•a•tion
ne•go•ti•a•tor
Ne•gro
Ne•groes
neigh (of horse; cf. *nay, née*)
neigh•bor
neigh•bor•hood
neigh•bor•ing
neigh•bor•ly

nei•ther
nem•a•tode
nem•e•sis
neo•lith•ic
ne•ol•o•gism
ne•ol•o•gist
ne•ol•o•gy
neo•phyte
neo•plasm
ne•o•ter•ic
ne•pen•the
neph•ew
ne•phri•tis
nep•o•tism
Nep•tune
Ne•ro•ni•an
nerve
nerve•less
nerve–rack•ing
ner•vous
nervy
ne•science
ne•scient
nest egg
nes•tle
nes•tling v.
nest•ling n.
neth•er•most
net•ting
net•tle
net•work
neu•ral
neu•ral•gia
neur•as•the•nia

neu•ri•tis
neu•rol•o•gist
neu•rol•o•gy
neu•ron
neu•ro•sis
neu•rot•ic
neu•ter
neu•tral
neu•tral•i•ty
neu•tral•iza•tion
neu•tral•ize
neu•tral•ly
neu•tron
Ne•va•da
nev•er
nev•er•the•less
new (recent; cf. *gnu, knew*)
New•ark N.J., N.Y., Ohio
new•born
New Bruns•wick
new•com•er
new•el
new•fan•gled
new–fash•ioned
New•found•land
New Hamp•shire
New Jer•sey
new•ly
new•mar•ket
New Mex•i•co
new•ness
news•boy

news•break
news•cast
news•cast•er
news•girl
news•hound
news•let•ter
news•man
news•mon•ger
news•pa•per
news•pa•per•man
news•pa•per•
   wom•an
news•print
news•reel
news re•lease
news•stand
news•wom•an
news•wor•thy
newsy
New Year
New York
next door adv.
next–door adj.
nib•ble
nice•ly
Ni•cene
nice•ness
nice•ty
niche
nick
nick•el
nick•el•if•er•ous
nick•el•ode•on
nick•er

nick•name
nic•o•tine
niece
nig•gard
nig•gard•ly
nig•gling
night (darkness; cf.
   knight)
night and day
night•cap
night•clothes
night•club
night•dress
night•fall
night•gown
night•hawk
night•in•gale
night key
night latch
night let•ter
night•long
night•ly
night•mare
night owl
night rid•er
night–robe
night•shade
night shift
night•shirt
night•stick
night ta•ble
night•time
night•walk•er
ni•gres•cent

ni•gri•tude
ni•hil•ism
ni•hil•ist
ni•hil•is•tic
Ni•ke
nim•ble
nim•bus
Nim•rod
nin•com•poop
nine•pin
nine•teen
nine•teenth
nine•ti•eth
nine•ty
nin•ny
ninth
nip•per
nip•ping
nip•ple
Nip•pon•ese
nir•va•na
ni•sei
ni•trate
ni•tric
ni•tride
ni•tri•fi•ca•tion
ni•tri•fy
ni•trite
ni•tro•gen
ni•trog•e•nous
ni•tro•glyc•er•in
ni•trous
nit•ty–grit•ty
ni•zam

No•ah
no•bil•i•ty
no•ble•man
no•ble•wom•an
no•bly
no•body
noct•am•bu•list
noc•tur•nal
noc•turne
nod•ded
nod•ding
nod•u•lar
nod•ule
no–fault
noise•less
nois•i•ly
noi•some
noisy
no•mad
no•mad•ic
no•mad•ism
nom de guerre
nom de plume
no•men•cla•ture
nom•i•nal
nom•i•nal•ly
nom•i•nate
nom•i•na•tion
nom•i•na•tive
nom•i•na•tor
nom•i•nee
non•agen•da
non•bio•de•grad•
  able

non•cha•lance
non•cha•lant
non•com•ba•tant
non•com•mis•sioned
non•com•mit•tal
non•com•pet•i•tive
non•com•pli•ance
non com•pos men•
  tis
non•con•duc•tor
non•con•form•ist
non•con•for•mi•ty
non•co•op•er•a•tion
non•de•script
non•dis•crim•i•na•
  tion
non•en•ti•ty
non•es•sen•tial
none•the•less
non•ex•empt
non•ex•is•tent
non•fea•sance
non•fic•tion
non•im•pact
  print•er
non•in•ter•ven•tion
non•join•der
non•me•tal•lic
non•pa•reil
non•par•ti•san
non•pay•ment
non•prof•it
non•re•im•burs•able
non•res•i•dent

non•re•sis•tance
non•re•sis•tant
non•re•stric•tive
non•re•turn•able
non•sched•uled
non•sense
non•sen•si•cal
non se•qui•tur
non•sked
non•skid
non•spe•cif•ic
non•stan•dard
non•stick
non•stop
non•suit
non•sup•port
non•union
non•ver•bal
non•vi•o•lence
non•vi•o•lent
non•vot•ing
noo•dle
noon•day
noon•tide
noon•time
nor•mal
nor•mal•i•ty
nor•mal•iza•tion
nor•mal•ize
nor•mal•ly
nor•ma•tive
Norse•man
North Car•o•li•na
North Da•ko•ta

north•east
north•east•er•ly
north•east•ern
north•east•ward
north•er•ly
north•ern
North•ern•er
north•land
north•ward
north•west
north•west•er•ly
north•west•ern
Nor•we•gian
nose•bleed
nose cone
nose–dive v.
nose•dive n.
nose drops
nose•gay
nose•piece
nose ring
nose•wheel
no–show
no•sog•ra•phy
no•sol•o•gy
nos•tal•gia
nos•tal•gic
nos•tril
nos•trum
not (negative; cf. *knot*)
no•ta•bil•i•ty
no•ta•ble
no•ta•ble•ness
no•ta•bly

no•tar•i•al
no•ta•ri•za•tion
no•ta•rize
no•ta•ry
no•ta•tion
note•book
not•ed
note•less
note•pa•per
note•tak•er n.
note–tak•ing n.
note•wor•thi•ness
note•wor•thy
noth•ing
noth•ing•ness
no•tice
no•tice•able
no•ti•fi•ca•tion
no•ti•fy
no•tion
no•to•ri•e•ty
no•to•ri•ous
not•with•stand•ing
nour•ish
nour•ish•ment
No•va Sco•tia
no•va•tion
nov•el
nov•el•ette
nov•el•is•tic
nov•el•ist
nov•el•ize
no•vel•la
nov•el•ty

No•vem•ber
no•ve•na
nov•ice
no•vi•ti•ate
No•vo•cain
now•a•days
no•way
no•ways
no•where
no–win
no•wise
nox•ious
noz•zle
nu•ance
nu•cle•ar
nu•cle•ate
nu•cle•ation
nu•cle•us
nu•di•ty
nu•ga•to•ry
nug•get
nui•sance
nul•li•fi•ca•tion
nul•li•fi•er
nul•li•fy
num•ber
num•ber•less
numb•ness
nu•mer•al
nu•mer•ate
nu•mer•a•tion
nu•mer•a•tor
nu•mer•i•cal
nu•mer•ol•o•gy

nu·mer·ous
nu·mis·mat·ic
nu·mis·ma·tist
num·skull
nun·cu·pa·tive
nun·nery
nup·tial
nurse·maid
nurs·ery
nurs·ery·man
nurs·ling

nur·ture
nut·crack·er
nut·meg
nut·pick
nu·tria
nu·tri·ent
nu·tri·ment
nu·tri·tion
nu·tri·tion·al
nu·tri·tion·ist
nu·tri·tious

nu·tri·tious·ly
nu·tri·tious·ness
nu·tri·tive
nut·shell
nut·ti·ness
nut·ty
nuz·zle
nuz·zling
ny·lon
nymph

oa·kum
oar (of a boat; cf. *or,* *ore*)
oar·lock
oars·man
oa·ses pl.
oa·sis sing.
oat·cake
oat·meal
ob·bli·ga·to
ob·du·ra·cy
ob·du·rate
obe·di·ence
obe·di·ent
obei·sance
obe·lisk
obese

obe·si·ty
obey
ob·fus·cate
ob·fus·ca·tion
obi·ter dic·tum
obit·u·ary
ob·ject
ob·jec·tion
ob·jec·tion·able
ob·jec·tive
ob·jec·tive·ly
ob·jec·tive·ness
ob·jec·tiv·i·ty
ob·jet d'art
ob·jur·ga·tion
ob·la·tion
ob·li·gate

ob·li·ga·tion
oblig·a·to·ry
oblige
oblig·ing
oblique
obliq·ui·ty
oblit·er·ate
oblit·er·a·tion
obliv·i·on
obliv·i·ous
ob·long
ob·lo·quy
ob·nox·ious
oboe
obo·ist
ob·scene
ob·scen·i·ty

ob·scur·ant
ob·scu·ra·tion
ob·scure
ob·scure·ness
ob·scu·ri·ty
ob·se·quies
ob·se·qui·ous
ob·se·quy
ob·serv·able
ob·ser·vance
ob·ser·vant
ob·ser·va·tion
ob·ser·va·tion·al
ob·ser·va·to·ry
ob·serve
ob·serv·er
ob·sess
ob·ses·sion
ob·ses·sive
ob·so·lesce
ob·so·les·cence
ob·so·les·cent
ob·so·lete
ob·sta·cle
ob·stet·ri·cal
ob·ste·tri·cian
ob·stet·rics
ob·sti·na·cy
ob·sti·nate
ob·strep·er·ous
ob·struct
ob·struc·tion
ob·struc·tion·ist
ob·struc·tive

ob·tain
ob·tain·able
ob·trud·er
ob·tru·sion
ob·tru·sive
ob·tu·rate
ob·tuse
ob·verse
ob·vi·ate
ob·vi·ous
oc·a·ri·na
oc·ca·sion
oc·ca·sion·al
oc·ca·sion·al·ly
Oc·ci·dent
oc·ci·den·tal
Oc·ci·den·tal·ism
oc·ci·den·tal·ize
oc·cip·i·tal
oc·ci·put
oc·clude
oc·clu·sion
oc·cult
oc·cul·ta·tion
oc·cult·ism
oc·cult·ist
oc·cu·pan·cy
oc·cu·pant
oc·cu·pa·tion·al
oc·cu·py
oc·cur
oc·curred
oc·cur·rence
oc·cur·ring

ocean·go·ing
oce·an·ic
ocean·og·ra·pher
o'clock
oc·ta·gon
oc·tag·o·nal
oc·tan·gu·lar
oc·tave
oc·ta·vo
Oc·to·ber
oc·to·ge·nar·i·an
oc·to·pus
oc·u·lar
oc·u·list
odd·i·ty
odd·ly
odd·ness
odds and ends
ode (poem; cf. *owed*)
odi·ous
odi·um
odor
odor·if·er·ous
odor·less
odor·ous
Odys·seus
od·ys·sey
of·fal
off and on
off–bal·ance adj.,
    adv.
off·beat
off·cast
off–cen·ter

off–col•or
of•fend
of•fend•er
of•fense
of•fen•sive
of•fer
of•fer•ing
of•fer•to•ry
off•hand
off–hour
of•fice
of•fice•hold•er
of•fi•cer
of•fi•cial (authorized;
  cf. *officious*)
of•fi•cial•ism
of•fi•cial•ly
of•fi•ci•ary
of•fi•ci•ate
of•fi•ci•a•tion
of•fi•ci•nal•ly
of•fi•cious
  (meddlesome; cf.
  official)
off•ing
off•ish
off–key
off–lim•its
off–line
off–peak
off•print
off•scour•ing
off–sea•son
off•set

off•shoot
off•shore
off•side
off•spring
off•stage
off–the–rec•ord
off–white
off year
of•ten
of•ten•times
oft•times
Ohio
ohm
ohm•me•ter
oil cake
oil•cloth
oil•er
oil field
oil•i•ness
oil pan
oil•skin
oil slick
oil•stone
oil well
oily
oint•ment
okay
Okla•ho•ma
old age n.
old–age adj.
old•en
old–fash•ioned
old•ish
old–line

Old Nick
old•ster
old–time adj.
old–tim•er n.
old–world adj.
oleo•graph
oleo•mar•ga•rine
ol•fac•tion
ol•fac•to•ry
oli•garch
oli•gar•chy
ol•ive
olym•pi•ad
Olym•pi•an
Olym•pic
Olym•pus
om•elet
om•i•nous
omis•si•ble
omis•sion
omit
omit•ted
omit•ting
om•ni•bus
om•ni•di•rec•tion•al
om•nip•o•tence
om•nip•o•tent
om•ni•pres•ent
om•ni•science
om•ni•scient
om•niv•o•rous
on–again, off–again
once–over n.
on•col•o•gy

on•com•ing
one (single thing; cf. *won*)
one–horse adj.
one–lin•er
one•ness
one–on–one
oner•ous
one•self
one–sid•ed
one–step n.
one•time
one–to–one
one–track adj.
one–up•man•ship
one–way adj.
on•go•ing
on•ion
on•ion•skin
on–line
on•look•er
on•ly
on•rush
on•set
on•slaught
On•tar•io
on–the–job
on•to
on•tog•e•ny
on•to•log•i•cal
on•tol•o•gy
onus
on•ward
on•yx

oozy
opac•i•ty
opal•es•cent
opaque
open
open air n.
open–air adj.
open–and–shut
open–end adj.
open•er
open–eyed
open•hand•ed
open•heart•ed
open–hearth
open house
open•ing
open mar•ket n.
open–mar•ket adj.
open–mind•ed
open–mouthed
open•ness
open•work
op•era
op•er•a•ble
op•er•ate
op•er•at•ic
op•er•a•tion•al
op•er•a•tive
op•er•a•tor
op•er•et•ta
op•er•ose
Ophe•lia
oph•thal•mol•o•gy
oph•thal•mo•scope

opi•ate
opine
opin•ion
opin•ion•at•ed
opi•um
op•po•nent
op•por•tune
op•por•tun•ism
op•por•tun•ist
op•por•tu•ni•ty
op•pos•able
op•pose
op•po•site
op•po•si•tion
op•press
op•pres•sion
op•pres•sive
op•pres•sor
op•pro•bri•ous
op•pro•bri•um
op•ta•tive
op•ti•cal
op•ti•cal char•ac•ter read•er
op•ti•cian
op•tics
op•ti•mism
op•ti•mist
op•ti•mis•tic
op•ti•mize
op•ti•mum
op•tion
op•tion•al
op•tom•e•trist

op•tom•e•try
op•u•lence
op•u•lent
or (conjunction; cf. *oar, ore*)
or•a•cle
orac•u•lar
oral (spoken; cf. *aural*)
or•ange
or•ange•ade
or•ange•wood
ora•tion
or•a•tor
or•a•tor•i•cal
or•a•to•rio
or•a•to•ry
or•bic•u•lar
or•bit
or•chard
or•ches•tra
or•ches•tral
or•ches•trate
or•ches•tra•tion
or•chid
or•dain
or•deal
or•der
or•der•li•ness
or•der•ly
or•di•nal
or•di•nance (law; cf. *ordnance*)
or•di•nari•ly
or•di•nary

or•di•nate
or•di•na•tion
ord•nance (munitions; cf. *ordinance*)
ore (mineral; cf. *oar, or*)
Or•e•gon
or•gan
or•gan•ic
or•gan•ism
or•gan•ist
or•gan•iz•able
or•ga•ni•za•tion
or•ga•nize
or•gy
ori•ent
ori•en•tal
ori•en•tal•ism
ori•en•tal•ize
ori•en•tate
ori•en•ta•tion
or•i•fice
ori•ga•mi
or•i•gin
orig•i•nal
orig•i•nal•i•ty
orig•i•nal•ly
orig•i•nate
orig•i•na•tion
orig•i•na•tive
orig•i•na•tor
ori•ole
Ori•on
or•i•son

or•na•ment
or•na•men•tal
or•na•men•ta•tion
or•nate
or•ni•thol•o•gy
oro•tund
or•phan
or•phan•age
Or•pheus
or•tho•dox
or•tho•graph•ic
or•thog•ra•phy
or•tho•pe•dic
os•cil•late (back and forth; cf. *osculate*)
os•cil•la•tion
os•cil•la•tor
os•cu•late (kiss; cf. *oscillate*)
os•cu•la•tion
os•cu•la•to•ry
Osi•ris
os•mi•um
os•mo•sis
os•prey
os•si•fi•ca•tion
os•si•fy
os•su•ary
os•ten•si•ble
os•ten•sive
os•ten•sive•ly
os•ten•ta•tion
os•ten•ta•tious
os•teo•path

os•teo•path•ic
os•te•op•a•thy
os•tra•cism
os•tra•cize
os•trich
oth•er
oth•er•wise
Ot•ta•wa
ot•to•man
ought (should; cf.
    aught)
our (possessive; cf.
    hour)
our•self
our•selves
oust•er
out–and–out
out•bal•ance
out•bid
out•board
out•bound
out•break
out•build•ing
out•burst
out•cast
out•class
out•come
out•crop
out•cry
out•curve
out•dat•ed
out•dis•tance
out•do

out•door adj.
out•doors
out•er
out•er–di•rect•ed
out•er•most
out•face
out•field
out•fit
out•fit•ter
out•flank
out•fox
out•gen•er•al
out•go
out•go•ing
out•grow
out•growth
out•guess
out•house
out•ing
out•land•er
out•land•ish
out•last
out•law
out•law•ry
out•lay
out•let
out•line
out•live
out•look
out•ly•ing
out•ma•neu•ver
out•match
out•mod•ed

out•num•ber
out–of–date
out–of–door
out–of–the–way
out•pa•tient
out•play
out•point
out•post
out•pour•ing
out•put
out•rage
out•ra•geous
out•reach
out•rid•er
out•rig•ger
out•right
out•run
out•sell
out•set
out•side
out•sid•er
out•sit
out•skirt
out•smart
out•soar
out•speak
out•spo•ken
out•spread
out•stand•ing
out•stay
out•stretch
out•ward
out•ward•ly

out•wear
out•weigh
out•wit
out•work
oval
oval•ly
ova•ry
ova•tion
ov•en
over
over•abun•dance
over•achiev•er
over•all
over and over
over•arm
over•awe
over•bal•ance
over•bear•ing•ly
over•board
over•build
over•bur•den
over•cap•i•tal•iza•
   tion
over•cast
over•charge
over•coat
over•come
over•com•mit
over•do (too much; cf.
   overdue)
over•dose
over•draft
over•draw

over•drawn
over•due (past due; cf.
   overdo)
over•em•pha•sis
over•flow
over•grow
over•hand
over•hang
over•haul
over•head
over•hear
over•heat
over•laid
over•land
over•lay
over•look
over•lord
over•ly
over•night
over•paid
over•pass
over•pay•ment
over•pop•u•la•tion
over•pow•er
over•price
over•pro•duc•tion
over•qual•i•fied
over•rat•ed
over•reach
over•ride
over•rule
over•run
over•seas

over•see
over•see•ing
over•seer
over•shad•ow
over•shoe
over•sight
over•size
over•sized
over•sleep
over•spread
over•stay
over•step
over•sub•scribe
over•sup•ply
overt
over•take
over–the–count•er
over•throw
over•time
overt•ly
over•tone
over•ture
over•turn
over•weigh
over•weight
over•whelm•ing•ly
over•work
owed (did owe; cf. *ode*)
owl•et
owl•ish
own•er•ship
ox•al•ic ac•id
ox•bow

ox•eye
ox•ford
ox•heart
ox•i•da•tion
ox•ide

ox•i•dize
ox•tail
ox•tongue
ox•y•gen
ox•y•gen•ate

oys•ter
oys•ter bed
oys•ter•man
ozone

P

pace•mak•er
pac•er
pachy•derm
pach•ys•an•dra
pa•cif•ic
pac•i•fi•ca•tion
pa•cif•i•ca•tor
pa•cif•i•ca•to•ry
pa•cif•i•cist
pac•i•fi•er
pac•i•fism
pac•i•fy
pack•age
pack•age deal
pack•er
pack•et
pack•horse
pack•ing
pack•ing•house
pack•man
pack rat
pack•sack
pack•sad•dle

pack•thread
pad•ding
pad•dle
pad•dler
pad•dock
pad•lock
pa•dre
pa•gan
pa•gan•ism
pa•gan•ize
pag•eant
pag•eant•ry
pag•i•na•tion
pa•go•da
paid
pail (bucket; cf. *pale*)
pain (hurt; cf. *pane*)
pain•ful
pain•kill•er
pain•less
pains•tak•ing
paint box
paint•brush

paint•er
paint•ing
paint•pot
pair (two; cf. *pare,
    pear*)
pa•ja•mas
pal•ace
pa•lan•quin
pal•at•able
pal•a•tal
pal•a•tal•iza•tion
pal•a•tal•ize
pal•ate (roof of the
    mouth; cf. *palette,
    pallet*)
pa•la•tial
pal•a•tine
pa•la•ver
pale (white; cf. *pail*)
pale•face
pal•ette (for paint; cf.
    palate, pallet)
pal•frey

pal•i•mony
pal•ing
pal•i•sade
Pal•la•di•an
pal•la•di•um
pall•bear•er
pal•let (couch; cf.
   palate, palette)
pal•li•ate
pal•li•a•tion
pal•lia•tive
pal•lid
pal•lor
pal•met•to
palm•ist•ry
pal•o•mi•no
pal•pa•ble
pal•pate (examine by
   touch)
pal•pi•tate (throb)
pal•pi•ta•tion
pal•sied
pal•sy
pal•try (trivial; cf.
   poultry)
pam•per
pam•phlet
pam•phle•teer
pan•a•cea
Pan–Amer•i•can
pan•a•tela
pan•cake
pan•chro•mat•ic
pan•cre•as

pan•cre•atin
pan•dem•ic
pan•de•mo•ni•um
pan•dow•dy
pane (of glass; cf. *pain*)
pan•e•gyr•ic
pan•e•gyr•i•cal
pan•e•gyr•ist
pan•el
pan•eled
pan•el•ing
pan•el•ist
pan•han•dle
pan•ic
pan•icked
pan•ic–strick•en
pan•ni•kin
pan•o•ply
pan•ora•ma
pan•oram•ic
pan•sy
pan•ta•loon
pan•the•ism
pan•the•ist
pan•the•is•ti•cal
pan•the•on
pan•ther
pan•to•graph
pan•to•mime
pan•try
pa•pa•cy
pa•pal
pa•pa•ya
pa•per

pa•per•back
pa•per•board
pa•per chase
pa•per clip
pa•per cut•ter
pa•per•hang•er
pa•per knife
pa•per•mill
pa•per–thin
pa•per•weight
pa•per•work
pa•pe•terie
pa•pier–mâ•ché
pa•poose
pa•pri•ka
pa•py•rus
par•a•ble
pa•rab•o•la
par•a•bol•ic
para•chute
pa•rade
par•a•dise
par•a•dox•i•cal
par•af•fin
par•a•gon
para•graph
par•al•lax
par•al•lel
par•al•leled
par•al•lel•ing
par•al•lel•ism
par•al•lel•o•gram
pa•ral•y•sis
par•a•lyt•ic

par•a•lyze
par•a•mount
para•noia
para•noi•ac
para•noid
par•a•pet
par•a•pher•na•lia
para•phrase
para•pro•fes•sion•al
par•a•site
par•a•sit•ic
par•a•sit•i•cide
para•sol
para•troop•er
par•boil
par•cel (bundle; cf. *partial*)
par•celed
par•cel•ing
parch•ment
par•don
par•don•able
par•don•er
pare (peel; cf. *pair, pear*)
par•e•go•ric
par•ent
par•ent•age
par•ent•er•al
pa•ren•the•ses pl.
pa•ren•the•sis sing.
par•en•thet•i•cal
par•ent•hood
pa•re•sis

par•fait
pa•ri•ah
pa•ri•etal
pari–mu•tu•el
par•ish (church; cf. *perish*)
pa•rish•io•ner
Pa•ri•sian
par•i•ty
park•way
par•lance
par•lay (gamble)
par•ley (conference)
par•lia•ment
par•lia•men•tar•i•an
par•lia•men•ta•ry
par•lor
par•lor car
par•lor•maid
par•lous
pa•ro•chi•al
par•o•dy
pa•role
par•ox•ysm
par•ox•ys•mal
par•quet
par•que•try
par•ra•keet
par•ri•cide
par•rot
parse
Par•si•fal
par•si•mo•ni•ous
par•si•mo•ny

pars•ley
pars•nip
par•son
par•son•age
par•take
par•tak•er
part•ed
par•terre
Par•the•non
par•tial (part; cf. *parcel*)
par•tial•i•ty
par•tial•ly
par•tic•i•pant
par•tic•i•pate
par•tic•i•pa•tion
par•tic•i•pa•tor
par•ti•cip•i•al
par•tic•i•ple
par•ti•cle
par•tic•u•lar
par•tic•u•lar•i•ty
par•tic•u•lar•iza•tion
par•tic•u•lar•ize
par•tic•u•lar•ly
par•ti•san
par•ti•san•ship
par•ti•tion
part•ly
part•ner
part•ner•ship
par•tridge
part–time

par•tu•ri•tion
par•ty
par•ty line
par•ve•nu
par•vis
pas•chal
pa•sha
pass•able
pas•sage
pas•sage•way
pass•book
pas•sé
passed (of movement; cf. *past*)
passe•men•terie
pas•sen•ger
passe–par•tout
pass•er•by
pas•si•ble
pass•ing
pas•sion
pas•sion•ate
pas•sion•flow•er
pas•sion•less
pas•sive
pass•key
pass•port
pass•word
past (of time; cf. *passed*)
paste•board
pas•tel
pas•tern
pas•teur•iza•tion

pas•teur•ize
pas•tiche
pas•tille
pas•time
pas•tor
pas•to•ral
pas•to•ral•ism
pas•to•ral•ly
pas•tor•ate
pas•tor•ship
pas•tra•mi
past•ry
pas•tur•age
pas•ture
pas•ty
pa•tchou•li
patch test
patch•work
patchy
pate (head; cf. *pâté*, *patty*)
pâ•té (spiced ground meat; cf. *pate*, *patty*)
pa•tel•la
pa•tent adj.
pat•ent n., v.
pat•ent•able
pat•en•tee
pa•ter•fa•mil•i•as
pa•ter•nal
pa•ter•nal•ism
pa•ter•nal•ly
pa•ter•ni•ty
Pat•er•son N.J.

pa•thet•ic
path•find•er
patho•log•ic
patho•log•i•cal
pa•thol•o•gy
pa•thos
path•way
pa•tience
pa•tient
pa•ti•na
pa•tio
pa•tri•arch
pa•tri•ar•chal
pa•tri•arch•ate
pa•tri•ar•chy
pa•tri•cian
pat•ri•cide
pat•ri•mo•ny
pa•tri•ot
pa•tri•ot•ic
pa•tri•o•tism
pa•trol
pa•trolled
pa•trol•ling
pa•trol•man
pa•trol•wom•an
pa•tron
pa•tron•age
pa•tron•ize
pat•ro•nym•ic
pa•troon
pat•ten
pat•ter
pat•tern

Pat•ter•son N.Y.
pat•ty (little pie; cf.
    pate, pâté)
pau•ci•ty
paunch•i•ness
pau•per
pau•per•ism
pau•per•ize
pave•ment
pa•vil•ion
pav•ing
pawn•bro•ker
pawn•bro•king
pawn•er
pawn•shop
pay•able
pay•check
pay•day
pay dirt
pay•ee
pay•er
pay•load
pay•mas•ter
pay•ment
pay off v.
pay•off n.
pay•roll
peace (calm; cf. *piece*)
peace•able
peace•ful
peace•mak•er
peace pipe
peace•time
peachy

pea•cock
pea•hen
peak (top; cf. *peek,*
    pique)
peal (loud ringing; cf.
    peel)
pea•nut
pear (fruit; cf. *pair,*
    pare)
pearly
pear–shaped
peas•ant•ry
peb•ble
pec•ca•dil•lo
pec•can•cy
pec•cant
pec•to•ral
pec•u•late
pec•u•la•tion
pec•u•la•tor
pe•cu•liar
pe•cu•liar•i•ty
pe•cu•liar•ly
pe•cu•ni•ary
ped•a•gog•ic
ped•a•gog•i•cal
ped•a•gogue
ped•a•go•gy
ped•al (of a bicycle; cf.
    peddle)
ped•aled
ped•al•ing
ped•ant
pe•dan•tic

ped•ant•ry
ped•dle (sell; cf.
    pedal)
ped•dler
ped•dling
ped•es•tal
pe•des•tri•an
pe•des•tri•an•ism
pe•di•a•tri•cian
pe•di•at•rics
ped•i•cure
ped•i•gree
ped•i•ment
pe•dom•e•ter
peek (look; cf. *peak,*
    pique)
peel (pare; cf. *peal*)
peep•hole
peep show
peep sight
peer (look; cf. *pier*)
peer•age
peer•ess
peer•less
pee•vish
Peg•a•sus
pegged
peg•ging
pe•jo•ra•tive
Pe•la•gian
pel•i•can
pe•lisse
pel•la•gra
pel•let

pell–mell
pel·lu·cid
pel·try
pel·vis
pe·nal
pe·nal·iza·tion
pe·nal·ize
pen·al·ty
pen·ance
pen·chant
pen·cil
pen·ciled
pen·cil·er
pen·dant
pen·den·cy
pen·dent
pend·ing
pen·drag·on
pen·du·lous
pen·du·lum
pen·e·tra·bil·i·ty
pen·e·tra·ble
pen·e·trate
pen·e·tra·tion
pen·e·tra·tive
pen·guin
pen·hold·er
pen·i·cil·lin
pen·in·su·la
pen·in·su·lar
pen·i·tence
pen·i·tent
pen·i·ten·tial
pen·i·ten·tia·ry

pen·i·tent·ly
pen·knife
pen·man
pen·man·ship
pen name
pen·nant
pen·nies
pen·ni·less
Penn·syl·va·nia
Penn·syl·va·nian
pen·ny
pen·ny·weight
pen·ny–wise
pen·ny·worth
pe·no·log·i·cal
pe·nol·o·gist
pe·nol·o·gy
pen·sile
pen·sion
pen·sion·ary
pen·sion·er
pen·sive
pen·stock
pen·ta·gon
pen·tag·o·nal
pen·tath·lon
Pen·te·cost
pent·house
pe·nult
pen·ul·ti·mate
pe·nu·ri·ous
pen·u·ry
pe·on
pe·on·age

pe·o·ny
peo·ple
pep·per
pep·per–and–salt
   adj.
pep·per·box
pep·per·corn
pep·per·mint
pep·pery
pep·sin
pep talk
per·ad·ven·ture
per·am·bu·la·tion
per·am·bu·la·tor
per an·num
per·cale
per cap·i·ta
per·ceiv·able
per·ceive
per·cent
per·cent·age
per·cen·tile
per·cept
per·cep·ti·ble
per·cep·tion
per·cep·tive
per·cep·tu·al
per·chance
Per·che·ron
per·cip·i·ence
per·cip·i·ent
per·co·late
per·co·la·tor
per·cus·sion

per•cus•sive
per di•em
per•di•tion
per•e•gri•na•tion
pe•remp•to•ri•ly
pe•remp•to•ri•ness
pe•remp•to•ry
pe•ren•ni•al
per•fect
per•fect•ible
per•fec•tion
per•fec•tion•ism
per•fect•ly
per•fec•to
per•fid•i•ous
per•fi•dy
per•fo•rate
per•fo•ra•tion
per•fo•ra•tor
per•force
per•form
per•for•mance
per•form•er
per•fume
per•fum•er
per•fum•ery
per•func•to•ry
per•haps
per•il•ous
pe•rim•e•ter
pe•ri•od
pe•ri•od•ic
pe•ri•od•i•cal

pe•riph•er•al
pe•riph•ery
pe•riph•ra•sis
peri•phras•tic
peri•scope
peri•scop•ic
per•ish (die; cf.
    parish)
per•ish•able
peri•to•ni•tis
per•i•win•kle
per•jure
per•jur•er
per•ju•ry
per•ma•nence
per•ma•nen•cy
per•ma•nent
per•me•abil•i•ty
per•me•able
per•me•ate
per•me•ation
per•mis•si•ble
per•mis•sion
per•mis•sive
per•mit
per•mit•ted
per•mit•ting
per•mu•ta•tion
per•ni•cious
per•nick•e•ty
per•ora•tion
per•ox•ide
per•pen•dic•u•lar

per•pe•trate
per•pe•tra•tion
per•pe•tra•tor
per•pet•u•al
per•pet•u•al•ly
per•pet•u•ate
per•pet•u•a•tion
per•pet•u•a•tor
per•pe•tu•ity
per•plex
per•plexed
per•plexed•ly
per•plex•i•ty
per•qui•site
per•ry
per se
per•se•cute (harass;
    cf. *prosecute*)
per•se•cu•tion
per•se•cu•tor
Per•seus
per•se•ver•ance
per•se•vere
Per•sian
per•si•flage
per•sim•mon
per•sist
per•sis•tence
per•sis•ten•cy
per•sis•tent
per•son
per•son•able
per•son•age

per•son•al (not public; cf. *personnel*)

per•son•al•i•ty (disposition; cf. *personalty*)

per•son•al•ize

per•son•al•ly

per•son•al•ty (property; cf. *personality*)

per•son•i•fi•ca•tion

per•son•i•fy

per•son•nel (employees; cf. *personal*)

per•spec•tive (appearance to the eye; cf. *prospective*)

per•spi•ca•cious

per•spi•cac•i•ty

per•spi•cu•ity

per•spic•u•ous

per•spi•ra•tion

per•spi•ra•to•ry

per•spire

per•suade

per•sua•si•ble

per•sua•sion

per•sua•sive

per•tain

per•ti•na•cious

per•ti•nac•i•ty

per•ti•nence

per•ti•nen•cy

per•ti•nent

per•turb

per•turb•able

per•tur•ba•tion

pe•rus•al

pe•ruse

pe•rus•er

Pe•ru•vi•an

per•vade

per•va•sive

per•verse

per•ver•sion

per•ver•si•ty

per•ver•sive

per•vert

per•vert•ed

per•vert•er

per•vi•ous

pes•si•mism

pes•si•mist

pes•si•mis•tic

pes•ter

pest•hole

pest•house

pes•ti•cide

pes•tif•er•ous

pes•ti•lence

pes•ti•lent

pes•ti•len•tial

pes•tle

pet•al

pet•cock

pet•it (petty)

pe•tite (small)

pe•ti•tion

pe•ti•tion•er

pet•it point

pet•ri•fac•tion

pet•ri•fac•tive

pet•ri•fy

pet•ro•chem•i•cal

pet•rol

pet•ro•la•tum

pe•tro•leum

pet•ro•log•ic

pe•trol•o•gy

pet•ti•coat

pet•ti•fog

pet•ti•fog•gery

pet•ti•ly

pet•ti•ness

pet•ty

pet•u•lance

pet•u•lan•cy

pet•u•lant

pe•tu•nia

pew•ter

pew•ter•er

pha•lan•ges pl.

pha•lanx sing.

phan•tasm

phan•tas•ma•go•ria

phan•tom

pha•raoh

phar•i•see

phar·ma·ceu·ti·cal
phar·ma·cist
phar·ma·co·poe·ia
phar·ma·cy
phase out v.
phase·out n.
pheas·ant
phe·nom·e·na pl.
phe·nom·e·nal
phe·nom·e·nol·o·gy
phe·nom·e·non sing.
phi·al
phi·lan·der
phi·lan·der·er
phil·an·throp·ic
phil·an·throp·i·cal
phi·lan·thro·pist
phi·lan·thro·py
phil·a·tel·ic
phi·lat·e·ly
Phil·har·mon·ic
phi·lip·pic
Phil·ip·pine
phi·lis·tine
phil·o·log·i·cal
phi·lol·o·gist
phi·lol·o·gy
phi·los·o·pher
philo·soph·ic
philo·soph·i·cal
phi·los·o·phy
phil·ter (drug; cf. *filter*)

phlegm
phleg·mat·ic
pho·bia
Phoe·ni·cian
phoe·nix
pho·net·ic
pho·ne·ti·cian
pho·nics
pho·no·graph
phos·phate
phos·pho·resce
phos·pho·res·cence
phos·pho·res·cent
phos·pho·ric
phos·pho·rous adj.
phos·pho·rus n.
pho·to·cell
pho·to·cop·i·er
pho·to·copy
pho·to·elec·tric
pho·to·en·grav·ing
pho·to·ge·nic
pho·to·graph
pho·tog·ra·pher
pho·to·graph·ic
pho·tog·ra·phy
pho·to·gra·vure
pho·to·li·thog·ra·phy
pho·to·mu·ral
pho·to·play
pho·to·re·con·nais·sance

pho·to·stat
phrase·ol·o·gy
phre·net·ic
phre·nol·o·gist
phre·nol·o·gy
phys·ic (medicine; cf. *physique, psychic*)
phys·i·cal (of the body; cf. *fiscal*)
phy·si·cian
phys·i·cist
phys·ics
phys·i·og·no·my
phys·i·og·ra·phy
phys·i·ol·o·gist
phys·i·ol·o·gy
phy·sique (of the body; cf. *physic, psychic*)
pi·a·nis·si·mo
pi·a·nist
pi·ano n.
pi·anos pl.
pi·as·ter
pi·az·za
pi·ca
pic·a·dor
pic·a·resque
pic·a·yune
pic·ca·lil·li
pic·co·lo
pic·co·lo·ist
pick·ax

pick·er·el
pick·et
pick·le
pick·lock
pick over
pick·pock·et
pick up v.
pick·up n.
pic·nic n., v.
pic·nicked
pic·nick·er
pic·nick·ing
pi·cot
pic·to·graph
pic·tog·ra·phy
pic·to·ri·al
pic·ture
pic·tur·esque
pid·gin (language; cf. *pigeon*)
pie·bald
piece (part; cf. *peace*)
piece goods
piece·meal
piece·work
pie chart
pie·plant
pier (dock; cf. *peer*)
pi·ety
pi·geon (bird; cf. *pidgin*)
pi·geon·hole
pi·geon–toed

pi·geon·wing
pig·fish
pig·gery
pig·gish
pig·gy·back
pig·head·ed
pig iron
pig·ment
pig·men·tary
pig·men·ta·tion
pigmy
pig·pen
pig·skin
pig·sty
pig·tail
pig·tailed
pig·weed
pike·man
pike perch
pik·er
pike·staff
pi·las·ter
pil·chard
pil·fer
pil·grim
pil·grim·age
pil·ing
pil·lage
pil·lar
pill·box
pil·lion
pil·lo·ry
pil·low

pil·low·case
pi·lot
pi·lot·house
pi·lot light
pim·ple
pin·afore
pince–nez
pinch hit n.
pinch–hit v.
pin curl
pin·cush·ion
pine·ap·ple
pin·feath·er
pin·fold
Ping–Pong
pin·head
pin·head·ed
pin·hole
pin·ion
pink·eye
pin·na·cle
pi·noch·le
pin·point
pin·prick
pin·stripe
pin·up
pin·wheel
pi·o·neer
pi·ous
pipe clay n.
pipe–clay v.
pipe dream
pipe·line

pip•er
pipe•stone
pipe wrench
pi•quan•cy
pi•quant
pique (provoke; cf. *peak, peek*)
pi•ra•cy
pi•ra•nha
pi•rate
pi•rat•i•cal
pir•ou•ette
pis•ca•to•ry
pis•ta•chio
pis•til (of plant)
pis•tol (weapon)
pis•tole (old coin)
pis•tol–whip
pis•ton
pitch–black
pitch–dark
pitch•er
pitch•fork
pitch•man
pitch pipe
pitch•stone
pit•e•ous
pit•fall
pit•head
pith•i•ly
pith•i•ness
pithy
piti•able
piti•ful

piti•less
pit•man
pit saw
pit•tance
pit•ter–pat•ter
Pitts•burg Calif.,
    Kans.
Pitts•burgh Pa.
pi•tu•itary
pity
piv•ot
piv•ot•al
piz•za
piz•ze•ria
piz•zi•ca•to
pla•ca•bil•i•ty
pla•ca•ble
plac•ard
pla•cate
pla•ca•to•ry
pla•ce•bo
place•kick
place mat
place•ment
plac•id
pla•cid•i•ty
pla•gia•rism
pla•gia•rist
pla•gia•rize
pla•gia•ry
plague
plain (simple; cf. *plane*)
plain•clothes•man
plain•ness

plains•man
plain•spo•ken
plain•tiff (complainant)
plain•tive (mournful)
plait (fold; cf. *plat,*
    plate, pleat)
plane (airplane; cf.
    plain)
plan•et
plan•e•tar•i•um
plan•e•tary
plan•gent
plank•ing
plank•ton
plan•ner
plan•tain
plan•tar (of the sole;
    cf. *planter*)
plan•ta•tion
plant•er (farmer; cf.
    plantar)
plaque
plas•ter
plas•ter•board
plas•ter•er
plas•tic
plas•tic•i•ty
plat (map; cf. *plait,*
    plate, pleat)
plate (dish; cf. *plait,*
    plat, pleat)
pla•teau
plate•ful
plate glass

plat•en
plat•er
plat•form
plat•ing
plat•i•num
plat•i•tude
plat•i•tu•di•nous
pla•ton•ic
Pla•to•nism
pla•toon
plat•ter
plau•dit
plau•si•bil•i•ty
plau•si•ble
play back v.
play•back n.
play•bill
play•boy
play•er
play•ful
play•girl
play•go•er
play•ground
play•house
play•let
play off v.
play–off n.
play•pen
play•room
play school n.
play•suit
play•thing
play•time
play•wright

play yard
pla•za
plea
plead•able
plead•er
plead•ing
pleas•ant
pleas•ant•ry
pleas•ing
plea•sur•able
plea•sure
pleat (arrange in pleats; cf. *plait*, *plat*, *plate*)
ple•be•ian
pleb•i•scite
plec•trum
pledge
pledg•ee
pled•get
ple•na•ry
pleni•po•ten•tia•ry
plen•i•tude
plen•te•ous
plen•ti•ful
plen•ty
ple•num
ple•o•nasm
pleth•o•ra
pleu•ri•sy
pli•abil•i•ty
pli•able
pli•an•cy
pli•ant
pli•ers

plod•ded
plod•der
plod•ding
plot•ted
plot•ter
plot•ting
plow•boy
plow•man
plow•share
plug
plugged
plug•ging
plug–ug•ly
plum (fruit)
plum•age
plumb (weight)
plumb bob
plumb•er
plumb•ing
plumb line
plum•met
plump•ness
plun•der
plun•der•er
plung•er
plu•per•fect
plu•ral
plu•ral•ism
plu•ral•is•tic
plu•ral•i•ty
plu•ral•iza•tion
plu•ral•ize
plu•toc•ra•cy
plu•to•crat

plu•to•crat•ic
plu•to•ni•um
ply•wood
pneu•mat•ic
pneu•mat•ics
pneu•mo•nia
pneu•mon•ic
poach•er
pock•et
pock•et•book
pock•et•ful
pock•et–
   hand•ker•chief
pock•et•knife
pock•mark
po•di•a•try
po•di•um
po•em
po•esy
po•et
po•et•as•ter
po•et•ic
po•et•i•cal
po•et•ry
po•grom
poi•gnan•cy
poi•gnant
poin•set•tia
point–blank
point•ed
point•er
point•less
point of view
poi•son

poi•son•ous
poi•son–pen adj.
pok•er
po•lar
po•lar•i•ty
po•lar•iza•tion
po•lar•ize
Po•lar•oid
pole (rod; cf. *poll*)
pole•ax
pole•cat
po•lem•ic
po•lem•i•cal
pole•star
pole vault n.
pole–vault v.
pole–vault•er n.
po•lice•man
po•lice•wom•an
poli•clin•ic
   (dispensary; cf.
   polyclinic)
pol•i•cy
pol•i•cy•hold•er
pol•ish
Pol•ish
pol•ish•er
po•lit•bu•ro
po•lite
po•lite•ness
po•lit•ic
po•lit•i•cal
po•lit•i•cal•ly
pol•i•ti•cian

pol•i•tics
pol•i•ty
pol•ka
pol•ka dot n.
pol•ka–dot adj.
poll (vote; cf. *pole*)
pol•len
pol•li•nate
pol•li•wog
poll tax
pol•lut•ant
pol•lute
pol•lu•tion
po•lo•naise
pol•ter•geist
pol•troon
poly•an•dry
poly•an•thus
poly•chro•mat•ic
poly•chrome
poly•clin•ic (hospital;
   cf. *policlinic*)
poly•eth•yl•ene
po•lyg•a•mist
po•lyg•a•mous
po•lyg•a•my
poly•glot
poly•gon
poly•graph
poly•graph•ic
pol•yp
poly•phon•ic
poly•syl•lab•ic
poly•syl•la•ble

poly•tech•nic
poly•un•sat•u•rat•ed
po•made
pome•gran•ate
pom•mel
pom•pa•dour
pom•pa•no
pom•pos•i•ty
pomp•ous
pon•cho sing.
pon•chos pl.
pon•der
pon•der•a•ble
pon•der•ous
pon•gee
pon•iard
pon•tiff
pon•tif•i•cal
pon•tif•i•cate
pon•toon
po•ny
po•ny•tail
poo•dle
pooh–pooh
pool•room
poor box
poor farm
poor•house
poor•ly
poor–spir•it•ed
pop•corn
pop–eyed
pop•gun
pop•in•jay

pop•lar (tree; cf.
  popular)
pop•lin
pop•over
pop•py
pop•py•cock
pop•u•lace (people;
  cf. *populous*)
pop•u•lar (widely
  liked; cf. *poplar*)
pop•u•lar•i•ty
pop•u•lar•iza•tion
pop•u•lar•ize
pop•u•late
pop•u•la•tion
pop•u•lous (thickly
  populated; cf.
  populace)
por•ce•lain
por•cu•pine
pore (study; cf. *pour*)
pork•er
po•ros•i•ty
po•rous
por•phy•ry
por•poise
por•ridge
por•rin•ger
por•ta•bil•i•ty
por•ta•ble
por•tage
por•tal
por•tend
por•tent

por•ten•tous
por•ter
por•ter•house
port•fo•lio
port•hole
por•ti•co
por•tiere
por•tion
port•li•ness
port•ly
port•man•teau
por•trait
por•trai•ture
por•tray
por•tray•al
Por•tu•guese
por•tu•laca
pos•it
po•si•tion
pos•i•tive
pos•i•tron
pos•se
pos•sess
pos•sessed
pos•ses•sion
pos•ses•sive
pos•sess•or
pos•si•bil•i•ty
pos•si•ble
post•age
post•al
post•box
post•boy
post•card

post·clas·si·cal
post·date
post·doc·tor·al
post·er
pos·te·ri·or
pos·ter·i·ty
pos·tern
post·grad·u·ate
post·haste
post·hole
post horn
post–horse
post·hu·mous
post·hyp·not·ic
pos·til·ion
post·lude
post·man
post·mark
post·mas·ter
post·mis·tress
post·mor·tem
post·na·sal
post–obit
post of·fice n.
post–of·fice adj.
post–of·fice box
post·paid
post·pone
post·pone·ment
post·pran·di·al
post·re·tire·ment
post·script
post·test
pos·tu·lant

pos·tu·late
pos·ture
post·war
post·wom·an
po·ta·ble
pot·ash
po·tas·si·um
po·ta·tion
po·ta·to
po·ta·toes
pot·bel·lied
pot·bel·ly
pot·boil·er
pot·boy
pot cheese
po·ten·cy
po·ten·tate
po·ten·tial
po·ten·ti·al·i·ty
po·tent·ly
pot·hole
pot·hook
pot·house
po·tion
pot·latch
pot·luck
pot·pie
pot·pour·ri
pot roast
pot·sherd
pot·shot
pot still
pot·tage
pot·ter

pot·tery
pouch
Pough·keep·sie N.Y.
poul·ter·er
poul·tice
poul·try (fowl; cf.
  paltry)
poul·try·man
pound·age
pound cake
pour (rain; cf. *pore*)
pov·er·ty–strick·en
pow·der
pow·dery
pow·er·boat
pow·er·ful
pow·er·less
pow·er pack
pow·er play
pow·wow
prac·ti·ca·bil·i·ty
prac·ti·ca·ble
  (feasible)
prac·ti·cal (useful)
prac·ti·cal·i·ty
prac·ti·cal·ly
prac·tice
prac·tic·er
prac·ti·cum
prac·ti·tio·ner
prag·mat·ic
prag·mat·i·cal
prag·ma·tism
prag·ma·tist

prai•rie
praise•wor•thi•ness
praise•wor•thy
pra•line
prank•ish
prat•tle
pray (beseech; cf. *prey*)
prayer
prayer book
prayer•ful
preach•er
preach•ment
pre•ad•mis•sion
pre•am•ble
pre•ar•ranged
pre•as•signed
pre•can•cel
pre•car•i•ous
pre•cau•tion
pre•cau•tion•ary
pre•cede (go before;
  cf. *proceed*)
pre•ce•dence
  (priority; cf.
  precedents)
pre•ce•den•cy
pre•ce•dent adj.
prec•e•dent n.
prec•e•dents
  (previous acts; cf.
  precedence)
pre•ced•ing
pre•cept
pre•cep•tive

pre•cep•tor
pre•cep•to•ry
pre•ces•sion
pre•ces•sion•al
pre•cinct
pre•cious
prec•i•pice
pre•cip•i•tance
pre•cip•i•tan•cy
pre•cip•i•tant
pre•cip•i•tate
pre•cip•i•tate•ly
pre•cip•i•tate•ness
pre•cip•i•ta•tion
pre•cip•i•ta•tor
pre•cip•i•tous
pre•cise
pre•ci•sion
pre•clude
pre•clu•sion
pre•clu•sive
pre•co•cious
pre•coc•i•ty
pre•con•ceive
pre•con•cep•tion
pre•con•cert
pre•cook
pre•cur•sor
pre•cur•so•ry
pred•a•to•ry
pre•de•cease
pre•de•ces•sor
pre•des•ti•nar•i•an
pre•des•ti•na•tion

pre•des•tine
pre•de•ter•mine
pre•dic•a•ment
pred•i•cate
pred•i•ca•tion
pred•i•ca•tive
pre•dict
pre•dict•able
pre•dic•tion
pre•dic•tive
pre•dic•tor
pre•di•lec•tion
pre•dis•pose
pre•dis•po•si•tion
pre•dom•i•nance
pre•dom•i•nant
pre•dom•i•nate
pre•dom•i•na•tion
pre•em•i•nence
pre•em•i•nent
pre•empt
pre•emp•tive
pre•ex•ist•ing
pre•fab
pre•fab•ri•cate
pref•ace
pref•a•to•ry
pre•fect
pre•fec•ture
pre•fer
pref•er•a•ble
pref•er•ence
pref•er•en•tial
pre•ferred

pre•fer•ring
pre•fix
pre•flight
preg•nan•cy
preg•nant
pre•heat
pre•his•tor•ic
pre•judge
prej•u•dice
prej•u•di•cial
prel•a•cy
prel•ate
pre•lim•i•nary
pre•lude
pre•ma•ture
pre•ma•tu•ri•ty
pre•med•i•tate
pre•med•i•ta•tion
pre•mier
pre•miere
prem•ise
prem•is•es (real
   estate; cf. *promises*)
pre•mi•um
pre•mo•ni•tion
pre•mon•i•to•ry
pre•na•tal
pre•oc•cu•pan•cy
pre•oc•cu•pa•tion
pre•oc•cu•pied
pre•oc•cu•py
pre•or•dain
pre•paid

prep•a•ra•tion
pre•par•a•tive
pre•pa•ra•to•ry
pre•pare
pre•pared
pre•pared•ness
pre•pay
pre•pay•ment
pre•plan•ning
pre•pon•der•ance
pre•pon•der•ant
pre•pon•der•ate
prep•o•si•tion
prep•o•si•tion•al
pre•pos•sess
pre•pos•sess•ing
pre•pos•ses•sion
pre•pos•ter•ous
pre•po•ten•cy
pre•pro•gram
pre•re•cord
pre•reg•is•ter
pre•req•ui•site
pre•rog•a•tive
pres•age n.
pre•sage v.
Pres•by•te•ri•an
pre•school
pre•scient
pre•scribe (order as a
   remedy; cf. *proscribe*)
pre•scrip•ti•ble
pre•scrip•tion

pre•scrip•tive
pres•ence (of mind;
   cf. *presents*)
pre•sent v.
pres•ent adj., n.
pre•sent•able
pre•sen•ta•tion
pre•sen•ta•tive
pres•ent–day
pre•sen•tee
pre•sen•ti•ment
   (foreboding; cf.
   presentment)
pres•ent•ly
pre•sent•ment (from
   grand jury; cf.
   presentiment)
pres•ents (gifts; cf.
   presence)
pre•serv•able
pres•er•va•tion
pre•ser•va•tive
pre•serve
pre•side
pres•i•den•cy
pres•i•dent
pres•i•den•tial
pre•sid•er
press agent n.
press•board
press box
pressed
press•er

press–gang
press•ing
press•man
press•mark
press•room
press•run
pres•sure
pres•sur•ize
press•work
pres•ti•dig•i•ta•tion
pres•ti•dig•i•ta•tor
pres•tige
pres•ti•gious
pres•tis•si•mo
pre•sum•able
pre•sume
pre•sump•tion
pre•sump•tive
pre•sump•tu•ous
pre•sup•pose
pre•tend
pre•tend•ed
pre•tend•er
pre•tense
pre•ten•sion
pre•ten•tious
pret•er•it
pre•ter•nat•u•ral
pre•test
pre•text
pret•ti•ly
pret•ti•ness
pret•ty

pret•zel
pre•vail
pre•vail•ing
prev•a•lence
prev•a•lent
pre•var•i•cate
pre•var•i•ca•tion
pre•var•i•ca•tor
pre•vent
pre•vent•able
pre•ven•ta•tive
pre•ven•tion
pre•ven•tive
pre•view
pre•vi•ous
pre•vi•sion
prey (victim; cf. *pray*)
price–cut•ter
price–fix•ing
price in•dex
price•less
price tag
prick•le
prick•li•ness
prick•ly
priest•ess
priest•hood
priest•ly
pri•ma•cy
pri•ma don•na
pri•ma fa•cie
pri•mar•i•ly
pri•ma•ry

pri•mate
prim•er
prime time
pri•me•val
prim•i•tive
pri•mo•gen•i•ture
pri•mor•di•al
prim•rose
Prince Ed•ward
  Is•land
prince•ly
prin•cess
prin•ci•pal (chief; cf.
  principle)
prin•ci•pal•i•ty
prin•ci•pal•ly
prin•ci•ple (rule; cf.
  principal)
print•able
print•er
print•ery
print•ing
print out v.
print•out n.
pri•or
pri•or•ess
pri•or•i•ty
pri•or•ship
prism
pris•mat•ic
pris•on
pris•on•er
pris•tine

pri•va•cy
pri•vate
pri•va•teer
pri•vate•ly
pri•va•tion
priv•et
priv•i•lege
priv•i•ly
priv•i•ty
privy
prize•fight
prize ring
prob•a•bil•i•ty
prob•a•ble
prob•a•bly
pro•bate
pro•ba•tion
pro•ba•tion•al
pro•ba•tion•ary
pro•ba•tion•er
pro•ba•tive
pro•ba•to•ry
pro•bi•ty
prob•lem
prob•lem•at•ic
prob•lem•at•i•cal
pro•bos•cis
pro•ca•the•dral
pro•ce•dur•al
pro•ce•dure
pro•ceed (move
   forward; cf. *precede*)
pro•ceed•ing

pro•cess
pro•ces•sion
pro•ces•sion•al
pro•ces•sor
pro•claim
proc•la•ma•tion
pro•cliv•i•ty
pro•con•sul
pro•cras•ti•nate
pro•cras•ti•na•tion
pro•cras•ti•na•tor
pro•cre•ation
pro•cre•ative
pro•crus•te•an
proc•tor
proc•to•ri•al
pro•cur•able
proc•u•ra•tion
proc•u•ra•tor
pro•cure
pro•cure•ment
prod•i•gal
prod•i•gal•i•ty
pro•di•gious
prod•i•gy
pro•duce
pro•duc•er
prod•uct
pro•duc•tion
pro•duc•tive
pro•duc•tiv•i•ty
pro•fa•na•tion
pro•fa•na•to•ry

pro•fane
pro•fan•i•ty
pro•fess
pro•fessed•ly
pro•fes•sion
pro•fes•sion•al
pro•fes•sion•al•ism
pro•fes•sion•al•ly
pro•fes•sor
pro•fes•so•ri•al
pro•fes•sor•ship
prof•fer
prof•fer•ing
pro•fi•cien•cy
pro•fi•cient
pro•file
prof•it (gain; cf.
   prophet)
prof•it•able
prof•i•teer
prof•it•less
prof•li•ga•cy
prof•li•gate
pro for•ma
pro•found
pro•fun•di•ty
pro•fuse
pro•fu•sion
pro•gen•i•tor
prog•e•ny
prog•no•sis
prog•nos•tic
prog•nos•ti•cate

prog•nos•ti•ca•tion
pro•gram
pro•gram•ma•ble
pro•gram•mat•ic
pro•grammed
pro•gram•mer
pro•gram•ming
prog•ress n.
pro•gress v.
pro•gres•sion
pro•gres•sive
pro•hib•it
pro•hi•bi•tion•ist
pro•hib•i•tive
pro•hib•i•to•ry
proj•ect n.
pro•ject v.
pro•jec•tile
pro•jec•tion•ist
pro•jec•tive
pro•jec•tor
pro•le•tar•i•an
pro•le•tar•i•at
pro•lif•er•ate
pro•lif•ic
pro•lix
pro•logue
pro•long
pro•lon•gate
prom•e•nade
prom•i•nence
prom•i•nent
pro•mis•cu•ity

pro•mis•cu•ous
prom•ise
prom•is•es (pledges;
 cf. *premises*)
prom•i•sor
prom•is•so•ry
prom•on•to•ry
pro•mote
pro•mot•er
pro•mo•tion
pro•mo•tion•al
prompt
prompt•book
prompt•er
promp•ti•tude
prompt•ly
prompt•ness
pro•mul•gate
pro•mul•ga•tion
pro•nom•i•nal
pro•noun
pro•nounce
pro•nounce•able
pro•nounced
pro•nounce•ment
pro•nounc•ing
pro•nun•ci•a•men•
 to
pro•nun•ci•a•tion
proof•read•er
proof•room
prop•a•ga•ble
pro•pa•gan•da

pro•pa•gan•dist
pro•pa•gan•dize
prop•a•gate
prop•a•ga•tion
prop•a•ga•tive
pro•pane
pro•pel
pro•pel•lant
pro•pelled
pro•pel•ler
pro•pel•ling
pro•pense
pro•pen•si•ty
prop•er•ly
prop•er•tied
prop•er•ty
proph•e•cy n. (a
 prediction; cf.
 prophesy)
proph•e•si•er
proph•e•sy v. (to
 predict; cf. *prophecy*)
proph•et (predicts
 future; cf. *profit*)
pro•phet•ic
pro•phet•i•cal
pro•phy•lac•tic
pro•pin•qui•ty
pro•pi•ti•ate
pro•pi•ti•a•tion
pro•pi•ti•ator
pro•pi•tia•to•ry
pro•pi•tious

pro•po•nent
pro•por•tion
pro•por•tion•al
pro•por•tion•ate
pro•pos•al
pro•pose (to state; cf. *purpose*)
prop•o•si•tion
pro•pound
pro•pri•etary
pro•pri•etor
pro•pri•ety
pro•pul•sion
pro•pul•sive
pro ra•ta
pro•rate
pro•sa•ic
pro•sce•ni•um
pro•scribe (outlaw; cf. *prescribe*)
pro•scrip•tion
pro•scrip•tive
prose
pros•e•cute (legal trial; cf. *persecute*)
pros•e•cu•tion
pros•e•cu•tor
pros•e•lyte
pro•sit
pros•pect
pro•spec•tive (expected; cf. *perspective*)
pro•spec•tus

pros•per
pros•per•i•ty
pros•per•ous
pros•tate
pros•the•sis
pros•thet•ics
pros•ti•tute
pros•ti•tu•tion
pros•trate
pros•tra•tion
prosy
pro•tag•o•nist
pro•te•an
pro•tect
pro•tec•tion
pro•tec•tion•ism
pro•tec•tion•ist
pro•tec•tive
pro•tec•tor
pro•tec•tor•ate
pro•té•gé
pro•tein
pro tem
pro•test
prot•es•tant
Prot•es•tant•ism
pro•tes•ta•tion
pro•to•col
pro•to•plasm
pro•to•type
pro•tract
pro•trac•tile
pro•trac•tion
pro•trac•tor

pro•trude
pro•tru•sion
pro•tru•sive
pro•tu•ber•ance
pro•tu•ber•ant
prov•able
proved
prov•en
prov•e•nance
prov•en•der
prov•erb
pro•ver•bi•al
pro•vide
pro•vid•ed
prov•i•dence
prov•i•dent
prov•i•den•tial
pro•vid•er
prov•ince
pro•vin•cial
pro•vin•cial•ism
pro•vi•sion
pro•vi•sion•al
pro•vi•sion•ary
pro•vi•sion•er
pro•vi•so
pro•vi•so•ry
prov•o•ca•tion
pro•voc•a•tive
pro•voke
pro•vok•ing
prow•ess
prox•i•mal
prox•i•mate

prox·im·i·ty
prox·i·mo
proxy
prude
pru·dence
pru·dent
pru·den·tial
prud·ish
pru·ri·ence
pru·ri·ent
pry·ing
psalm
psalm·book
psalm·ist
psalm·o·dy
pseud·onym
pseud·on·y·mous
psit·ta·co·sis
pso·ri·a·sis
Psy·che
psy·chi·at·ric
psy·chi·a·trist
psy·chi·a·try
psy·chic (of the mind;
   cf. *physic, physique*)
psy·cho·anal·y·sis
psy·cho·an·a·lyst
psy·cho·an·a·lyze
psy·cho·log·i·cal
psy·chol·o·gist
psy·chol·o·gize
psy·chol·o·gy
psy·cho·path
psy·cho·path·ic

psy·cho·sis
psy·cho·so·mat·ic
psy·cho·ther·a·py
pu·ber·ty
pub·lic
pub·lic–
   ad·dress sys·tem
pub·li·ca·tion
pub·li·cist
pub·lic·i·ty
pub·li·cize
pub·lic·ly
pub·lic·ness
pub·lic re·la·tions
pub·lic–spir·it·ed
pub·lish
pub·lish·er
puck·ery
pud·ding
pud·dle
pud·dling
pu·den·cy
pudg·i·ness
pueb·lo
pu·er·ile
Puer·to Ri·co
puff·i·ness
puffy
pu·gi·lism
pu·gi·list
pu·gi·lis·tic
pug·na·cious
pug·nac·i·ty
pug nose

pug–nosed
puis·sance
puis·sant
pul·chri·tude
pul·chri·tu·di·nous
pul·let
pul·ley
Pull·man
pull over v.
pull·over adj., n.
pul·mo·nary
pul·mo·tor
pulp·i·ness
pul·pit
pulp·wood
pulpy
pul·sate
pul·sa·tion
pul·ver·ize
pum·ice
pum·mel
pum·meled
pum·mel·ing
pum·per·nick·el
pump·kin
punch·board
punch card
punch–drunk
pun·cheon
punch line
punc·til·io
punc·til·i·ous
punc·tu·al
punc·tu·al·i·ty

punc·tu·al·ly
punc·tu·ate
punc·tu·a·tion
punc·tu·a·tor
punc·ture
pun·dit
pun·gen·cy
pun·gent
pun·ish
pun·ish·able
pun·ish·er
pun·ish·ment
pu·ni·tive
pun·ster
punt·er
pu·ny
pu·pil
pup·pet
pup·pet·ry
pup·py
pup tent
pur·blind
pur·chas·able
pur·chase
pur·dah
pure·ly
pur·ga·tion
pur·ga·tive
pur·ga·to·ri·al
pur·ga·to·ry
purge
pu·ri·fi·ca·tion
pu·ri·fi·er

pu·ri·fy
pur·ist
pu·ri·tan
pu·ri·tan·i·cal
pu·ri·ty
pur·lieu
pur·loin
pur·ple
pur·plish
pur·port
pur·port·ed·ly
pur·pose (intention;
    cf. *propose*)
pur·pose·ly
pur·po·sive
purr
purse–proud
purs·er
pur·su·ance
pur·su·ant
pur·sue
pur·suit
pu·ru·lent
pur·vey
pur·vey·ance
pur·vey·or
pur·view
push·ball
push broom
push but·ton n.
push–but·ton adj.
push·cart
push·i·ness

push·ing
push·over n.
push·pin
push–pull adj.
push–up n.
pu·sil·la·nim·i·ty
pu·sil·lan·i·mous
pus·tu·lant
pus·tu·lar
pus·tu·late
pus·tu·la·tion
pus·tule
pu·ta·tive
put down v.
put–down n.
put off
put–on adj., n.
pu·tre·fac·tion
pu·tre·fac·tive
pu·tre·fy
pu·tres·cence
pu·tres·cent
pu·trid
put·ter
put·ty
put up v.
put–up adj.
puz·zle
puz·zle·ment
puz·zler
pyg·my
py·lon
py·lo·rus

py•or•rhea
pyr•a•mid
py•ra•mi•dal

pyre
py•ro•ma•nia
py•ro•ma•ni•ac

py•rox•y•lin
pyr•rhic
py•thon

quack•ery
quad•ran•gle
qua•dran•gu•lar
quad•rant
qua•dran•tal
qua•drat•ic
qua•dren•ni•al
qua•dren•ni•um
quad•ri•lat•er•al
qua•drille
qua•dril•lion
quad•ru•ped
qua•dru•pe•dal
qua•dru•ple
qua•dru•plet
qua•dru•pli•cate
quaff
quag•mire
qual•i•fi•ca•tion
qual•i•fied
qual•i•fy
qual•i•ta•tive
qual•i•ty
qualm

quan•da•ry
quan•ti•fy
quan•ti•ta•tive
quan•ti•ty
quan•tum
quar•an•tine
quark
quar•rel
quar•reled
quar•rel•ing
quar•rel•some
quar•ry
quar•ry•ing
quar•ter
quar•ter•back
quar•ter•deck
quar•ter•ly
quar•ter•mas•ter
quar•tet
quar•to
quarts (measures)
quartz (mineral)
qua•sar
qua•si

qua•si–ju•di•cial
qua•si–pub•lic
qua•train
qua•tre•foil
qua•ver•ing•ly
quay (wharf; cf. *key*)
quea•si•ness
quea•sy
Que•bec
queen–size
queer
quench•less
quer•u•lous
que•ry
ques•tion
ques•tion•able
ques•tion•er
ques•tion•naire
queue (waiting line; cf.
    cue)
quib•ble
quib•bling
quick•en
quick fire n.

quick–fire adj.
quick–freeze n., v.
quick•ie
quick•lime
quick–lunch n.
quick•sand
quick•sil•ver
quick•step
quick–tem•pered
quick–wit•ted
quid•di•ty
quid•nunc
qui•es•cence
qui•es•cent
qui•et (silent; cf. quit, quite)
qui•et•ness
qui•etude

qui•etus
qui•nine
quin•tes•sence
quin•tet
quin•tu•plet
quin•tu•pli•cate
quip
quipped
quip•ping
quire (24 sheets; cf. choir)
quit (leave; cf. quiet, quite)
quit•claim
quite (completely; cf. quiet, quit)
quit•tance
quit•ter

quiv•er
qui vive
quix•ot•ic
quiz
quizzed
quiz•zi•cal
quiz•zing
quoin (printing; cf. coign, coin)
quoit
quon•dam
quo•rum
quo•ta
quot•able
quo•ta•tion
quote
quo•tid•i•an
quo•tient

R

rab•bet (groove; cf. rabbit)
rab•bi
rab•bit (animal; cf. rabbet)
rab•bit•ry
rab•ble
rab•ble–rous•er
ra•bid
ra•bies

rac•coon
race•course
race•horse
rac•er
race•track
race•way
ra•cial
rac•i•ly
rac•i•ness
rac•ing

rac•ism
rac•ist
rack•et
rack•et•ball
rack•e•teer
ra•con•teur
ra•dar
ra•dar•scope
ra•di•al
ra•di•ance

ra•di•an•cy

ra•di•ant

ra•di•ant•ly

ra•di•ate

ra•di•a•tion

ra•di•a•tor

rad•i•cal

rad•i•cal•ism

rad•i•cal•ly

ra•dii (sing.: *radius*)

ra•dio

ra•dio•ac•tive

ra•dio•gram

ra•dio•graph

ra•di•og•ra•phy

ra•dio•iso•tope

ra•di•om•e•ter

ra•dio•phone

ra•dio•sonde

ra•dio•tele•graph

ra•dio•tele•phone

ra•dio•ther•a•py

rad•ish

ra•di•um

ra•di•us (pl.: *radii*)

raf•fle

raf•ter

rafts•man

rag•a•muf•fin

rag•ged adj.

ragged v.

rag•ing

rag•lan

rag•man

ra•gout

rag•pick•er

rag•time

rag•weed

rail•bird

rail fence

rail•head

rail•ing

rail•lery

rail•road

rail–split•ter

rail•way

rai•ment

rain (water; cf. *reign*, *rein*)

rain•bow

rain check

rain•coat

rain dance

rain•drop

rain•fall

rain gauge

rain•mak•ing

rain•proof

rain•spout

rain•squall

rain•storm

rain•wa•ter

rain•wear

rainy

raise (lift; cf. *rays*, *raze*)

rai•sin

rai•son d'être

ra•ja *or* ra•jah

rake•hell

rake–off

rak•ish

ral•ly

ram•ble

ram•bler

ram•bling

ram•bunc•tious

ram•e•kin

ram•i•fi•ca•tion

ram•i•fy

ram•pant

ram•part

ram•rod

ram•shack•le

ranch•er

ranch•man

ran•cid

ran•cor

ran•cor•ous

ran•dom

ran•dom–ac•cess mem•o•ry

rangy

ran•kle

ran•sack

ran•som

ra•pa•cious

ra•pac•i•ty

rap•id

rap•id–fire

ra•pid•i•ty

rap•id•ly

ra•pi•er
rap•ine
rapped (struck; cf.
   rapt, wrapped)
rap•port
rapt (engrossed; cf.
   rapped, wrapped)
rap•ture
rap•tur•ous
rare•bit
rar•efac•tion
rar•efied
rar•efy
rare•ly
rare•ness
rar•i•ty
ras•cal
ras•cal•i•ty
rash•ly
rash•ness
rasp•ber•ry
rasp•ing•ly
rat•able
ratch•et
rath•er
raths•kel•ler
rat•i•fi•ca•tion
rat•i•fy
rat•ing
ra•tio
ra•ti•o•ci•na•tion
ra•tion
ra•tio•nal
ra•tio•nale

ra•tio•nal•iza•tion
ra•tio•nal•ize
rat•like
rat•line
rat race
rat•tail
rat•tan
rat•tle
rat•tle-brained
rat•tler
rat•tle•snake
rat•tle•trap
rat•trap n.
rau•cous
rav•age
rav•el
rav•eled
rav•el•ing
ra•ven
rav•en•ing
rav•en•ous
ra•vine
rav•i•o•li
rav•ish•ing•ly
raw•boned
raw•hide
ray•on
rays (of light; cf. *raise,*
   raze)
raze (tear down; cf.
   raise, rays)
ra•zor
ra•zor•back
re•act

re•ac•tion
re•ac•tion•ary
re•ac•ti•vate
re•ac•tor
read•able
read•er•ship
readi•ly
readi•ness
re•ad•just•ment
read-on•ly mem•
   o•ry
ready-made
ready-to-wear
re•af•firm
re•agent
re•al (true; cf. *reel*)
re•al es•tate
re•alia
re•al•ism
re•al•ist
re•al•is•tic
re•al•is•ti•cal•ly
re•al•i•ty (real event;
   cf. *realty*)
re•al•iza•tion
re•al•ize
re•al•ly
realm
Re•al•tor
re•al•ty (property; cf.
   reality)
re•ap•point
re•ap•prais•al
rear guard

re•arm
re•ar•range
rea•son
rea•son•able
rea•son•ing
re•as•sem•ble
re•as•sur•ance
re•as•sure
re•bate
reb•el adj., n.
re•bel v.
re•belled
re•bel•ling
re•bel•lion
re•bel•lious
re•birth
re•buff
re•buke
re•bus
re•but•tal
re•cal•ci•tran•cy
re•cal•ci•trant
re•call
re•cant
re•ca•pit•u•late
re•ca•pit•u•la•tion
re•cap•ture
re•cede
re•ceipt
re•ceiv•able
re•ceive
re•ceiv•er•ship
re•cent
re•cep•ta•cle

re•cep•tion
re•cep•tive
re•cess
re•ces•sion
re•ces•sion•al
re•ces•sive
re•cid•i•vism
rec•i•pe
re•cip•i•ent
re•cip•ro•cal
re•cip•ro•cate
re•cip•ro•ca•tion
rec•i•proc•i•ty
re•cit•al
rec•i•ta•tion
rec•i•ta•tive
re•cite
reck•less
reck•on
re•claim
rec•la•ma•tion
re•cline
re•cluse
rec•og•ni•tion
re•cog•niz•able
re•cog•ni•zance
rec•og•nize
re•coil
re–col•lect (collect again)
rec•ol•lect (recall)
rec•ol•lec•tion
rec•om•mend
rec•om•men•da•tion

re•com•mit
rec•om•pense
rec•on•cile
rec•on•cil•i•a•tion
re•con•di•tion
re•con•firm
re•con•fir•ma•tion
re•con•nais•sance
re•con•noi•ter
re•con•sid•er
re•con•struc•tion
re•con•vene
re•cord v.
rec•ord n.
re•cord•er
re•coup
re•course
re•cov•er (regain)
re–cov•er (cover again)
re•cov•ery
rec•re•ant
rec•re•ation
re•crim•i•na•tion
re•cru•des•cence
re•cruit
rect•an•gle
rect•an•gu•lar
rec•ti•fi•ca•tion
rec•ti•fi•er
rec•ti•fy
rec•ti•lin•ear
rec•ti•tude
rec•to•ry

rec•tum
re•cum•bent
re•cu•per•ate
re•cu•per•a•tion
re•cur
re•curred
re•cur•rence
re•cur•rent
re•cur•ring
re•cy•cle
red—bait•ing
red•bird
red—blood•ed
red•breast
red•bud
red•cap
red—car•pet adj.
red•coat
Red Cross
re•dec•o•rate
re•deem
re•deem•able
re•deem•er
re•demp•tion
re•de•vel•op•ment
red—hand•ed adj.,
    adv.
red•head
red—hot
re•dis•count
re•dis•trib•ute
re•dis•trict
red lead
red—let•ter

red•o•lence
red•o•lent
re•dou•ble
re•doubt•able
re•dound
red—pen•cil v.
re•dress
red•skin
red tape
re•duce
re•duc•tion
re•dun•dan•cy
re•dun•dant
red•wing
red•wood
re•echo
re•ed•u•cate
reek (smell; cf. *wreak*,
    wreck)
reel (spool; cf. *real*)
re•elect
re•em•pha•size
re•em•ploy
re•en•act
re•en•grave
re•en•list
re•en•trance
re•en•try
re•es•tab•lish
re•ex•am•i•na•tion
re•ex•am•ine
re•fer
ref•er•ee
ref•er•ence

ref•er•en•dum
re•ferred
re•fer•ring
re•fine
re•fined
re•fine•ment
re•fin•er
re•fin•ery
re•flect
re•flec•tion
re•flec•tive
re•flec•tor
re•flex
re•flex•ive
re•for•es•ta•tion
re•form
ref•or•ma•tion
re•for•ma•to•ry
re•formed
re•frac•tion
re•frac•to•ry
re•frain
re•fresh
re•fresh•ment
re•frig•er•ant
re•frig•er•ate
re•frig•er•a•tion
re•frig•er•a•tor
ref•uge
ref•u•gee
re•ful•gent
re•fur•bish
re•fus•al
re•fuse (reject)

ref•use (garbage)
re•fut•able
ref•u•ta•tion
re•fute
re•gain
re•gal
re•gale
re•ga•lia
re•gard
re•gard•ful
re•gard•less
re•gat•ta
re•gen•cy
re•gen•er•ate
re•gen•er•a•tive
re•gent
reg•i•cide
re•gime
reg•i•men
reg•i•ment
reg•i•men•tal
reg•i•men•ta•tion
re•gion
re•gion•al
re•gis•seur
reg•is•ter (to enroll;
  cf. *registrar*)
reg•is•tered
reg•is•trar (record
  keeper; cf. *register*)
reg•is•tra•tion
reg•is•try
reg•nant
re•gress

re•gres•sion
re•gres•sive
re•gret
re•gret•ful
re•gret•ta•ble
re•gret•ted
re•gret•ting
reg•u•lar
reg•u•lar•i•ty
reg•u•lar•ize
reg•u•late
reg•u•la•tion
reg•u•la•to•ry
re•gur•gi•tate
re•ha•bil•i•tate
re•hash
re•hear•ing
re•hears•al
re•hearse
reign (sovereignty; cf.
  rain, rein)
re•im•burs•able
re•im•burse
rein (of a horse; cf.
  rain, reign)
re•in•car•na•tion
rein•deer
re•in•force
re•in•force•ment
re•in•sert
re•in•state
re•in•sur•ance
re•in•sure
re•in•vest

re•in•vig•o•rate
re•is•sue
re•it•er•ate
re•it•er•a•tion
re•ject
re•jec•tion
re•joice
re•join
re•join•der
re•ju•ve•nate
re•kin•dle
re•lapse
re•late
re•la•tion•ship
rel•a•tive
rel•a•tiv•i•ty
re•lax
re•lax•ation
re•laxed
re•lay
re•lease
rel•e•gate
re•lent
re•lent•less
rel•e•vance
rel•e•vant
re•li•able
re•li•ance
re•li•ant
rel•ic
rel•ict
re•lief
re•lieve
re•li•gion

re•li•gious
re•lin•quish
rel•i•quary
rel•ish
re•luc•tance
re•luc•tant
re•ly
re•main
re•main•der
re•mand
re•mark
re•mark•able
re•mar•riage
re•me•di•a•ble
re•me•di•al
rem•e•dy
re•mem•ber
re•mem•brance
re•mind
re•mind•er
rem•i•nisce
rem•i•nis•cence
rem•i•nis•cent
re•mis•sion
re•mit•tance
re•mit•tent
rem•nant
re•mon•e•tize
re•mon•strance
re•mon•strate
re•mon•stra•tion
re•morse
re•morse•less

re•mote
re•mov•able
re•mov•al
re•move
re•mu•ner•ate
re•mu•ner•a•tion
re•mu•ner•a•tive
re•nais•sance
ren•der
ren•dez•vous
ren•di•tion
ren•e•gade
re•nege
re•ne•go•tia•ble
re•ne•go•ti•ate
re•new
re•new•able
re•new•al
ren•net
re•nom•i•nate
re•nounce
ren•o•vate
ren•o•va•tion
re•nown
rent•al
re•nun•ci•a•tion
re•open
re•or•der
re•or•ga•ni•za•tion
re•pair
re•pair•er
re•pair•man
rep•a•ra•tion

rep•ar•tee
re•past
re•pa•tri•ate
re•pa•tri•a•tion
re•pay
re•peal
re•peat
re•peat•er
re•pel
re•pelled
re•pel•lent
re•pel•ling
re•pent
re•pen•tance
re•pen•tant
re•per•cus•sion
rep•er•toire
rep•er•to•ry
rep•e•ti•tion
rep•e•ti•tious
re•pet•i•tive
re•pine
re•place
re•place•able
re•place•ment
re•plen•ish•ment
re•plete
re•plev•in
rep•li•ca
rep•li•cate
re•ply
re•port
re•port•er

re•pose
re•pos•i•to•ry
re•pos•sess
re•pous•sé
rep•re•hend
rep•re•hen•si•ble
rep•re•sent
rep•re•sen•ta•tion
rep•re•sen•ta•tive
re•press
re•pressed
re•pres•sion
re•pres•sive
re•prieve
rep•ri•mand
re•print
re•pri•sal
re•proach
re•proach•ful
rep•ro•bate
re•pro•duce
re•pro•duc•tion
re•pro•duc•tive
re•pro•graph•ics
re•proof
re•prove
rep•tile
rep•til•ian
re•pub•lic
re•pub•li•can
re•pu•di•ate
re•pu•di•a•tion
re•pug•nance

re•pug•nant
re•pulse
re•pul•sion
re•pul•sive
re•pur•chase
rep•u•ta•ble
rep•u•ta•tion
re•pute
re•quest
re•qui•em
re•quire
re•quire•ment
req•ui•site
req•ui•si•tion
re•quit•al
re•quite
rere•dos
re•run
re•sal•able
re•scind
re•scis•sion
re•script
res•cue
re•search
re•sem•blance
re•sem•ble
re•sent
re•sent•ful
re•sent•ment
res•er•va•tion
re•serve
re•served
res•er•voir

re•shuf•fle
re•side
res•i•dence (home; cf. *residents*)
res•i•dent
res•i•den•tial
res•i•dents (those who reside; cf. *residence*)
re•sid•u•al
re•sid•u•ary
res•i•due
re•sid•u•um
re•sign
res•ig•na•tion
re•sil•ience
re•sil•ient
res•in
res•in•ous
re•sist
re•sis•tance
re•sis•tant
re•sis•tiv•i•ty
re•sis•tor
res•o•lute
res•o•lu•tion
re•solve
res•o•nance
res•o•nant
res•o•na•tor
re•sort
re•sound
re•source
re•source•ful

re•spect
re•spect•abil•i•ty
re•spect•able
re•spect•ful
re•spect•ful•ly (with deference; cf. *respectively*)
re•spec•tive
re•spec•tive•ly (in that order; cf. *respectfully*)
res•pi•ra•tion
res•pi•ra•tor
re•spi•ra•to•ry
re•spite
re•splen•dent
re•spond
re•spon•dent
re•sponse
re•spon•si•bil•i•ty
re•spon•si•ble
re•spon•sive
rest (repose; cf. *wrest*)
res•tau•rant
res•tau•ra•teur
rest home
rest house
res•ti•tu•tion
res•tive
rest•less
res•to•ra•tion
re•stor•ative
re•store
re•strain

re•straint
re•strict
re•stric•tion
re•stric•tive
re•sult
re•sul•tant
re•sume v.
ré•su•mé n.
re•sump•tion
re•sur•face
re•sur•gence
res•ur•rect
res•ur•rec•tion
re•sus•ci•tate
re•sus•ci•ta•tion
re•tail
re•tain
re•tain•er
re•tal•i•ate
re•tal•i•a•tion
re•tal•ia•to•ry
re•tard
re•tar•da•tion
re•ten•tion
re•ten•tive
re•ten•tiv•i•ty
ret•i•cence
ret•i•cent
ret•i•cule
ret•i•na
ret•i•nene
re•tire
re•tire•ment
re•tool

re•tort
re•touch
re•trace
re•tract
re•trac•tile
re•trac•tion
re•treat
re•trench
ret•ri•bu•tion
re•triev•able
re•trieve
re•triev•er
ret•ro•ac•tive
ret•ro•ces•sion
ret•ro•fit
ret•ro•grade
ret•ro•gres•sion
ret•ro–rock•et
ret•ro•spect
ret•ro•spec•tive
re•trous•sé
re•turn
re•turn•able
re•union
re•unite
re•us•able
re•use
re•val•ue
re•vamp
re•veal
rev•eil•le
rev•el
rev•e•la•tion
rev•eled

rev•el•ing
re•venge
rev•e•nue
re•ver•ber•ate
re•ver•ber•a•tion
re•ver•ber•a•to•ry
re•vere
rev•er•ence
rev•er•end
rev•er•ent
rev•er•en•tial
rev•er•ie
re•ver•sal
re•verse
re•vers•ible
re•ver•sion
re•ver•sion•ary
re•vert
re•vert•ed
re•vet•ment
re•vict•ual
re•view (restudy; cf. *revue*)
re•view•er
re•vile
re•vise
re•vi•sion
re•vi•tal•ize
re•viv•al
re•vive
re•viv•i•fy
re•vo•ca•ble
re•vo•ca•tion
re•voke

re•volt
rev•o•lu•tion
rev•o•lu•tion•ary
rev•o•lu•tion•ist
rev•o•lu•tion•ize
re•volve
re•volv•er
re•vue (theatrical performance; cf. *review*)
re•vul•sion
re•ward
re•wind
re•word
re•work
re•write
re•zon•ing
rhap•sod•ic
rhap•so•dist
rhap•so•dize
rhap•so•dy
rheo•stat
rhe•sus
rhet•o•ric
rhe•tor•i•cal
rheum (watery discharge; cf. *room*)
rheu•mat•ic
rheu•ma•tism
rhine•stone
rhi•ni•tis
rhi•noc•er•os
Rhode Is•land
rhom•boid

rhu•barb
rhyme (verse; cf. *rime*)
rhythm
rhyth•mic
rib•ald
rib•ald•ry
rib•bon
ric•er
rick•ets
rick•ety
ric•o•chet
rid•dle
rid•er•less
ridge•pole
rid•i•cule
ri•dic•u•lous
rif•fle (shuffle; cf. *rifle*)
riff•raff
ri•fle (gun; cf. *riffle*)
ri•fle•man
ri•fle•scope
ri•fling
right (correct; cf. *rite, write*)
righ•teous•ness
right•ful
right hand n.
right–hand adj.
right–hand•ed
right–of–way
right wing n.
right–wing•er n.
rig•id
ri•gid•i•ty

rig·or·ous

rime (frost; cf. *rhyme*)

ring (a bell; cf. *wring*)

ring·bolt

ring·bone

ring·dove

ring·lead·er

ring·mas·ter

ring·side

ring·worm

rinse

ri·ot·ous

ri·par·i·an

rip·en

rip off v.

rip–off n.

ri·poste

rip·ple

rip·rap

rip–roar·ing

rip·saw

rip·snort·er

rip·tide

ris·i·bil·i·ty

risk·i·ness

ris·qué

rite (ceremony; cf. *right, write*)

rit·u·al

ri·val

ri·valed

ri·val·ing

ri·val·ry

riv·er·bed

riv·er·boat

riv·er·side

riv·et

riv·u·let

road (highway; cf. *rode, rowed*)

road·bed

road·block

road hog

road·house

road·stead

road·ster

road test

road·way

road·work

robbed

rob·bery

rob·bing

rob·in

ro·bot

ro·bot·ics

ro·bust

ro·bus·tious

rock bot·tom n.

rock·bound

rock·et

rock·et·ry

rock 'n' roll

rock–ribbed

rock salt

rock·slide

rock snake

rock wool

rock·work

ro·co·co

rode (did ride; cf. *road, rowed*)

ro·dent

ro·deo

rod·man

roe (fish eggs; cf. *row*)

roent·gen

rogue

rogu·ish

role (part)

roll (turn over)

roll back v.

roll·back n.

roll bar

roll call

roll·er coast·er

ro·maine

ro·mance

ro·man·tic

ro·man·ti·cism

rood (crucifix; cf. *rude, rued*)

roof·less

roof·top

rook·ery

rook·ie

room (of a house; cf. *rheum*)

room and board

room·er (lodger; cf. *rumor*)

room·ette

room·ful

room•i•ness
room•mate
roost•er
root (of a tree; cf. *rout*, *route*)
root beer
root•less
root•let
rope•danc•er
rope•walk
Ror•schach
ro•sa•ry
ro•se•ate
rose•bud
rose•bush
rose–col•ored
rose•mary
ro•se•o•la
ro•sette
rose wa•ter n.
rose–wa•ter adj.
rose•wood
ros•in
ros•ter
ros•trum
ro•ta•ry
ro•tate
ro•ta•tion
rote (memory; cf. *wrote*)
ro•tis•ser•ie
ro•to•gra•vure
ro•tor
rot•ten•stone

ro•tund
ro•tun•da
ro•tun•di•ty
rouge
rough (rude; cf. *ruff*)
rough•age
rough–and–ready
rough–and–tum•ble
rough•cast
rough–dry
rough•en
rough–hew
rough•house
rough•neck
rough•rid•er
rough•shod
rou•lade
rou•leau
rou•lette
round•about
roun•de•lay
round•house
round–shoul•dered
rounds•man
round–the–clock
round–trip
round up v.
round•up n.
roust•about
rout (disperse; cf. *root*, *route*)
route (highway; cf. *root*, *rout*)

route•man
rou•tine
rou•tin•ize
row (a boat; cf. *roe*)
row•boat
row•di•ness
row•dy
rowed (did row; cf. *road*, *rode*)
row•el
row house
row•lock
roy•al
roy•al•ist
roy•al•ty
ru•ba•to
rubbed
rub•ber
rub•ber band
rub•ber•ize
rub•ber•neck
rub•ber stamp n.
rub•ber–stamp v.
rub•bing
rub•bish
rub•ble
rub•ble•work
rub down v.
rub•down n.
ru•bel•la
Ru•bi•con
ru•bi•cund
ru•bric
ruck•sack

ruck•us
rud•der
rud•dy
rude (rough; cf. *rood,*
   rued)
ru•di•ment
ru•di•men•ta•ry
rued (regretted; cf.
   rood, rude)
rue•ful
ruff (collar; cf. *rough*)
ruf•fi•an
ruf•fle
rug•ged
rug•ged•iza•tion
ru•in•ous
rule of thumb
rule out
rum•ba
rum•ble
ru•mi•nant
ru•mi•nate
ru•mi•na•tion

rum•mage
ru•mor (gossip; cf.
   roomer)
ru•mor•mon•ger
rum•ple
rum•pus
rum•run•ner
run•about
run•around n.
run away v.
run•away adj., n.
run down v.
run–down adj.
run•down n.
rung (a bell; cf. *wrung*)
run in v.
run–in n.
run•ner
run•ner–up
run off v.
run•off n.
run–of–the–mill
run–of–the–mine

run on v.
run–on adj., n.
run over v.
run–over adj.
run•over n.
run•proof
run through v.
run–through n.
run•way
ru•pee
rup•ture
ru•ral
ru•ral•ly
rush hour
rus•set
rus•tic
rus•ti•cate
rus•tle
rust–proof v.
rust•proof adj.
ru•ta•ba•ga
ruth•less
rye (grain; cf. *wry*)

Sab•bath
sab•bat•i•cal
sa•ber
sa•ble
sab•o•tage

sab•o•teur
sa•bra
sac (pouch in animal; cf.
   sack)
sac•cha•rin n.

sac•cha•rine adj.
sac•er•do•tal
sa•chem
sack (bag; cf. *sac*)
sack•cloth

sack coat
sack•ful
sack race
sac•ra•ment
sac•ra•men•tal
sa•cred
sac•ri•fice
sac•ri•fi•cial
sac•ri•lege
sac•ri•le•gious
sac•ris•tan
sac•ris•ty
sac•ro•sanct
sa•crum
sad•den
sad•der
sad•dest
sad•dle
sad•dle•bag
sad•dle•bow
sad•dle•cloth
sad•dler
sad•iron
sa•dism
sa•dist
sa•dis•tic
sad•ness
safe–con•duct
safe•crack•er
safe–de•pos•it box
safe•guard
safe•keep•ing
safe•ty
saf•fron

sa•ga
sa•ga•cious
sa•gac•i•ty
sag•a•more
sage•brush
sa•hib
sail (of a ship; cf. *sale*)
sail•boat
sail•cloth
sail•fish
sail•or
saint•li•ness
saint•ly
sa•laam
sal•abil•i•ty
sal•able
sa•la•cious
sal•ad
sal•a•man•der
sa•la•mi
sal•a•ried
sal•a•ry
sale (selling; cf. *sail*)
sales
sales check
sales•clerk
sales•man
sales•man•ship
sales•per•son
sales•room
sales•wom•an
sal•i•cyl•ic
sa•lience
sa•lient

sa•line
sa•li•va
sal•i•vary
sal•low
sal•ma•gun•di
salm•on
sa•lon (shop)
sa•loon (tavern)
sal•ta•to•ry
salt•box
salt•cel•lar
sal•tine
salt•i•ness
salt marsh
salt•pe•ter
salt•shak•er
salt wa•ter n.
salt•wa•ter adj.
salt•works
salty
sa•lu•bri•ous
sal•u•tary
sal•u•ta•tion
sa•lu•ta•to•ri•an
sa•lute
sal•vage
sal•va•tion
Sa•mar•i•tan
same•ness
sa•mite
sam•o•var
sam•pan
sam•ple
sam•pler

sam•pling

sam•u•rai

san•a•to•ri•um

san•a•to•ry (healing;
  cf. *sanitary*)

sanc•ti•fi•ca•tion

sanc•ti•fy

sanc•ti•mo•nious

sanc•tion

sanc•ti•ty

sanc•tu•ary

sanc•tum

san•dal

san•dal•wood

sand•bag

sand•bank

sand•bar

sand•blast

sand•box

sand•er

sand•glass

sand•hog

sand•lot

sand•man

sand•pa•per

sand•pile

sand•pip•er

sand•soap

sand•stone

sand•storm

sand ta•ble

sand trap

sand•wich

sand•worm

sang•froid

san•gui•nary

san•guine

san•i•tary (hygienic;
  cf. *sanatory*)

san•i•ta•tion

san•i•ty

sans-cu•lotte

sap•ling

sa•pon•i•fy

sap•phire

sap•suck•er

sap•wood

sar•a•band

sar•casm

sar•cas•tic

sar•co•ma

sar•coph•a•gi pl.

sar•coph•a•gus sing.

sar•dine

sar•don•ic

sard•onyx

sar•gas•so

sa•rong

sar•sa•pa•ril•la

sar•to•ri•al

Sas•katch•e•wan

sas•sa•fras

sa•tan•ic

satch•el

sa•teen

sat•el•lite

sa•tia•ble

sa•tiate adj.

sa•ti•ate v.

sa•ti•ety

sat•in

sat•in•wood

sat•ire

sa•tir•ic

sa•tir•i•cal

sat•i•rize

sat•is•fac•tion

sat•is•fac•to•ri•ly

sat•is•fac•to•ry

sat•is•fy

sa•trap

sat•u•rate

sat•u•rat•ed

sat•u•ra•tion

Sat•ur•day

sat•ur•nine

sa•tyr

sauce•pan

sau•cer

sau•er•bra•ten

sau•er•kraut

Sault Sainte Ma•rie

sau•na

saun•ter

sau•sage

sau•té

sau•terne

sav•age

sav•age•ry

sa•van•na

sa•vant

sav•ings bond

sav•ior
sa•vory
saw•dust
sawed–off
saw•horse
saw•mill
saw–toothed
saw•yer
sax•o•phone
say–so
scab•bard
scaf•fold
scaf•fold•ing
scal•a•wag
scale–down
scal•lion
scal•lop
scal•pel
scam•per
scan•dal
scan•dal•ize
scan•dal•ous
Scan•di•na•vian
scan•ner
scan•ning
scan•sion
scant•i•ly
scant•ling
scanty
scape•goat
scap•u•la
scap•u•lar
scar•ab
scarce•ly

scar•ci•ty
scare•crow
scar•i•fy
scar•la•ti•na
scar•let
scath•ing
scat•ter
scat•ter•brain
scav•en•ger
sce•nar•io
scen•ery
scene•shift•er
sce•nic
scent (odor; cf. *cent,*
    sent)
scep•ter
sched•ule
sche•mat•ic
scheme
scher•zo
schism
schist
schmaltz
schnook
schol•ar
schol•ar•ly
schol•ar•ship
scho•las•tic
scho•las•ti•cism
school–age
school•bag
school board
school•boy
school bus

school•child
school dis•trict
school•girl
school•house
school•man
school•mas•ter
school•mate
school•mis•tress
school•room
school•teach•er
school•work
schoo•ner
sci•at•ic
sci•at•i•ca
sci•ence
sci•en•tif•ic
sci•en•tist
scim•i•tar
scin•til•la
scin•til•late
sci•on
scis•sors
scle•ro•sis
scoff•law
scor•bu•tic
score•board
score•card
score•keep•er
scorn•ful
scor•pi•on
scot–free
scoun•drel
scourge
scout•mas•ter

scrap·book
scrap·per
scrap·ple
scratch
scratch·i·ness
scratchy
screech
screed
screen
screen·play
screw·ball
screw·driv·er
scrib·ble
scrim·mage
scrim·shaw
scrip (paper money)
script (manuscript)
scrip·tur·al
scrip·ture
scriv·en·er
scrof·u·la
scroll·ing
scroll·work
scrubbed
scrub·bing
scrump·tious
scru·ple
scru·pu·lous
scru·ti·nize
scru·ti·ny
scuf·fle
scuf·fling
scull (boat; cf. *skull*)
scul·lery

scul·lion
sculp·tor
sculp·tur·al
sculp·ture
scur·ril·i·ty
scur·ri·lous
scur·vy
scut·tle
scut·tle·butt
scut·tling
scythe
sea (ocean; cf. *see*)
sea·bag
sea bass
sea·beach
sea·bird
sea·board
sea·boot
sea·borne
sea breeze
sea chest
sea·coast
sea dog
sea·drome
sea·far·er
sea·far·ing
sea fight
sea·food
sea·fowl
sea·front
sea·girt
sea·go·ing
sea green
sea gull

sea horse
sea–lane
seal·ant
sea legs
seal ring
seal·skin
seam (sewn; cf. *seem*)
sea·man
sea·man·like
sea·man·ship
seam·less
seam·ster mas.
seam·stress fem.
sé·ance
sea·plane
sea·port
sear (burn; cf. *seer*)
search·light
sea room
sea·scape
Sea Scout
sea·shell
sea·shore
sea·sick
sea·side
sea·son
sea·son·able
sea·son·al
seat belt
seat·ed
seat·ing
sea·wall
sea·ward
sea·wa·ter

sea•way
sea•weed
sea•wor•thi•ness
sea•wor•thy
se•ba•ceous
se•cant
se•cede
se•ces•sion
se•clude
se•clu•sion
sec•ond
sec•ond•ari•ly
sec•ond•ary
sec•ond class n.
sec•ond–class adj.
sec•ond–guess v.
sec•ond•hand adj.
sec•ond–rate adj.
sec•ond thought
se•cre•cy
se•cret
sec•re•tari•al
sec•re•tary
se•crete
se•cre•tion
se•cre•tive
se•cre•to•ry
sec•tar•i•an
sec•ta•ry
sec•tion
sec•tion•al•ly
sec•tor
sec•u•lar
sec•u•lar•ism

se•cure
se•cu•ri•ty
se•dan
se•date
se•da•tion
sed•a•tive
sed•en•tary
sed•i•ment
sed•i•men•ta•ry
se•di•tion
se•di•tious
se•duce
se•duc•er
se•duc•tion
se•duc•tive
sed•u•lous
see (perceive; cf. *sea*)
seed (of a plant; cf.
   cede)
seed•i•ness
seed•ling
seed•pod
seedy
seem (appear; cf. *seam*)
seem•li•ness
seem•ly
seep•age
seer (prophet; cf. *sear*)
seer•suck•er
see–saw
see–through adj.
seg•ment
seg•re•gate
seg•re•gat•ed

seg•re•ga•tion
seg•re•ga•tion•ist
seis•mic
seis•mo•graph
seis•mo•log•i•cal
seis•mom•e•ter
seize
seiz•ing
sei•zure
sel•dom
se•lect
se•lec•tion
se•lec•tive
se•lect•man
Se•lect•ric
se•le•ni•um
self–abase•ment
self–ad•dressed
self–ag•gran•dize•
   ment
self–as•sured
self–cen•tered
self–clean•ing
self–com•posed
self–con•fi•dence
self–con•scious
self–con•tained
self–con•trol
self–de•fense
self–de•struc•tion
self–de•ter•mi•
   na•tion
self–dis•ci•pline
self–ed•u•cat•ed

self•ef•face•ment
self•em•ployed
self•es•teem
self•ev•i•dent
self•ex•e•cut•ing
self•ex•plan•a•to•ry
self•ex•pres•sion
self•glo•ri•fi•ca•tion
self•gov•ern•ment
self•help
self•im•age
self•im•por•tance
self•im•posed
self•im•prove•ment
self•in•crim•i•na•tion
self•in•dul•gence
self•in•flict•ed
self•in•sured
self•in•ter•est
self•ish
self•less
self•liq•ui•dat•ing
self•made
self•mo•ti•vat•ed
self•paced
self•pity
self•pos•sessed
self•pos•ses•sion
self•pres•er•va•tion
self•pro•tec•tion
self•re•gard
self•re•li•ance
self•re•spect

self•ris•ing
self•sac•ri•fice
self•same
self•sat•is•fac•tion
self•start•er
self•suf•fi•cien•cy
self•suf•fi•cient
self•sup•port
self•taught
self•teach
self•willed
self•wind•ing
sell•er (one who sells;
    cf. *cellar*)
sell out v.
sell•out n.
selt•zer
sel•vage
se•man•tic
sema•phore
sem•blance
se•mes•ter
semi•an•nu•al
semi•ar•id
semi•au•to•mat•ed
semi•au•to•mat•ic
semi•au•ton•o•mous
semi•cir•cle
semi•civ•i•lized
semi•clas•si•cal
semi•co•lon
semi•con•duc•tor
semi•con•scious
semi•crys•tal•line

semi•dark•ness
semi•de•tached
semi•fi•nal
semi•fin•ished
semi•in•de•pen•dent
semi•in•di•rect
semi•month•ly
sem•i•nar
sem•i•nary
semi•per•ma•nent
semi•pre•cious
semi•pri•vate
semi•pro
semi•pro•fes•sion•al
semi•pub•lic
semi•skilled
semi•sweet
semi•trans•lu•cent
semi•trans•par•ent
semi•vow•el
semi•week•ly
semi•year•ly
sem•pi•ter•nal
sen•ate
sen•a•tor
sen•a•to•ri•al
send•off n.
se•nes•cent
se•nile
se•nil•i•ty
se•nior
se•nior•i•ty
sen•sa•tion

sen•sa•tion•al
sense•less
sens•es (sensations; cf. *census*)
sen•si•bil•i•ty
sen•si•ble
sen•si•tive
sen•si•tiv•i•ty
sen•si•tize
sen•so•ry
sen•su•al
sen•su•ous
sent (dispatched; cf. *cent, scent*)
sen•tence
sen•ten•tious
sen•tient
sen•ti•ment
sen•ti•men•tal
sen•ti•men•tal•ism
sen•ti•men•tal•i•ty
sen•ti•nel
sen•try
sep•a•ra•ble
sep•a•rate
sep•a•ra•tion
sep•a•rat•ist
sep•a•ra•tor
se•pia
Sep•tem•ber
sep•tet
sep•tic
sep•ti•ce•mia
sep•tu•a•ge•nar•i•an

sep•ul•cher
se•pul•chral
sep•ul•ture
se•quel
se•quence
se•quen•tial
se•ques•ter
se•ques•trate
se•quin
se•quoia
se•ra•glio
ser•aph
se•raph•ic
ser•e•nade
ser•en•dip•i•ty
se•rene
se•ren•i•ty
serf (peasant; cf. *surf*)
serge (cloth; cf. *surge*)
ser•geant
se•ri•al (series; cf. *cereal*)
se•ri•al•iza•tion
se•ri•al•ize
se•ri•a•tim
se•ries (related group; cf. *serious, serous*)
ser•if
seri•graph
se•rio•com•ic
se•ri•ous (grave; cf. *series, serous*)
se•ri•ous–mind•ed
ser•mon

ser•mon•ize
se•rous (like serum; cf. *series, serious*)
ser•pent
ser•pen•tine
ser•ra•tion
se•rum
ser•vant
ser•vice
ser•vice•able
ser•vice charge
ser•vile
ser•vil•i•ty
ser•vi•tor
ser•vi•tude
ser•vo•mech•a•nism
ser•vo•mo•tor
ses•a•me
ses•qui•cen•ten•ni•al
ses•qui•pe•da•lian
ses•sion (a meeting; cf. *cession*)
set•back n.
set off v.
set•off n.
set out v.
set•out n.
set piece
set•screw
set•tee
set•ter
set•tle•ment
set•tling
set to v.

set–to n.
set up v.
set•up n.
sev•en•teenth
sev•en–up
sev•er
sev•er•al
sev•er•al•fold
sev•er•al•ty
sev•er•ance
se•vere
se•ver•i•ty
sew (stitch; cf. *so, sow*)
sew•age
sew•er
sew•er•age
sex•tant
sex•tet
sex•ton
sex•u•al•i•ty
shab•bi•ness
shab•by
shack•le
shad•ow
shad•ow box n.
shad•ow•box v.
shad•ow•box v.
shad•owy
shag•bark
shag•gi•ness
sha•green
shake•down adj., n.
shake•out n.
shake up v.
shake–up n.

shak•i•ly
shal•lop
shal•lot
shal•low
sham
sham•ble
shame
shame•faced
shame•ful
shame•less
sham•ing
sham•poo
sham•rock
shang•hai
shan•ty
shan•ty•town
shape•less
shape•li•ness
shape•ly
shape–up n.
share•crop•per
shared log•ic sys•
    tem
shared re•source
    sys•tem
share•hold•er
shark•skin
sharp•en•er
sharp•er
sharp–eyed
sharp•shoot•er
sharp–sight•ed
sharp–tongued
sharp–wit•ted

shat•ter•proof
shave•tail
shawl
sheaf
shear (cut; cf. *sheer*)
sheath n.
sheathe v.
sheath•ing
sheath knife
sheen
sheep–dip
sheep•dog
sheep•fold
sheep•herd•er
sheep•ish
sheep•skin
sheer (thin; cf. *shear*)
sheet met•al
Sheet•rock
shel•lac
shel•lacked
shel•lack•ing
shell•back
shell•fire
shell•fish
shell game
shell•proof
shell shock n.
shel•ter
she•nan•i•gan
shep•herd
sher•bet
sher•iff
sher•ry

shib·bo·leth
shield
shift·i·ly
shift·i·ness
shift key
shift·less
shifty
shil·ling
shimmed
shim·mer
shim·my
shin·gle
ship·board
ship·build·ing
ship·fit·ter
ship·mas·ter
ship·mate
ship·ment
ship·pa·ble
shipped
ship·per
ship·ping
ship·shape
ship·wreck
ship·wright
ship·yard
shirr·ing
shirt·ing
shirt·mak·er
shirt·tail
shirt·waist
shish ke·bab
shiv·er
shock·proof

shod
shod·di·ly
shod·di·ness
shod·dy
shoe
shoed
shoe·horn
shoe·ing
shoe·lace
shoe·mak·er
shoe·string
shoe tree
sho·gun
shone (gave light; cf.
   shown)
shook–up
shoot (to fire; cf. *chute*)
shop·keep·er
shop·lift·er
shop·lift·ing
shop·per
shop·talk
shop·worn
shore·line
short·age
short·bread
short·cake
short·change
short cir·cuit n.
short–cir·cuit v.
short·com·ing
short·cut
short·en·ing
short·fall

short·hand
short·hand·ed
short haul n.
short–haul adj.
short·horn
short–lived
short–range adj.
short ribs
short·sight·ed
short–spo·ken
short·stop
short–tem·pered
short–term
short·wave
short weight n.
short–weight v.
short–wind·ed
shot·gun
shot put
shot–put·ter
shoul·der
shov·el
shov·eled
shov·el·ful
shov·el·ing
show·boat
show·case
show·down
show·er
show·i·er
show·i·est
show·i·ly
show·i·ness
show·man

shown (displayed; cf. *shone*)
show off v.
show–off n.
show•piece
show•place
show•room
showy
shrap•nel
shred
shred•der
shred•ding
shrewd
shrew•ish
shriek
shrimp
shrink•age
shriv•el
shriv•eled
shriv•el•ing
shrub•bery
shud•der
shuf•fle
shuf•fle•board
shut down v.
shut•down n.
shut–eye
shut–in adj., n.
shut off v.
shut•off n.
shut out v.
shut•out n.
shut•ter
shut•ter•bug

shut•tle•cock
shy•ster
sib•i•lant
sib•ling
sib•yl
sib•yl•line
sick bay
sick•bed
sick call
sick•en•ing
sick•ish
sick•le
sick leave
sick•li•ness
sick•ness
sick•room
side•band
side•board
side•burns
side•car
side•light
side•line
side•long
si•de•re•al
side•sad•dle
side•show
side•slip
side•spin
side•split•ting
side step n.
side•step v.
side•swipe
side•track
side•walk

side•wall
side•ways
side•wise
si•dle
siege
si•en•na
si•es•ta
sieve
sigh
sight (vision; cf. *cite*, *site*)
sight•less
sight•li•ness
sight•ly
sight–read v.
sight–see•ing
sig•moid
sig•nal
sig•naled
sig•nal•ing
sig•nal•ize
sig•nal•man
sig•na•to•ry
sig•na•ture
sign•board
sig•net
sig•nif•i•cance
sig•nif•i•cant
sig•ni•fi•ca•tion
sig•ni•fy
sign•post
si•lage
si•lence
si•lenc•er

si·lent
si·le·sia
si·lex
sil·hou·ette
sil·i·ca
sil·i·cate
sil·i·con (element)
sil·i·cone (compound)
sil·i·co·sis
silk·en
silk·i·ness
silk–stock·ing adj.
silk·weed
silk·worm
silky
sil·ly
si·lo
si·los
sil·ver
sil·ver·smith
sil·ver–tongued
sil·ver·ware
sil·very
sim·i·an
sim·i·lar
sim·i·lar·i·ty
sim·i·le
si·mil·i·tude
sim·mer
si·mon–pure
sim·per
sim·ple
sim·ple·mind·ed
sim·ple·ton

sim·plex
sim·plic·i·ty
sim·pli·fi·ca·tion
sim·pli·fy
sim·plis·tic
sim·ply
sim·u·la·crum
sim·u·late
sim·u·la·tion
si·mul·ta·neous
sin·cere
sin·cer·i·ty
si·ne·cure
sin·ew
sin·ewy
sin·ful
singe
singed
singe·ing
sin·gle
sin·gle–breast·ed
sin·gle–hand·ed
sin·gle–mind·ed
sin·gle·ness
sin·gle–space v.
sin·gle·ton
sin·gle–track adj.
sin·gly
sing·song
sin·gu·lar
sin·gu·lar·i·ty
sin·is·ter
sink·age
sink·er

sink·hole
sin·u·os·i·ty
sin·u·ous
si·nus
Sioux City Iowa
si·phon
si·ren
sir·loin
si·roc·co
sis·ter–in–law
sit–down n.
site (place; cf. *cite*, *sight*)
sit–in n.
sit·u·at·ed
sit·u·a·tion
sit up v.
sit–up n.
six–pack
sixth
six·ti·eth
siz·able
siz·zle
siz·zling
skate·board
skat·er
skein
skel·e·ton
skep·tic
skep·ti·cal
skep·ti·cism
sketch
sketch·book
sketch·i·ly

sketchy
skew•er
ski
skid
skid•ded
skid•ding
skid row
ski•ing
ski jump
ski lift
skilled
skil•let
skill•ful
skimpy
skin
skin•flint
skinned
skin•ning
skin•tight
skip
skipped
skip•per
skip•ping
skir•mish
skit•tish
skiv•er
skulk
skull (bone of head; cf.
    scull)
skull•cap
skunk
sky blue n.
sky–blue adj.
sky•cap

sky•coach
sky div•er
sky–high
sky•lark
sky•light
sky•line
sky•rock•et
sky•scrap•er
sky•ward
sky wave
sky•way
sky•writ•er
sky•writ•ing
slack•en
sla•lom
slam
slammed
slam•ming
slan•der
slan•der•ous
slap•dash
slap•hap•py
slap•jack
slapped
slap•ping
slap•stick
slat•tern
slat•tern•li•ness
slaugh•ter
slaugh•ter•house
slav•ery
slav•ish
slay (kill; cf. *sleigh*)
slea•zi•ness

slea•zy
sledge
sledge•ham•mer
sleep•er
sleep•i•ness
sleep•less
sleep•walk•er
sleep•wear
sleepy
sleeve•less
sleigh (winter vehicle;
    cf. *slay*)
sleigh bell
slen•der
sleuth
sleuth•hound
slide rule
slight
slime
sling•shot
slip
slip•case
slip•cov•er
slip•knot
slip noose
slip–on n.
slip•over n.
slip•page
slipped
slip•per
slip•peri•ness
slip•pery
slip•ping
slip sheet n.

slip–sheet v.

slip•shod

slip up v.

slip•up n.

slith•er

sliv•er

sloe (fruit; cf. *slow*)

sloe–eyed

slo•gan

sloop

slope

slop•pi•ness

slop•py

sloth•ful

slouch

slouch•i•ness

slouchy

slo•ven•li•ness

slov•en•ly

slow (not fast; cf. *sloe*)

slow•down n.

slow•poke

slow–wit•ted

sloyd

sludge

slug•gard

slug•gish

sluice

sluice•way

slum•ber

slum•lord

slush

small•pox

smart•en

smash•up n.

smat•ter•ing

smi•lax

smith•er•eens

smoke•house

smoke•jack

smoke•less

smok•er

smoke•stack

smok•ing room n.

smok•ing–room adj.

smoky

smol•der

smooth

smooth•bore

smooth–tongued

smor•gas•bord

smoth•er

smudge

smug•gle

smut•ty

snaf•fle

sna•fu

snag

snagged

snag•ging

snail–paced

snake pit

snake•root

snake•skin

snaky

snap•drag•on

snap•shot

snare drum

sneak•er

sneak thief

sneer

sneeze

snick•er

snip

snipped

snip•pety

snip•pi•ness

snip•ping

snip•py

sniv•el

sniv•eled

sniv•el•ing

snob

snob•bery

snob•bish

snor•kel

snow•ball

snow•bank

snow–blind

snow•blow•er

snow•bound

snow•capped

snow•drift

snow•drop

snow•fall

snow•flake

snow line

snow•man

snow•mo•bile

snow•plow

snow•shed

snow•shoe

snow•storm
snow•suit
snow tire
snow–white adj.
snowy
snub
snubbed
snub•bing
snub–nosed
snuff•box
snuff•er
snuf•fle
so (thus; cf. *sew*, *sow*)
soap•box
soap•i•ness
soap•stone
soap•suds
soapy
soar (rise aloft; cf. *sore*)
soared (did soar; cf.
  sward, *sword*)
so•ber
so•ber•sides
so•bri•ety
so•bri•quet
so–called
soc•cer
so•cia•bil•i•ty
so•cia•ble
so•cial
so•cial•ism
so•cial•ist
so•cial•ite
so•cial•ize

so•cial•ly
so•cial–mind•ed
so•ci•etal
so•ci•ety
so•cio–eco•nom•ic
so•cio•log•i•cal
so•ci•ol•o•gist
so•ci•ol•o•gy
so•cio•po•lit•i•cal
sock•et
so•da
so•dal•i•ty
sod•den
so•di•um
soft•ball
soft–boiled
soft copy
soft•en
soft•head•ed
soft•heart•ed
soft–shoe
soft soap n.
soft–soap v.
soft–spo•ken
soft•ware
soft•wood
sog•gi•ness
sog•gy
soi–di–sant
so•journ
so•lace
so•lar
sol•der
sol•dier

sold–out
sole (only; cf. *soul*)
so•le•cism
sole•ly
sol•emn
so•lem•ni•ty
sol•em•ni•za•tion
sol•em•nize
sol•e•noid
sol•feg•gio
so•lic•it
so•lic•i•ta•tion
so•lic•it•ed
so•lic•it•ing
so•lic•i•tor
so•lic•i•tous
so•lic•i•tude
sol•id
sol•i•dar•i•ty
so•lid•i•fi•ca•tion
so•lid•i•fy
so•lid•i•ty
sol•id–state
so•lil•o•quies
so•lil•o•quize
so•lil•o•quy
sol•i•taire
sol•i•tary
sol•i•tude
so•lo
sol•stice
sol•u•bil•i•ty
sol•u•ble
so•lu•tion

solv•able

sol•ven•cy

sol•vent

som•ber

som•bre•ro

some (part; cf. *sum*)

some•body

some•day adv.

some•how

some•one

some•place adv.

som•er•sault

some•thing

some•time adv.

some•times

some•what

some•where

som•me•lier

som•nam•bu•lism

som•no•lent

son (child; cf. *sun*)

so•na•ta

song•bird

song•book

song•fest

song•writ•er

son–in–law

son•net

son•ne•teer

so•nor•i•ty

so•no•rous

soothe

sooth•ing•ly

sooth•say•er

soot•i•ness

sooty

soph•ism

so•phis•ti•cate

so•phis•ti•cat•ed

so•phis•ti•ca•tion

soph•ist•ry

soph•o•more

so•po•rif•ic

so•pra•no

sor•cer•er

sor•cery

sor•did

sore (painful; cf. *soar*)

sore•head

sor•ghum

so•ror•i•ty

sor•rel

sor•ri•ly

sor•row

sor•row•ful

sor•ry

sou•brette

souf•flé

soul (spirit; cf. *sole*)

soul•ful

soul•less

soul mate

soul–search•ing

sound•proof adj., v.

soup•çon

soup du jour

sour•dough

sour grapes

south•bound

South Car•o•li•na

South Da•ko•ta

south•east

south•er•ly

south•ern

South•ern•er

south•land

south•paw

south pole

south•side

south•west

sou•ve•nir

sov•er•eign

sov•er•eign•ty

so•vi•et

sow (plant; cf. *sew, so*)

soy

soya

soy•bean

space–age

space•craft

space•flight

space•man

space•ship

space shut•tle

space suit

space•wom•an

spa•cious

spade•work

spa•ghet•ti

spal•peen

span•drel

span•gle

span•iel
span•ner
spare•ribs
spar•kle
spark plug
spar•row
spas•mod•ic
spas•tic
spa•tial
spat•ter
spat•u•la
spav•ined
speak•easy
speak•er
spear•fish
spear•head
spear•mint
spe•cial
spe•cial•ist
spe•cial•iza•tion
spe•cial•ize
spe•cial•ty
spe•cie (coin)
spe•cies (variety)
spe•cif•ic
spec•i•fi•ca•tion
spec•i•fy
spec•i•men
spe•cious
spec•ta•cle
spec•tac•u•lar
spec•ta•tor
spec•ter
spec•tral

spec•tro•scope
spec•trum
spec•u•late
spec•u•la•tion
spec•u•la•tive
spec•u•lum
speech
speech•less
speed•boat
speed•i•ly
speed lim•it
speed•om•e•ter
speed•up n.
speed•way
spe•le•ol•o•gy
spell•bind•er
spell•bound
spe•lunk•er
spend•thrift
sphag•num
spher•i•cal
sphinx
spick–and–span adj.
spic•ule
spicy
spi•der
spig•ot
spike•nard
spill•way
spin•ach
spi•nal
spin•dle
spine•less
spin•et

spin off v.
spin–off n.
spin•ster
spi•ral
spi•raled
spi•ral•ing
spi•ral•ly
spi•rea
spir•it•ed
spir•it•less
spir•i•tu•al
spir•i•tu•al•ism
spir•i•tu•al•i•ty
spir•i•tu•ous
spit•ball
spit curl
spite•ful
spit•fire
spit•toon
splash•board
splash•down
splash guard
splen•did
splen•dor
sple•net•ic
splin•ter
split–lev•el adj., n.
splotch
splurge
spoil•age
spoils•man
spoil•sport
spo•ken
spoke•shave

spokes•man

spokes•per•son

spokes•wom•an

spo•li•a•tion

spon•dee

sponge

spongy

spon•sor

spon•sor•ship

spon•ta•ne•ity

spon•ta•ne•ous

spoon–feed v.

spoon•ful

spo•rad•ic

sport•ive

sports•cast

sport shirt

sports•man

sports•man•ship

sports•wear

sports•writ•er

spot check n.

spot–check v.

spot•less

spot•light n., v.

spot•ted

spot•ter

sprawl

spread ea•gle n.

spread–ea•gle adj.,
   v.

spree

spright•li•ness

spright•ly

spring•board

spring•bok

spring–clean•ing n.

spring•house

spring•i•ness

spring•time

sprin•kle

sprin•kler

sprin•kling

sprock•et

sprout

spruce

spu•mo•ni *or*
   spu•mo•ne

spur

spu•ri•ous

spurn

spur–of–the–
   mo•ment

spurred

spur•ring

spurt

spur track

sput•nik

sput•ter

spu•tum

spy•glass

squab

squab•ble

squad•ron

squad room

squal•id

squall

squa•lor

spring•board

square dance

square deal

square knot

square–rigged

square root

squash

squat•ter

squaw

squawk

squeak

squea•mish

squee•gee

squir•rel

squirt

sta•bil•i•ty

sta•bi•li•za•tion

sta•bi•lize

sta•bi•liz•er

sta•ble

stac•ca•to

sta•di•um

staff•er

stage•coach

stage•craft

stage fright

stage•hand

stage•struck

stag•ger

stag•nant

stag•nate

stag•na•tion

staid (sedate; cf. *stayed*)

stain•less

stair (steps; cf. *stare*)
stair•case
stair•way
stair•well
stake (marker; cf. *steak*)
stake•hold•er
stake out v.
stake•out n.
sta•lac•tite (hangs down)
sta•lag•mite (stands up)
stale•mate
stalk•ing–horse n.
stal•lion
stal•wart
sta•men
stam•i•na
stam•mer
stam•pede
stamp•er
stanch
stan•chion
stand–alone
stan•dard
stan•dard–bear•er n.
stan•dard•bred n.
stan•dard•iza•tion
stan•dard•ize
stand by v.
stand•by n.
stand•ee
stand in v.

stand–in n.
stand off v.
stand•off adj., n.
stand•off•ish
stand out v.
stand•out n.
stand•pat•ter
stand•pipe
stand•point
stand•still
stand up v.
stand–up adj.
stan•za
sta•ple
star•board
star–cham•ber adj.
starch•i•ness
starchy
star–crossed
star•dom
star•dust
stare (look; cf. *stair*)
star•fish
star•gaz•er
star•let
star•light
star•ling
star•lit
star•ry–eyed
star shell
star–span•gled
star•tle
star•tling
star•va•tion

starve
state•craft
state•hood
state•house
state•less
state•li•ness
state•ly
state•ment
state of the art
state•room
states•man
states' right•er
state•wide
stat•ic
sta•tion
sta•tion•ary (fixed; cf. *stationery*)
sta•tio•ner
sta•tio•nery (paper; cf. *stationary*)
stat•ism
sta•tis•ti•cal
sta•tis•ti•cian
sta•tis•tics
stat•u•ary
stat•ue (sculpture; cf. *stature, statute*)
stat•u•esque
stat•u•ette
stat•ure (height; cf. *statue, statute*)
sta•tus
stat•ute (law; cf. *statue, stature*)

stat•u•to•ry
stay–at–home
   adj., n.
stayed (remained; cf. *staid*)
stay•sail
stead•fast
steadi•ly
steak (meat; cf. *stake*)
steal (rob; cf. *steel*)
stealth
steam•boat
steam•er
steam fit•ter
steam–heat•ed
steam•roll•er
steam•ship
steam ta•ble
steel (metal; cf. *steal*)
steel wool
steel•work
steel•yard
stee•ple
stee•ple•chase
stee•ple•jack
steer•age
steer•age•way
steers•man
stem
stemmed
stem•ware
stem–wind•er
sten•cil
sten•ciled

sten•cil•ing
ste•nog•ra•pher
steno•graph•ic
ste•nog•ra•phy
sten•to•ri•an
step (walk; cf. *steppe*)
step•broth•er
step•child
step•daugh•ter
step down v.
step–down n.
step•fa•ther
step in v.
step–in n.
step•lad•der
step•moth•er
step•par•ent
steppe (plain; cf. *step*)
step•ping–off place
step•ping–stone
step•sis•ter
step•son
step stool
step up v.
step–up adj., n.
step•wise
ste•reo
ste•reo•phon•ic
ste•re•op•ti•con
ste•reo•scope
ste•reo•type
ster•ile
ste•ril•i•ty
ster•il•ize

ster•ling
ster•num
ster•nu•ta•tion
ster•to•rous
stetho•scope
ste•ve•dore
stew•ard
stew•pan
stick•ful
stick•i•ness
stick•ler
stick•pin
stick–to–it•ive•ness
stick up v.
stick•up n.
stiff•en
stiff–necked
sti•fle
stig•ma sing.
stig•ma•ta pl.
stig•ma•tize
stile (fence; cf. *style*)
sti•let•to
still•birth
still•born
still hunt n.
still–hunt v.
still life
stilt•ed
stim•u•lant
stim•u•late
stim•u•lat•ing
stim•u•la•tion
stim•u•li pl.

stim•u•lus sing.

stin•gi•ness

stin•gy

stink•er

stink•weed

sti•pend

sti•pen•di•ary

stip•ple

stip•u•late

stip•u•la•tion

stir

stirred

stir•ring

stir•rup

stock•ade

stock•bro•ker

stock car (for
   livestock)

stock•car (for racing)

stock clerk

stock•hold•er

stock•ing

stock–in–trade n.

stock•job•ber

stock•man

stock•pile n., v.

stock•pot

stock•proof

stock•room

stock•yard

stodg•i•ness

stodgy

sto•ic

stoke•hold

stok•er

stol•id

stom•ach

stom•ach•ache

stone–blind

stone–broke

stone–cut•ter

stone–deaf

stone•ma•son

stone•ware

stone•work

ston•i•ly

stony•heart•ed

stop–and–go

stop•light

stop•watch

stor•able

stor•age

store•front n., adj.

store•house

store•keep•er

store•room

store•wide

storm•bound

storm cloud

storm door

stormy

sto•ry

sto•ry•book

sto•ry•tell•er

stout•heart•ed

stove•pipe

stove•top

stow•age

stow away v.

stow•away n.

stra•bis•mus

strad•dle

strad•dling

strag•gle

strag•gly

straight (direct; cf.
   strait)

straight•away

straight•edge

straight•for•ward

straight–line adj.

straight man

strait (narrow; cf.
   straight)

strait•jack•et

strait•laced *or*
   straight•laced

strang•er

stran•gle•hold

stran•gu•late

strap•hang•er

strap•less

strapped

strap•ping

strat•a•gem

stra•te•gic

strat•e•gist

strat•e•gy

strat•i•fy

strato•sphere

stra•tum

straw•ber•ry

straw•board
straw man
stream
stream•lined
street•car
street•light
strength
strength•en
stren•u•ous
strep•to•coc•ci pl.
strep•to•coc•cus
   sing.
stress•ful
stretch•er–bear•er
stretch–out n.
stri•a•tion
stric•ture
stri•dent
strike•bound
strike•break•er
strike out v.
strike•out n.
strike over v.
strike•over n.
string along
strin•gent
string•i•ness
strip•ling
stro•bo•scope
strong–arm adj., v.
strong•hold
strong–mind•ed
strong room
strong suit

stron•tium
stro•phe
struc•tur•al
struc•ture
strug•gle
strug•gling
strych•nine
stub
stubbed
stub•bing
stub•born
stub•by
stuc•co
stuc•co•work
stuck–up adj.
stud•book
stu•dent
stud•ied
stu•dio
stu•dios
stu•di•ous
study
stuff
stuff•i•ness
stuff•ing
stuffy
stul•ti•fy
stum•ble•bum
stu•pe•fy
stu•pen•dous
stu•pid
stu•pid•i•ty
stu•por
stur•dy

stur•geon
stut•ter
sty•gian
style (fashion; cf. *stile*)
style•book
styl•ish
styl•ist
styl•iza•tion
styl•ize
sty•lo•graph•ic
sty•lus
sty•mie
styp•tic
sua•sion
suave
sua•vi•ty
sub•al•tern
sub•as•sem•bly
sub•av•er•age
sub•base•ment
sub•com•mit•tee
sub•con•scious
sub•con•ti•nent
sub•con•tract
sub•con•trac•tor
sub•cul•ture
sub•cu•ta•ne•ous
sub•deb
sub•deb•u•tante
sub•di•vide
sub•di•vi•sion
sub•due
sub•ed•i•tor
sub•head

sub•ject
sub•jec•tion
sub•jec•tive
sub•ju•gate
sub•junc•tive
sub•lease
sub•let
sub•li•mate
sub•li•ma•tion
sub•lime
sub•lim•i•nal
sub•lim•i•ty
sub•ma•rine
sub•merge
sub•merg•ible
sub•mers•ible
sub•mer•sion
sub•mis•sion
sub•mis•sive
sub•mit
sub•mit•ting
sub•nor•mal
sub•or•di•nate
sub•or•di•na•tion
sub•orn
sub•poe•na
sub•scribe
sub•scrip•tion
sub•se•quent
sub•ser•vi•ence
sub•ser•vi•ent
sub•side
sub•si•dence
sub•sid•iary

sub•si•dize
sub•si•dy
sub•sist
sub•sis•tence
sub•son•ic
sub•stance
sub•stan•dard
sub•stan•tial
sub•stan•ti•ate
sub•stan•tive
sub•sti•tute
sub•sur•face
sub•ter•fuge
sub•ter•ra•nean
sub•ti•tle
sub•tle
sub•tle•ty
sub•tly
sub•to•tal
sub•tract
sub•trac•tion
sub•tra•hend
sub•trea•sury
sub•trop•i•cal
sub•urb
sub•ur•ban•ite
sub•ur•bia
sub•ven•tion
sub•ver•sion
sub•ver•sive
sub•vert
sub•way
suc•ceed
suc•cess

suc•cess•ful
suc•ces•sion
suc•ces•sive
suc•ces•sor
suc•cinct
suc•cor (help; cf. *sucker*)
suc•co•tash
suc•cu•lent
suc•cumb
suck•er (fish; cf. *succor*)
suc•tion
sud•den
su•do•rif•ic
sue
sued
suede
su•et
suf•fer
suf•fer•ance
suf•fer•ing
suf•fice
suf•fi•cien•cy
suf•fi•cient
suf•fix
suf•fo•cate
suf•fo•ca•tion
suf•fra•gan
suf•frage
suf•frag•ette
suf•frag•ist
suf•fuse
suf•fu•sion

sug•ar
sug•ar beet
sug•ar•cane
sug•ar•coat
sug•ar•loaf
sug•ar•plum
sug•gest
sug•ges•tion
sug•ges•tive
sui•cid•al
sui•cide
su•ing
suit (garment; cf. *suite*, *sweet*)
suit•abil•i•ty
suit•able
suit•case
suite (a group; cf. *suit*, *sweet*)
suit•or
sul•fate
sul•fur
sulk•i•ness
sulky
sul•len
sul•tan
sul•ta•na
sul•try
sum (total; cf. *some*)
su•mac
sum•ma cum lau•de
sum•mari•ly
sum•ma•rize

sum•ma•ry (brief account; cf. *summery*)
sum•ma•tion
sum•mer•house
sum•mer•time
sum•mery (like summer; cf. *summary*)
sum•mit
sum•mons
sump pump
sump•tu•ary
sump•tu•ous
sun (in the sky; cf. *son*)
sun•baked
sun•bath n.
sun•bathe v.
sun•beam
sun•bon•net
sun•burn
sun•burst
sun•dae
Sun•day
sun deck
sun•di•al
sun•down
sun•dries
sun•dry
sun•fast
sun•fish
sun•flow•er
sun•glass•es
sun•glow
sun–god
sunk•en

sun•lamp
sun•light
sun•lit
sun•ni•ly
sun•ny
sun•ny–side up
sun par•lor
sun porch
sun•rise
sun•roof
sun–room
sun•screen
sun•set
sun•shade
sun•shine
sun•shiny
sun•spot
sun•stroke
sun•suit
sun•tan
sun–up
su•per•abun•dant
su•per•an•nu•ate
su•perb
su•per•cal•en•der
su•per•car•go
su•per•cil•ious
su•per•cool
su•per•ego
su•per•er•o•ga•tion
su•per•erog•a•to•ry
su•per•fi•cial
su•per•fi•ci•al•i•ty
su•per•flu•ity

su•per•flu•ous
su•per•heat
su•per•hu•man
su•per•im•pose
su•per•in•duce
su•per•in•tend
su•per•in•ten•dent
su•pe•ri•or
su•pe•ri•or•i•ty
su•per•la•tive
su•per•man
su•per•mar•ket
su•per•nal
su•per•nat•u•ral
su•per•nu•mer•ary
su•per•scrip•tion
su•per•sede
su•per•son•ic
su•per•sti•tion
su•per•sti•tious
su•per•struc•ture
su•per•tank•er
su•per•vene
su•per•vise
su•per•vi•sion
su•per•vi•sor
su•per•wom•an
su•pi•nate
su•pine
sup•per
sup•plant
sup•ple
sup•ple•ment
sup•ple•men•tal

sup•ple•men•ta•ry
sup•pli•ance
sup•pli•ant
sup•pli•cant
sup•pli•cate
sup•pli•ca•tion
sup•pli•er
sup•ply
sup•port
sup•port•er
sup•port•ive
sup•pose
sup•pos•ed•ly
sup•po•si•tion
sup•pos•i•ti•tious
sup•press
sup•pres•sion
sup•pu•ra•tion
su•pra
su•pra•re•nal
su•prem•a•cist
su•prem•a•cy
su•preme
su•preme•ly
sur•base
sur•cease
sur•charge
sur•cin•gle
sure•fire
sure•foot•ed
sure•ly
sure•ty
surf (waves; cf. *serf*)
sur•face

surf•board
sur•feit
surf•er
surf–rid•ing n.
surge (wave; cf. *serge*)
sur•geon
sur•gery
sur•gi•cal
sur•li•ness
sur•ly
sur•mise
sur•mount
sur•name
sur•pass
sur•plice (garment)
sur•plus (excess)
sur•plus•age
sur•prise
sur•re•al•ism
sur•re•but•tal
sur•ren•der
sur•rep•ti•tious
sur•ro•gate
sur•round
sur•tax
sur•veil•lance
sur•vey
sur•vey•or
sur•viv•al
sur•vive
sur•vi•vor
sus•cep•ti•bil•i•ty
sus•cep•ti•ble
sus•pect

sus•pend

sus•pense

sus•pen•sion

sus•pi•cion

sus•pi•cious

sus•tain

sus•te•nance

sut•ler

sut•tee

su•ture

su•zer•ain

svelte

swad•dle

swag•ger

swal•low

swamp

swamp•i•ness

swamp•land

swans•down

swan song

sward (grass; cf. *soared, sword*)

swar•thi•ness

swar•thy

swash•buck•ler

swas•ti•ka

swatch

swear•word

sweat•band

sweat•box

sweat•er

sweat gland

sweat•i•ly

sweat•i•ness

sweat•pants

sweat•shirt

sweat•shop

sweat suit

sweaty

sweep•stakes

sweet (not sour; cf. *suit, suite*)

sweet•bread

sweet•bri•er

sweet corn

sweet•en

sweet fern

sweet flag

sweet•heart

sweet•meat

sweet pea

sweet•shop

sweet tooth

sweet wil•liam

swelled–head•ed adj.

swelled–head•ed•ness n.

swel•ter

swel•ter•ing

swerve

swim•ming•ly

swim•suit

swin•dle

swin•dler

swin•dling

swine•herd

swin•ish

switch•back

switch•blade knife

switch•board

switch•er•oo

switch knife

switch•man

switch•yard

swiv•el

swoon

swoop

sword (weapon; cf. *soared, sward*)

sword•fish

sword grass

sword knot

sword•play

swords•man

syc•a•more

sy•co•phant

syl•lab•ic

syl•lab•i•cate

syl•la•ble

syl•la•bus

syl•lo•gism

sylph

syl•van

sym•bi•o•sis

sym•bol (emblem; cf. *cymbal*)

sym•bol•ic

sym•bol•ism

sym•bol•ize

sym•met•ri•cal

sym•me•try

sym•pa•thet•ic
sym•pa•thize
sym•pa•thiz•er
sym•pa•thy
sym•phon•ic
sym•pho•ny
sym•po•sium
symp•tom
syn•a•gogue
syn•chro•mesh
syn•chro•ni•za•tion
syn•chro•nize
syn•chro•nous

syn•co•pate
syn•co•pa•tion
sny•co•pe
syn•dic
syn•di•cal•ism
syn•di•cate
syn•drome
syn•ec•do•che
syn•er•gism
syn•er•gis•tic
syn•od
syn•onym

syn•on•y•mous
syn•op•sis
syn•tax
syn•the•sis
syn•the•size
syn•thet•ic
sy•ringe
syr•up
sys•tem•at•ic
sys•tem•atize
sys•tem•wide
sys•tol•ic

tab•ard
Ta•bas•co
tab•er•na•cle
ta•ble
tab•leau sing.
tab•leaux pl.
ta•ble•cloth
ta•ble d'hôte
ta•ble–hop
ta•ble•land
ta•ble•spoon•ful
tab•let
ta•ble•ware
tab•loid
ta•boo

ta•bor
tab•o•ret
tab•u•lar
tab•u•late
tab•u•la•tor
ta•chis•to•scope
ta•chom•e•ter
ta•chyg•ra•phy
tac•it
tac•i•turn
tack•le
tac•o•nite
tact•ful
tac•ti•cal
tac•ti•cian

tac•tics
tac•tile
tact•less
tad•pole
taf•fe•ta
taff•rail
tag•board
tag day
tag end
tagged
tag•ging
tag line
tail (end; cf. *tale*)
tail•board
tail•coat

tail•gate n., v.
tail•light
tai•lored
tai•lor–made
tail•piece
tail pipe
tail•race
tail•spin
tail•stock
tail wind
take down v.
take•down adj., n.
take–home pay
take off v.
take•off n.
take–out adj.
take•out n.
take over v.
take•over n.
take up v.
take–up n.
talc
tale (story; cf. *tail*)
tale•bear•er
tal•ent
tales•man (chosen for jury)
tal•is•man (a charm object)
talk•ative
talk•ing–to
Tal•la•has•see Fla.
tal•low
Tal•mud

tal•on
ta•ma•le
tam•a•rack
tam•a•rind
tam•bou•rine
tam•per
tam•pon
tan•a•ger
tan•bark
tan•dem
tan•gent
tan•ger•ine
tan•gi•ble
tan•gle
tan•go
tan•kard
tan•nery
tan•nic
tan•ta•lize
tan•ta•lus
tan•ta•mount
tap dance n.
tap–dance v.
tape deck
tape•line
tape mea•sure
tape play•er
ta•per (diminish; cf. *tapir*)
tape–re•cord v.
tape re•cord•er n.
tap•es•try
tape•worm
tap•i•o•ca

ta•pir (animal; cf. *taper*)
tap•room
tap•root
tar•an•tel•la
ta•ran•tu•la
tar•di•ness
tar•dy
tare (weight; cf. *tear*)
tar•get
tar•iff
tar•la•tan
tar•nish
tar•pau•lin
tar•pon
tar•ra•gon
tar•tan
tar•tar
tar•tar•ic
Tar•ta•rus
task force
task•mas•ter
tas•sel
taste•ful
taste•less
tast•i•ly
tasty
tat•ter•de•ma•lion
tat•ter•sall
tat•ting
tat•too
taught (instructed; cf. *taut*)
taunt

taut (tight; cf. *taught*)
tau·tol·o·gy
tav·ern
taw·dri·ness
taw·dry
taw·ny
tax·able
tax·a·tion
tax–ex·empt
taxi
taxi·cab
taxi danc·er
taxi·der·mist
taxi·der·my
tax·ied
taxi·ing
taxi·man
taxi·me·ter
tax·pay·er
T–bill
T–bone
tea (a drink; cf. *tee*)
tea bag
tea ball
teach·able
teach·er
tea·cup
tea dance
tea gown
tea·house
tea·ket·tle
teak·wood
team (in sports; cf. *teem*)

team·mate
team·ster
team·work
tea·pot
tear (rip; cf. *tare*)
tear (weep; cf. *tier*)
tear·drop
tear·ful
tear gas n.
tear·gas v.
tea·room
tear sheet
tear·stain
tea·spoon·ful
tea·time
tea tray
tea wag·on
tech·ni·cal
tech·ni·cal·i·ty
tech·ni·cian
Tech·ni·col·or
tech·nique
tech·noc·ra·cy
tech·no·log·i·cal
tech·nol·o·gy
te·dious
te·di·um
tee (in golf; cf. *tea*)
teem (abound with; cf. *team*)
teen·age
teen·ag·er
teens
tee·ter

tee·to·tal·er
Tel·Au·to·graph
tele·cast
tele·com·mu·ni·ca·tions
tele·com·mut·ing
tele·con·fer·ence
tele·course
tele·fac·sim·i·le
tele·gram
tele·graph
te·leg·ra·pher
tele·graph·ic
te·leg·ra·phy
tele·me·ter
tele·path·ic
te·lep·a·thy
tele·phone
tele·phon·ic
te·le·pho·ny
tele·pho·to
tele·print·er
tele·pro·cess·ing
Tele·Promp·Ter
tele·scope
tele·scop·ic
tele·text
tele·thon
Tele·type
Tele·type·set·ter
tele·type·writ·er
tele·vi·sion
tell·tale
tel·pher

tem•blor
te•mer•i•ty
tem•per
tem•per•a•ment
tem•per•ance
tem•per•ate
tem•per•a•ture
tem•pered
tem•pest
tem•pes•tu•ous
tem•plate
tem•ple
tem•po
tem•po•ral
tem•po•rari•ly
tem•po•rary
tem•po•rize
tempt
temp•ta•tion
tempt•ress
ten•a•ble
te•na•cious
te•nac•i•ty
ten•an•cy
ten•ant
ten•ant•able
ten–cent store
ten•den•cy
ten•den•tious
ten•der
ten•der•foot
ten•der•heart•ed
ten•der•iz•er
ten•der•loin

ten•don
ten•dril
ten•e•ment
Ten•nes•see
ten•nis
ten•on
ten•or
ten•pin
ten•sile
ten•sion
ten–speed
ten–strike
ten•ta•cle
ten•ta•tive
ten•ter•hook
tenth–rate
tent•mak•er
te•nu•ity
ten•u•ous
ten•ure
te•pee
tep•id
te•qui•la
ter•cen•te•na•ry
ter•gi•ver•sate
ter•ma•gant
ter•mi•na•ble
ter•mi•nal
ter•mi•nate
ter•mi•na•tion
ter•mi•ni pl.
ter•mi•nol•o•gy
ter•mi•nus sing.
ter•mite

tern (bird; cf. *turn*)
terp•si•cho•re•an
ter•race
ter•ra–cot•ta
ter•ra fir•ma
ter•rain
ter•ra•pin
ter•rar•i•um
ter•raz•zo
Ter•re Haute Ind.
ter•res•tri•al
ter•ri•ble
ter•ri•er
ter•rif•ic
ter•ri•fy
ter•ri•to•ri•al
ter•ri•to•ri•al•i•ty
ter•ri•to•ry
ter•ror
ter•ror•ism
ter•ror•ist
ter•ror•ize
terse
ter•tia•ry
tes•sel•la•tion
tes•ta•ment
tes•ta•men•ta•ry
tes•ta•tor
test–drive
tes•ti•fy
tes•ti•mo•ni•al
tes•ti•mo•ny
test tube n.
test–tube adj.

tet•a•nus

tête-à-tête

teth•er•ball

te•tral•o•gy

Teu•ton•ic

Tex•as

text•book

text ed•it•ing

tex•tile

tex•tu•al

tex•ture

thank•ful

thank•less

thanks•giv•ing

thank-you adj., n.

the•ater

the•at•ri•cal

their (possessive; cf. *there, they're*)

the•ism

thence•forth

the•od•o•lite

theo•lo•gian

theo•log•i•cal

the•ol•o•gy

the•o•rem

the•o•ret•i•cal

the•o•rize

the•o•ry

the•os•o•phy

ther•a•peu•tics

ther•a•pist

ther•a•py

there (that place; cf. *their, they're*)

there•af•ter

there•by

there•for (for it)

there•fore (consequently)

there•in•af•ter

there•in•to

there•of

there•on

there•to•fore

there•up•on

there•with

ther•mal

ther•mo•dy•nam•ics

ther•mo•elec•tric

ther•mom•e•ter

ther•mo•nu•cle•ar

ther•mo•plas•tic

ther•mo•stat

the•sau•rus

the•sis

they're (they are; cf. *their, there*)

thick•et

thick•set

thick-skinned

thief

thieves

thiev•ish

thim•ble•ful

thin

thin•ner

thin-skinned

third class n.

third-class adj.

third-rate adj.

thirst•i•ly

thirsty

this•tle•down

thith•er

tho•rac•ic

tho•rax

tho•ri•um

thorn•i•ness

thorny

thor•ough (complete; cf. *threw, through*)

thor•ough•bred

thor•ough•fare

thor•ough•go•ing

thought•ful

thought-out

thou•sand

thou•sand-leg•ger

thrall•dom

thra•son•i•cal

thread•bare

thread•worm

threat•en•ing•ly

three•fold

three-piece

three-ply

three•score

three•some

thren·o·dy
thresh·old
threw (past tense of
   throw; cf. *thorough,*
   through)
thrift·i·ly
thrift·less
thrifty
thrive
throat·i·ness
throaty
throe (effort; cf. *throw*)
throm·bo·sis
throne (royal chair; cf.
   thrown)
throng
throt·tle·hold
through (by means of;
   cf. *thorough, threw*)
through·out
through·put
through·way
throw (hurl; cf. *throe*)
throw·away
throw back v.
throw·back n.
thrown (hurled; cf.
   throne)
thrum
thrummed
thrum·ming
thru·way
thumb·nail

thumb·print
thumb·screw
thumb·tack
thun·der·bolt
thun·der·clap
thun·der·cloud
thun·der·head
thun·der·ous
thun·der·show·er
thun·der·storm
Thurs·day
thwart
thyme (spice; cf. *time*)
thy·mus
thy·roid
tib·ia
tic (twitching)
tick (of a clock)
tick·er
tick·et
tick·le
tick·ler
tid·al
tide (ocean; cf. *tied*)
tide·land
tide·mark
tide·wa·ter
ti·di·ly
ti·dy
tied (fastened; cf. *tide*)
tie–in n.
tie·pin
tier (row; cf. *tear*)

tie up v.
tie–up n.
ti·ger
tight·fist·ed
tight–lipped
tight–mouthed
tight·rope
tight·wad
til·bury
tilt·yard
tim·bale
tim·ber (wood; cf.
   timbre)
tim·ber·land
tim·ber·line
tim·ber·man
tim·ber·work
tim·bre (of the voice;
   cf. *timber*)
time (duration; cf.
   thyme)
time and a half
time card
time clock
time–con·sum·ing
time draft
time–hon·ored
time·keep·er
time–lapse
time·less
time·li·ness
time lock
time·ly

time·piece
time–sav·er
time–sav·ing
time–shar·ing
time sheet
time·ta·ble
time·worn
time zone
tim·id
ti·mid·i·ty
tim·o·rous
tim·o·thy
tim·pa·ni
tinc·ture
tin·der·box
tin·foil
tin·gle
tin·ker
tin–plate v.
tin·plate n.
tin·sel
tin·seled
tin·smith
tin·type
tin·ware
tin·work
ti·ny
tip
tipped
tip·ping
tip·ple
tip·staff
tip·ster
tip·sy

tip·toe
tip–top
ti·rade
tire·some
tis·sue
ti·tan
ti·tan·ic
tit·bit
tithe
tith·ing
tit·il·late
tit·i·vate
ti·tle
ti·tle·hold·er
tit·mouse
ti·trate
ti·tra·tion
tit·u·lar
to (preposition; cf. *too, two*)
toad·stool
toast·mas·ter
to·bac·co
to·bac·co·nist
to·bog·gan
toc·ca·ta
toc·sin
to·day
tod·dy
toe (of foot; cf. *tow*)
toe cap
toed
toe dance n.
toe–dance v.

toe·hold
toe·ing
toe·nail
tof·fee
to·ga
to·geth·er
tog·gle
toi·let
toil·some
toil·worn
to·ken
tol·er·a·ble
tol·er·ance
tol·er·ant
tol·er·ate
tol·er·a·tion
toll·booth
toll bridge
toll call
toll·gate
toll·house
toll road
tom·a·hawk
to·ma·to
tom·boy
tomb·stone
tom·cat
tom·fool·ery
to·mor·row
tom–tom
ton·al
to·nal·i·ty
tone
tone·arm

tone–deaf adj.

tongue

tongue–lash v.

tongue–lash•ing n.

tongue–tied

ton•ic

to•night

ton•nage

ton•neau

ton•sil

ton•sil•lec•to•my

ton•sil•li•tis

ton•so•ri•al

ton•sure

ton•tine

too (also; cf. *to, two*)

tool•box

tool•hold•er

tool•house

tool•mak•er

tool•room

tooth•ache

tooth•brush

tooth•paste

tooth•pick

tooth•some

to•paz

top boot

top•coat

top flight

top hat

top–heavy adj.

to•pi•ary

top•ic

top•i•cal

top•knot

top•mast

top•most

top–notch adj.

top•notch n.

to•pog•ra•pher

to•pog•ra•phy (of geography; cf. *typography*)

top•ping

top•sail

top se•cret

top•side

top•soil

top•sy–tur•vi•ness

top•sy–tur•vy adj., adv.

toque

torch•bear•er

torch•light

to•re•ador

tor•ment

tor•men•tor

tor•na•do

tor•pe•do

tor•pid

tor•por

torque

tor•rent

tor•ren•tial

tor•rid

tor•sion

tor•so

tor•ti•lla

tor•toise•shell

tor•to•ni

tor•tu•ous (winding; cf. *torturous*)

tor•ture

tor•tur•ous (painful; cf. *tortuous*)

toss•pot

toss–up n.

to•tal

to•taled

to•tal•ing

to•tal•i•tar•i•an

to•tal•i•ty

to•tal•ize

to•tal•ly

to•tem

touch down v.

touch•down n.

tou•ché

touch•i•ly

touch•i•ness

touch•stone

touch up v.

touch–up n.

tough•en

tough–mind•ed

tou•pee

tour de force

tour•ism

tour•ist

tour•ma•line

tour•na•ment

tour•ney
tour•ni•quet
tow (pull; cf. *toe*)
tow•age
to•ward
to•wards
tow•boat
tow•el
tow•el•ing
tow•er
tow•head
tow•line
towns•folk
town•ship
towns•man
towns•peo•ple
towns•wom•an
tow•path
tow•rope
tox•emia
tox•ic
tox•ic•i•ty
tox•i•col•o•gy
tox•oph•i•ly
trace•able
trac•ery
tra•chea
tra•cho•ma
trac•ing
track (path; cf. *tract*)
track•age
track•less
track•walk•er

tract (treatise; area; cf. *track*)
trac•ta•ble
trac•tion
trac•tor
trade–in n.
trade–last
trade•mark
trade name
trade–off n.
trade school
trades•man
trade wind
tra•di•tion
tra•duce
traf•fic
trag•a•canth
tra•ge•di•an
tra•ge•di•enne
trag•e•dy
trag•ic
trail•blaz•er
trail•er
train•able
train•bear•er
train•ee
train•load
train•man
train•sick
trait
trai•tor
trai•tor•ous
trai•tress

tra•jec•to•ry
tram•car
tram•mel
tram•ple
tram•po•line
tram•way
tran•quil
tran•quil•iz•er
tran•quil•li•ty
trans•act
trans•ac•tion
trans•at•lan•tic
tran•scend
tran•scen•dent
tran•scen•den•tal
tran•scen•den•tal•
  ism
trans•con•ti•nen•tal
tran•scribe
tran•script
tran•scrip•tion
trans•duc•er
tran•sept
trans•fer
trans•fer•able
trans•fer•ence
trans•fig•u•ra•tion
trans•fig•ure
trans•fix
trans•form
trans•for•ma•tion
trans•form•er
trans•fuse

trans•fu•sion
trans•gress
trans•gres•sion
trans•gres•sor
tran•sient
tran•sis•tor
tran•sit
tran•si•tion
tran•si•tive
tran•si•to•ry
trans•late
trans•la•tion
trans•la•tor
trans•lit•er•ate
trans•lu•cent
trans•mi•grate
trans•mis•si•ble
trans•mis•sion
trans•mit
trans•mit•tal
trans•mit•ter
trans•mu•ta•tion
trans•mute
trans•oce•an•ic
tran•som
trans•par•en•cy
trans•par•ent
tran•spire
trans•plant
trans•port
trans•por•ta•tion
trans•pose
trans•po•si•tion

trans•ship
tran•sub•stan•ti•a•
    tion
trans•verse
trap•door
tra•peze
trap•nest
trap•per
trap•ping
Trap•pist
trashy
trau•ma
trau•mat•ic
tra•vail (toil)
trav•el (journey)
trav•el agent
trav•eled
trav•el•er
trav•el•ing
tra•verse
trav•er•tine
trav•es•ty
treach•er•ous
treach•ery
trea•cle
trea•dle
tread•mill
trea•son
trea•sure
trea•sur•er
trea•sury
treat
trea•tise

treat•ment
trea•ty
tre•ble
tree fern
tree•nail
tree•top
tre•foil
trel•lis
trem•ble
tre•men•dous
trem•o•lo
trem•or
trem•u•lous
trench
tren•chan•cy
tren•chant
tren•cher
tre•pan
tre•phine
trep•i•da•tion
tres•pass
tres•pass•er
tres•tle
tres•tle•work
tri•ad
tri•al
tri•an•gle
tri•an•gu•lar
tri•an•gu•la•tion
trib•al
tribe
tribes•man
trib•u•la•tion

tri•bu•nal
tri•bune
trib•u•tary
trib•ute
trick•ery
trick•i•ly
trick•i•ness
trick•le
trick•ster
tri•col•or
tri•cy•cle
tri•dent
tri•en•ni•al
tri•fle
tri•fo•cal
trig•ger
trig•ger–hap•py
trig•o•nom•e•try
tril•lion
tril•li•um
tril•o•gy
Trin•i•ty
trin•ket
tri•par•tite
trip–ham•mer
triph•thong
tri•ple
tri•ple–space v.
trip•let
tri•plex
trip•li•cate
trip•li•ca•tion
tri•pod
trip•tych

tri•reme
tri•sect
tri•state
trit•u•rate
tri•umph
tri•um•phal
tri•um•phant
tri•um•vi•rate
triv•et
triv•ia
triv•i•al
triv•i•al•i•ty
tro•che (lozenge)
tro•chee (poetic term)
trog•lo•dyte
trol•ley
trom•bone
troop (of soldiers; cf.
   troupe)
troop•ship
trope
tro•phy
trop•ic
trot
trot•ted
trot•ting
trou•ba•dour
trou•ble•mak•er
trou•ble•shoot•er
trou•ble•some
trou•blous
troupe (of actors; cf.
   troop)
trou•sers

trous•seau
tro•ver
trow•el
tru•an•cy
tru•ant
truck•le
truck•load
truck•man
tru•cu•lence
tru•cu•lent
true–blue adj.
true–born
true–heart•ed
true–life adj.
truf•fle
tru•ism
tru•ly
trum•pery
trum•pet
trum•pet•er
trun•cate
trun•cheon
trun•dle
trunk line
trun•nion
trust•bust•er
trust•ee
trust•ee•ship
trust•ful
trust fund
trust•wor•thi•ness
trust•wor•thy
truth•ful
try•out n.

try square
tryst
tset•se
T–shirt
T square
tu•ba
tu•ber
tu•ber•cu•lar
tu•ber•cu•lin
tu•ber•cu•lo•sis
tu•ber•cu•lous
tube•rose
tu•bu•lar
Tu•dor
Tues•day
tug•boat
tug–of–war
tu•ition
tu•la•re•mia
tu•lip
tu•lip•wood
tulle
tum•ble
tum•bler
tum•ble•weed
tum•bril
tu•mor
tu•mult
tu•mul•tu•ous
tune•ful
tune•less
tune–up n.
tung•sten
tu•nic

tun•nel
tun•neled
tun•nel•ing
tur•ban (headdress; cf. *turbine*)
tur•bid
tur•bine (engine; cf. *turban*)
tur•bo•jet
tur•bot
tur•bu•lence
tur•bu•lent
tur•gid
tur•key
tur•key–cock
tur•mer•ic
tur•moil
turn (rotate; cf. *tern*)
turn•about
turn around v.
turn•around n.
turn•around time
turn•buck•le
turn•coat
turn down v.
turn•down adj., n.
turn in v.
turn–in n.
tur•nip
turn•key
turn off v.
turn•off n.
turn out v.
turn•out n.

turn over v.
turn•over adj., n.
turn•pike
turn•spit
turn•stile
turn•ta•ble
turn up v.
turn•up adj., n.
turn•ver•ein
tur•pen•tine
tur•pi•tude
tur•quoise
tur•ret
tur•tle•dove
tur•tle•neck
tus•sle
tu•te•lage
tu•te•lar
tu•te•lary
tu•tor
tut•ti–frut•ti
twi•light
twin–size
twitch
two (one and one; cf. *to, too*)
two–ply
two–sid•ed
two•some
two–step n.
two–way
ty•coon
ty•ing
tym•pa•num

type·cast
type·face
type·found·er
type·script
type·set·ter
type·write
type·writ·er
type·writ·ing
ty·phoid
ty·phoon

ty·phus
typ·i·cal
typ·i·fy
typ·ist
ty·pog·ra·pher
ty·po·graph·i·cal
ty·pog·ra·phy (of printing; cf. *topography*)

ty·poth·e·tae
ty·ran·ni·cal
ty·ran·ni·cide
tyr·an·nize
tyr·an·nous
tyr·an·ny
ty·rant
ty·ro

ubiq·ui·tous
ubiq·ui·ty
ud·der
ug·li·ness
ug·ly
uh·lan
ukase
uku·le·le
ul·cer
ul·cer·ation
ul·cer·ative
ul·cer·ous
ul·ster
ul·te·ri·or
ul·ti·mate
ul·ti·ma·tum

ul·ti·mo
ul·tra·con·ser·va·tive
ul·tra·fash·ion·able
ul·tra·ma·rine
ul·tra·mod·ern
ul·tra·na·tion·al·ism
ul·tra·son·ic
ul·tra·vi·o·let
ul·u·la·tion
Ulys·ses
um·bil·i·cal
um·bi·li·cus
um·brage
um·bra·geous

um·brel·la
um·laut
um·pire
un·abashed
un·abat·ed
un·able
un·ac·cept·able
un·ac·com·pa·nied
un·ac·count·able
un·ac·cus·tomed
un·adorned
un·adul·ter·at·ed
un·af·fect·ed
un·aligned
un·al·loyed
un·al·ter·able

un–Amer·i·can
una·nim·i·ty
unan·i·mous
un·as·sum·ing
un·avoid·able
un·aware
un·bal·anced
un·be·com·ing
un·be·lief
un·be·liev·er
un·bend
un·bi·ased
un·bid·den
un·bo·som
un·bound·ed
un·but·ton
un·called–for
un·cer·tain
un·char·ac·ter·is·tic
un·char·i·ta·ble
un·civ·i·lized
un·clas·si·fied
un·cle
un·clean
un·com·fort·able
un·com·mit·ted
un·com·mu·ni·ca·tive
un·com·pli·men·ta·ry
un·com·pro·mis·ing

un·con·cerned
un·con·di·tion·al
un·con·quer·able
un·con·scio·na·ble
un·con·scious
un·con·trol·la·ble
un·con·ven·tion·al
un·con·vinc·ing
un·cor·rect·ed
un·couth
unc·tion
unc·tu·ous
un·de·ni·able
un·der·age
un·der·arm
un·der·brush
un·der·class·man
un·der·clothes
un·der·cov·er
un·der·cur·rent
un·der·de·vel·oped
un·der·dog
un·der·em·ploy·ment
un·der·glaze
un·der·go
un·der·grad·u·ate
un·der·ground
un·der·hand·ed
un·der·line
un·der·mine
un·der·neath

un·der·pass
un·der·priv·i·leged
un·der·rate
un·der·score
un·der·sell
un·der·shirt
un·der·side
un·der·signed
un·der·sized
un·der·slung
un·der·stand
un·der·stood
un·der·study
un·der·tak·er
un·der·tone
un·der·tow
un·der·val·ue
un·der·wa·ter
un·der way adv.
un·der·way adj.
un·der·wear
un·der·weight
un·der·went
un·der·world
un·der·write
un·di·vid·ed
un·do (unfasten; cf. *undue*)
un·doubt·ed·ly
un·due (excessive; cf. *undo*)
un·du·la·tion
un·du·ly

un•earned
un•earth•ly
un•eas•y
un•em•ployed
un•en•cum•bered
un•equal
un•equiv•o•cal
un•err•ing
un•ex•cep•tion•able
un•ex•pect•ed
un•fa•mil•iar
un•fa•vor•able
un•fore•seen
un•for•get•ta•ble
un•for•tu•nate
un•furl
un•gain•ly
un•god•ly
un•guent
un•heard–of
uni•cam•er•al
uni•fi•ca•tion
uni•form
uni•for•mi•ty
uni•fy
uni•lat•er•al
un•im•proved
un•in•hib•it•ed
un•in•tel•li•gent
un•in•tel•li•gi•ble
un•in•ter•est•ed
union

union•ize
unique
uni•son
unit
unite
Unit•ed States
uni•ty
uni•ver•sal
uni•ver•sal•i•ty
uni•verse
uni•ver•si•ty
un•kempt
un•kind•ly
un•know•ing
un•known
un•law•ful
un•leash
un•less
un•let•tered
un•like•ly
un•lim•it•ed
un•man•ly
un•manned
un•mind•ful
un•mit•i•gat•ed
un•nat•u•ral
un•nec•es•sary
un•nerve
un•oc•cu•pied
un•par•al•leled
un•pleas•ant
un•prec•e•dent•ed
un•prej•u•diced

un•prin•ci•pled
un•qual•i•fied
un•ques•tion•able
un•rav•el
un•re•al
un•rea•son•able
un•re•con•struct•ed
un•re•gen•er•ate
un•re•mit•ting
un•right•teous
un•rul•i•ness
un•ruly
un•sat•is•fac•to•ry
un•sa•vory
un•scathed
un•schooled
un•scru•pu•lous
un•seem•ly
un•skill•ful
un•so•cia•ble
un•so•phis•ti•cat•ed
un•speak•able
un•sprung
un•think•able
un•ti•dy
un•tie
un•til
un•time•li•ness
un•time•ly
un•told
un•touch•able
un•to•ward
un•truth•ful

un•tu•tored
un•usu•al
un•var•nished
un•want•ed
  (undesired; cf.
  unwonted)
un•wary
un•well
un•whole•some
un•wield•i•ness
un•wieldy
un•wont•ed
  (unaccustomed; cf.
  unwanted)
un•wor•thi•ness
un•wor•thy
un•writ•ten
up–and–com•ing
up•beat adj., n.
up•braid
up•bring•ing
up•com•ing
up–coun•try
up•date
up•draft
up–front adj.
up•grade
up•heav•al
up•hill adj., adv., n.
up•hold
up•hol•ster
up•hol•ster•er
up•hol•stery

up•keep
up•land
up•lift
up•on
up•per
up•per–class adj.
up•per•class•man
up•per•cut
up•per•most
up•right
up•ris•ing
up•roar•i•ous
up•root
up•set
up•shot
up•stage
up•stairs
up•start
up•state adj., n.
up•stream
up•stroke
up•swept
up•swing
up•tight
up–to–date
up•town
up•turn
up•ward
ura•ni•um
ur•ban (of city)
ur•bane (suave)
ur•ban•i•ty
ur•ban•iza•tion

ur•chin
ur•gen•cy
ur•gent
uric
urn (vase; cf. *earn*)
Ur•su•line
ur•ti•car•ia
us•able
us•age
use•ful
use•ful•ness
use•less
ush•er
usu•al
usu•fruct
usu•rer
usu•ri•ous
usurp
usur•pa•tion
usurp•er
usu•ry
Utah
uten•sil
uter•ine
util•i•tar•i•an
util•i•ty
uti•liz•able
uti•lize
ut•most
uto•pi•an•ism
ut•ter
ut•ter•ance
ux•o•ri•ous

va•can•cy
va•cant
va•cate
va•ca•tion
va•ca•tion•ist
vac•ci•nate
vac•ci•na•tion
vac•cine
vac•il•late
vac•il•la•tion
va•cu•ity
vac•u•ous
vac•u•um
va•de me•cum
vag•a•bond
va•ga•ry
va•gran•cy
va•grant
vague
vain (conceited; cf.
  vane, vein)
vain•glo•ri•ous
vain•glo•ry
va•lance (drapery; cf.
  valence)
vale (valley; cf. veil)
vale•dic•to•ri•an
vale•dic•to•ry
va•lence (combining
  power; cf. valance)

val•en•tine
val•et
val•e•tu•di•nar•i•an
Val•hal•la
val•iant
val•id
val•i•date
val•i•da•tion
va•lid•i•ty
va•lise
val•ley
val•or
val•o•ri•za•tion
val•or•ous
valu•able
val•u•a•tion
val•ue
val•ue•less
val•vu•lar
vam•pire
van•dal•ism
vane (weather; cf. vain,
  vein)
van•guard
va•nil•la
van•ish
van•i•ty
van•quish
van•tage
va•pid

va•por
va•por•iza•tion
va•por•ize
va•por•iz•er
va•por•ous
va•que•ro
vari•able
vari•ance
vari•ant
vari•a•tion
vari•col•ored
var•i•cose
var•ied
var•ie•gate
var•ie•ga•tion
va•ri•ety
var•i•o•rum
var•i•ous
var•nish
vary (diversify; cf. very)
vas•cu•lar
va•sec•to•my
Vas•e•line
vas•sal
Vat•i•can
vaude•ville
vaude•vil•lian
veg•e•ta•ble
veg•e•tar•i•an
veg•e•tar•i•an•ism

veg•e•tate

veg•e•ta•tion

veg•e•ta•tive

ve•he•mence

ve•he•ment

ve•hi•cle

ve•hic•u•lar

veil (garment; cf. *vale*)

vein (blood vessel; cf. *vain, vane*)

vel•lum

ve•loc•i•pede

ve•loc•i•ty

ve•lour

vel•vet

vel•ve•teen

ve•nal (mercenary; cf. *venial*)

vend•ee

ven•det•ta

ven•dor

ve•neer

ven•er•a•ble

ven•er•ate

ven•er•a•tion

Ve•ne•tian

ven•geance

venge•ful

ve•nial (forgivable; cf. *venal*)

ve•ni•re•man

ven•i•son

ven•om•ous

ve•nous

ven•ti•late

ven•ti•la•tion

ven•ti•la•tor

ven•tral

ven•tri•cle

ven•tril•o•quism

ven•tril•o•quist

ven•ture•some

ven•tur•ous

ven•ue

ve•ra•cious (truthful; cf. *voracious*)

ve•rac•i•ty

ve•ran•da

ver•bal

ver•bal•ism

ver•bal•iza•tion

ver•bal•ly

ver•ba•tim

ver•be•na

ver•biage

ver•bose

ver•dant

ver•dict

ver•di•gris

ver•dure

ver•i•fi•ca•tion

ver•i•fy

ver•i•ly

veri•si•mil•i•tude

ver•i•ty

ver•meil

ver•mi•cel•li

ver•mi•cide

ver•mic•u•late

ver•mi•form

ver•mi•fuge

ver•mil•ion *or* ver•mil•lion

ver•min

ver•min•ous

Ver•mont

ver•nac•u•lar

ver•nal

ver•ni•er

ver•sa•tile

ver•sa•til•i•ty

ver•si•fi•ca•tion

ver•si•fy

ver•sion

ver•sus

ver•te•bra sing.

ver•te•brae pl.

ver•te•bral

ver•te•brate

ver•tex

ver•ti•cal

ver•ti•cal•ly

ver•tig•i•nous

very (extremely; cf. *vary*)

ves•i•cle

ves•pers

ves•sel

ves•tal

ves•ti•bule

ves•tige

ves•ti•gial

vest•ment

vest–pock•et adj.

ves•try

ves•try•man

vet•er•an

vet•er•i•nary

ve•to

ve•toed

ve•toes

vex•a•tion

vex•a•tious

vi•a•bil•i•ty

vi•a•ble

via•duct

vi•al (bottle; cf. *vile*, *viol*)

vi•and

vi•brant

vi•bra•phone

vi•brate

vi•bra•tion

vi•bra•to

vi•bra•tor

vi•bra•to•ry

vic•ar

vic•ar•age

vi•car•i•ous

vice (sin; cf. *vise*)

vice ad•mi•ral

vice–chan•cel•lor

vice–con•sul

vice•ge•rent

vice pres•i•dent

vice•re•gal

vice•roy

vice ver•sa

vi•chys•soise

vic•i•nage

vi•cin•i•ty

vi•cious

vi•cis•si•tude

vic•tim

vic•tim•ize

vic•tor

vic•to•ria

Vic•to•ri•an

vic•to•ri•ous

vic•to•ry

vict•ual

vi•cu•ña

vid•eo

vid•eo•cas•sette

vid•eo•con•fer•ence

vid•eo•disk

vid•eo dis•play ter•mi•nal

vid•eo•phone

vid•eo•tape

vid•eo•tex

vig•il

vig•i•lance

vig•i•lant

vig•i•lan•te

vi•gnette

vig•or•ous

vile (odious; cf. *vial*, *viol*)

vil•i•fy

vil•lage

vil•lain

vil•lain•ous

vil•lainy

vin•ai•grette

vin•cu•lum

vin•di•cate

vin•di•ca•tion

vin•dic•a•tive (justifying)

vin•dic•tive (vengeful)

vin•e•gar

vin•e•gary

vine•yard

vin•tage

vint•ner

vi•nyl

vi•ol (instrument; cf. *vial*, *vile*)

vi•o•la

vi•o•late

vi•o•lence

vi•o•lent

vi•o•let

vi•o•lin•ist

VIP

vi•per

vi•ra•go

vir•eo

vir•gin

Vir•gin•ia

vir•ile

vi•ril•i•ty

vir•tu•al

vir•tue
vir•tu•os•i•ty
vir•tu•o•so
vir•tu•ous
vir•u•lence
vir•u•lent
vi•rus
vis•age
vis-à-vis
vis•cer•al
vis•cid
vis•cos•i•ty
vis•count
vis•cous
vise (tool; cf. *vice*)
vis•i•bil•i•ty
vis•i•ble
vi•sion
vi•sion•ary
vis•it
vis•i•ta•tion
vis•i•tor
vi•sor
vis•ta
vi•su•al
vi•su•al aid
vi•su•al•ize
vi•tal
vi•tal•i•ty
vi•tal•ize
vi•ta•min
vi•ti•ate
vit•re•ous
vit•ri•fy

vit•ri•ol
vi•tu•per•a•tion
vi•tu•per•a•tive
vi•va•cious
vi•vac•i•ty
viv•id
vi•vip•a•rous
vivi•sec•tion
vix•en
vi•zier
vo•cab•u•lary
vo•cal
vo•cal•ist
vo•cal•ize
vo•ca•tion (career; cf.
    avocation)
vo•ca•tion•al
voc•a•tive
vo•cif•er•ous
vo•der
vod•ka
voice•less
voice rec•og•ni•tion
void•able
voir dire
vol•a•tile
vol•a•til•i•ty
vol•ca•nic
vol•ca•no
vo•li•tion
vol•ley
vol•ley•ball
volt•age
vol•u•bil•i•ty

vol•u•ble
vol•ume
vol•u•met•ric
vo•lu•mi•nous
vol•un•tari•ly
vol•un•ta•rism
vol•un•tary
vol•un•teer
vo•lup•tu•ary
vo•lup•tuous
vom•it
voo•doo
vo•ra•cious (greedy;
    cf. *veracious*)
vo•rac•i•ty
vor•tex
vo•ta•ry
vo•tive
vouch
vouch•er
vouch•safe
vow•el
voy•age
vul•ca•ni•za•tion
vul•ca•nize
vul•gar
vul•gar•ism
vul•gar•i•ty
vul•gar•iza•tion
vul•ner•a•bil•i•ty
vul•ner•a•ble
vul•ture
vul•tur•ous
vy•ing

wad
wad•ded
wad•ding
wade (in water; cf. *weighed*)
wa•fer
waf•fle
wa•ger
Wag•ne•ri•an
wag•on
wain•scot
waist (blouse; cf. *waste*)
waist•band
waist•coat
waist•line
wait (delay; cf. *weight*)
wait•ress
waive (abandon; cf. *wave*)
waiv•er (abandonment; cf. *waver*)
walk•away
walk•ie–talk•ie
walk in v.
walk–in adj., n.
walk–on n.
walk out v.
walk•out n.
walk•over n.

walk–up n.
wal•let
wall•eyed
wall•flow•er
wal•low
wall•pa•per n., v.
wall–to–wall
wal•nut
wal•rus
wam•pum
wan•der
wan•der•lust
want (desire; cf. *wont*, *won't*)
wan•ton
war•bler
war cry
war dance
war•den
ward•robe
ward•room
ware (goods; cf. *wear*, *where*)
ware•house•man
ware•room
war•fare
war•head
war–horse
wari•ly

wari•ness
war•like
war•lord
warm–blood•ed
warmed–over
warm•heart•ed
war•mon•ger
warmth
warm up v.
warm–up n.
warp
war•path
war•plane
war•rant•able
war•ran•tee
war•ran•tor
war•ran•ty
war•ren
war•rior
War•saw Ind.
war•ship
wart•hog
war•time
war whoop
wary
war zone
wash•able
wash–and–wear adj.
wash•ba•sin

wash•board
wash•bowl
wash•cloth
washed–out
washed–up
wash•er
wash•house
Wash•ing•ton
wash out v.
wash•out n.
wash•room
wash•stand
wash•tub
was•sail
wast•age
waste (needless
  destruction; cf. *waist*)
waste•bas•ket
waste•ful
waste•land
waste•pa•per
waste•wa•ter
wast•rel
watch•band
watch•case
watch•dog
watch fire
watch•ful
watch•mak•er
watch•man
watch out v.
watch•out n.
watch•tow•er

watch•word
wa•ter
wa•ter•borne
wa•ter•col•or
wa•ter•course
wa•ter•craft
wa•ter•cress
wa•tered–down
wa•ter•fall
wa•ter•fowl
wa•ter•front
wa•ter•line
wa•ter•logged
wa•ter•man
wa•ter•mark
wa•ter•mel•on
wa•ter pipe
wa•ter po•lo
wa•ter•pow•er
wa•ter•proof
wa•ter–re•pel•lent
wa•ter–re•sis•tant
wa•ter•shed
wa•ter•side
wa•ter•spout
wa•ter•tight
wa•ter tow•er
wa•ter•way
wa•ter•wheel
wa•ter•works
wa•tery
watt•age
Wau•sau Wis.

wave (beckon; cf.
  waive)
wave band
wave•length
wa•ver (hesitate; cf.
  waiver)
wavy
wax•en
wax•work
way (direction; cf.
  weigh)
way•bill
way•far•er
way•lay
way•side
way•ward
weak adj. (feeble; cf.
  week)
weak•fish
weak•heart•ed
weak–kneed
weak•ling
weak–mind•ed
weak•ness
weal (state; welt; cf.
  we'll, wheal, wheel)
wealth
wealth•i•ness
wealthy
weap•on
wear (clothes; cf. *ware;*
  where)
wear•able

wea·ri·less
wea·ri·ly
wea·ri·ness
wea·ri·some
wear out
wea·ry
wea·sand
wea·sel
weath·er (atmospheric
   conditions; cf.
   whether)
weath·er–beat·en
weath·er·iza·tion
weath·er·proof
weav·er
web·foot n.
web–foot·ed adj.
wed
we'd (we would)
wed·ding
Wedg·wood
wed·lock
Wednes·day
week n. (7 days; cf.
   weak)
week·day
week·end
wee·vil
weigh (ponder; cf.
   way)
weighed (pondered;
   cf. *wade*)
weight (poundage; cf.
   wait)

weight·i·ly
weight·i·ness
weight·less
weight·less·ness
weighty
weird
wel·come
wel·fare
wel·far·ism
wel·kin
well
we'll (we will; cf. *weal,
   wheal, wheel*)
well–ad·vised
well–be·ing
well–be·loved
well·born
well–bred
well–con·di·tioned
well–de·fined
well–dis·posed
well–done
well–fa·vored
well–fixed
well–found·ed
well–groomed
well–ground·ed
well–han·dled
well·head
well–heeled
well–in·formed
well–knit
well–known
well–mean·ing

well–nigh
well–off
well–or·dered
well–read
well–round·ed
well–spo·ken
well·spring
well–thought–of
well–timed
well–to–do
well–turned
well–wish·er
well–worn
wel·ter
we're (we are)
weren't (were not)
were·wolf
West Ches·ter Pa.
West·ches·ter N.Y.
west·er·ly
west·ern
West·ern·er
West Vir·gin·ia
west·ward
wet (moist; cf. *whet*)
wet·back
wet blan·ket n.
wet–blan·ket v.
wet·land
wet nurse n.
wet–nurse v.
wet wash
we've (we have)
whale·back

whale•bone
wham•my
wharf
wharf•age
wharf•in•ger
wharves
what•ev•er
what•not
what•so•ev•er
wheal (welt; cf. *weal,*
    we'll, wheel)
wheat germ
whee•dle
wheel (turn; cf. *weal,*
    we'll, wheal)
wheel•bar•row
wheel•base
wheel•chair
wheel•horse
wheel•house
wheel•wright
whence
when•ev•er
when•so•ev•er
where (in what place;
    cf. *ware, wear*)
where•abouts
where•as
where•at
where•by
where•fore
where•in
where•of
where•so•ev•er

where•up•on
wher•ev•er
where•with
where•with•al
wher•ry
whet (sharpen; cf. *wet*)
wheth•er (if; cf.
    weather)
whet•stone
whey
which (pronoun; cf.
    witch)
which•ev•er
which•so•ev•er
while (during; cf. *wile*)
whi•lom
whim•per
whim•si•cal
whine (cry; cf. *wine*)
whip•cord
whip hand
whip•lash
whip•per•snap•per
whip•pet
whip•ping
whip•poor•will
whip•stitch
whirl•i•gig
whirl•pool
whirl•wind
whisk broom
whis•ker
whis•key
whis•per

whist
whis•tle
whis•tle–stop n., v.
white•bait
white•beard
white book
white•cap
white–col•lar
white•fish
white flag
white–head•ed
white–hot
white lead
white–liv•ered
whit•en
white sale
white•wash
white•wood
whith•er (where; cf.
    wither)
whit•low
whit•tle
who•dun•it
who•ev•er
whole (entire; cf. *hole*)
whole•heart•ed
whole•sale
whole•some
whole–souled
whol•ly (entirely; cf.
    holey, holly, holy)
whom•ev•er
whoop
who's (who is)

whose (possessive of *who*)
whose•so•ev•er
wick•ed•ness
wick•er•work
wick•et
wide–an•gle adj.
wide–awake adj.
wide–eyed
wide•mouthed
wide•spread
wid•ow
wid•ow•er
wid•ow•hood
wield
wife•like
wig•wag
wig•wam
wild•cat
wild•cat•ter
wil•der•ness
wild–eyed
wild•fire
wild•fowl
wild–goose chase
wild•life
wild•wood
wile (trick; cf. *while*)
will•ful
will–o'–the–wisp
wil•low•ware
will•pow•er
wind•age
wind•bag

wind•blown
wind•break
wind•burn
wind•fall
wind•jam•mer
wind•lass
wind•mill
win•dow
win•dow•pane
win•dow–shop v.
win•dow–shop•per n.
win•dow•sill
wind•pipe
wind•proof
wind•shield
wind•storm
wind•swept
wind up v.
wind•up adj., n.
wind•ward
wine (drink; cf. *whine*)
wine•glass
wine•grow•er
wine•press
wine•shop
wine•skin
wing chair
wing–foot•ed
wing nut
wing•span
wing•spread
win•ner
win•now

win•some
Win•ston–Sa•lem N.C.
win•ter
win•ter•green
win•ter•ize
win•ter–kill v.
win•ter•kill n.
wire•haired
wire•less
wire–pull•er n.
wire–pull•ing n.
wire•tap
wire•tap•per
Wis•con•sin
wis•dom
wise•acre
wise•crack
wise•ly
wish•bone
wish•ful
wishy–washy adj.
wis•te•ria
wist•ful
witch (hag; cf. *which*)
witch•craft
witch•ery
witch–hunt
with•al
with•draw
with•draw•al
with•er (shrivel; cf. *whither*)
with•hold

with•in
with•out
with•stand
with•stood
wit•ness
wit•ti•cism
wit•ti•ly
wit•ting•ly
wit•ty
wiz•ened
woe•be•gone
wolf•hound
wol•ver•ine
wom•an
wom•an•hood
wom•an•ish
wom•an•kind
wom•an•like
wom•an•li•ness
wom•an•ly
wom•en•folk
won (did win; cf. *one*)
won•der•ful
won•der•land
won•der•ment
won•der•work
won•drous
wont (custom; cf. *want*, *won't*)
won't (will not; cf. *want, wont*)
wood (lumber; cf. *would*)
wood•bin

wood•bine
wood–bor•ing adj.
wood–carv•er n.
wood carv•ing n.
wood•chop•per
wood•chuck
wood•craft
wood•cut
wood•cut•ter
wood•ed
wood•en
wood•en•head
wood•en•ware
wood•land
wood•lot
wood•man
wood•peck•er
wood•pile
wood pulp
wood•shed
woods•man
wood•turn•er n.
wood turn•ing n.
wood•wind
wood•work
wood•work•ing
wood•yard
wool•en
wool–gath•er v.
wool•gath•er•ing n.
wool•li•ness
wool•ly
wool•sack
Woos•ter Ohio

Worces•ter Mass.
word•age
word•book
word for word adv.
word–for–word
    adj.
word•i•ly
word•i•ness
word•ing
word–of–mouth adj.
word orig•i•na•tor
word pro•cess•ing
word pro•cess•ing
    op•er•a•tor
word pro•cess•ing
    spe•cial•ist
word pro•ces•sor
word•smith
word square
wordy
work•able
work•a•day
work•a•hol•ic
work•bag
work•bas•ket
work•bench
work•book
work•box
work camp
work•day
worked
work force
work•horse
work•house

work·ing
work·ing·man
work·ing·wom·an
work load
work·man
work·man·like
work·man·ship
work out v.
work·out n.
work·room
work·shop
work·sta·tion
work·ta·ble
work·week
world–beat·er n.
world·li·ness
world·ly
world·ly–mind·ed adj.
world·ly–wise
world–shak·ing adj.
world–wea·ri·ness
world·wide
worm–eat·en
worm gear
worm·hole
worm·wood
worn–out
wor·ri·ment
wor·ri·some
wor·ry·wart
wor·ship
wor·ship·ful

wor·sted
wor·thi·ly
wor·thi·ness
worth·less
worth·while adj.
worth·while·ness n.
wor·thy
would (auxiliary verb; cf. *wood*)
wound
wraith
wran·gle
wrap·around
wrapped (enveloped; cf. *rapped, rapt*)
wrap·per
wrap up v.
wrap–up n.
wrath·ful
wreak (inflict; cf. *reek, wreck*)
wreath n.
wreathe v.
wreck (ruin; cf. *reek, wreak*)
wreck·age
wreck·er
wren
wrench
wrest (pull away; cf. *rest*)
wres·tle
wres·tler

wres·tling
wretch·ed
wrig·gle
wrig·gly
wring (twist; cf. *ring*)
wring·er
wrin·kle
wrin·kling
wrist·band
wrist·let
wrist·lock
wrist pin
wrist·watch
writ
write (compose; cf. *right, rite*)
write down v.
write–down n.
write in v.
write–in adj., n.
write off v.
write–off n.
write out v.
writ·er
write up v.
write–up n.
writhe
writ·ing
writ·ten
wrong
wrong·do·er
wrong·do·ing
wrong·ful

wrong•head•ed
wrote (did write; cf.
   rote)
wrought

wrung (twisted; cf.
   rung)
wry (distorted; cf. *rye*)

wun•der•kind sing.
wun•der•kin•der pl.
Wy•o•ming

X

Xan•thip•pe
xe•bec
xe•non
xe•no•pho•bia

xe•rog•ra•phy
Xe•rox
X ray n.

X–ray adj., v.
X–ray tube
xy•lo•phone

Y

yacht
yachts•man
yak
yam
Yan•kee
yard•age
yard•arm
yard•bird
yard goods
yard•man
yard•mas•ter
yard•stick
yar•row

yaw
yawl
yawn
year•book
year•ling
year•ly
yearn
yeast
yel•low
yeo•man•ry
ye•shi•va *or*
   ye•shi•vah
yes–man

yes•ter•day
yes•ter•year
yew (tree; cf. *ewe, you*)
Yid•dish
yield
yo•del
yo•ga
yo•gurt
yoke (harness; cf. *yolk*)
yo•kel
yolk (of egg; cf. *yoke*)
Yom Kip•pur
yon•der

yore (past time)
you (pronoun; cf. *ewe*,
    yew)
young
young•ster

your (possessive of *you*)
you're (you are)
your•self
your•selves
youth•ful

yt•ter•bi•um
yt•tri•um
yule
yule•tide

Z

za•min•dar
za•ny
zar•zue•la
zeal
zeal•ot
zeal•ot•ry
zeal•ous
ze•bra
ze•bu
ze•na•na
ze•nith
zeph•yr
zep•pe•lin
ze•ro
zest

zig•gu•rat
zig•zag
zig•zagged
zig•zag•ging
zinc
zin•nia
Zi•on•ism
zip
ZIP Code
zipped
zip•per
zip•pered
zip•ping
zir•con
zir•co•ni•um

zith•er
zo•di•ac
zo•di•a•cal
zon•al
zoo•log•i•cal
zo•ol•o•gy
Zou•ave
zoy•sia
zuc•chet•to
zuc•chi•ni
Zu•ni
zwie•back
zy•mase
zy•mot•ic

REFERENCE SECTION

Most-Used Punctuation

Comma in a Series
Three or more items listed in a series are separated by commas.

Please purchase staples, paper clips, and tape.

The parking facilities will accommodate cars, trucks, buses, and motorcycles.

Comma With an Introductory Expression
Groups of words which introduce independent clauses are set off by commas.

As you know, the airplane arrived late.

If you care to join us for lunch, please give me a call.

Comma With a Parenthetical Expression
A parenthetical expression is often added to a sentence for emphasis. It is set off by commas where it interrupts the flow of the sentence.

The chairperson of the meeting should, by all means, follow the agenda.

Marylou Corsi, as you know, is the first person to receive this award.

Comma With an Appositive
An appositive is often interjected into a sentence to provide information about a noun or pronoun. Commas indicate where the appositive interrupts the flow of the sentence.

I would like you to meet my father, Edgar Johnson, who is visiting here this week.

Please take your complaint to the dean, Emily Hannaford.

Comma With a Conjunction

A comma is used to separate two independent clauses which are joined with a conjunction.

Today the weather is fantastic, and I am going to the beach.

All members of the team did their best, but they lost the game.

Semicolon in Place of a Conjunction

Sometimes two independent clauses are joined as a single sentence without a conjunction. In these instances, a semicolon indicates where the clauses join.

Apparently, the students studied; they all received good grades.

Fire struck at 2 a.m.; the building was in ruins by daybreak.

Semicolon in a Series

When one or more of the items in a series contains a comma, the items in the series are separated by semicolons.

The dates of the interviews will be Wednesday, September 5; Tuesday, October 16; and Wednesday, November 14.

The new officers will be Lillian Perez, President; George Meyers, Vice President; and Alice Milton, Secretary-Treasurer.

Colon With Lists

When a list of items is introduced with an abrupt or anticipatory expression, a colon follows that introduction.

Here are the materials needed: file folders, carbon ribbons, and correction tape.

Please observe the following guidelines:
1. **Leave one-inch side margins.**
2. **Center the main headings.**
3. **Use single-space typing.**

Direct Quotations

Quotations are capitalized, usually set off from the remainder of the sentence by a comma, and enclosed with quotation marks.

Mike asked, "Where is the library?"
"Was your flight pleasant?" inquired Ellen.

Numbers

Number expression is an area of English style about which even the experts sometimes disagree. Basically, numbers may be expressed as either figures or spelled words.

A number expressed in figures is readily recognized and quickly comprehended, and it is considered informal. A number expressed as a spelled word, on the other hand, is less obvious, and is considered formal. The degree of formality of the document may govern, to a certain extent, the number expression that is selected.

While English style manuals provide many rules governing the use of numbers in written material, the following four simplified statements provide guidelines for the most frequent uses of numbers.

The Basic Number Rule

Most occurrences of numbers in written material may be covered by the basic rule which specifies that numbers one through ten are spelled, while numbers larger than ten are expressed in figures. Numbers used with units of measure should be expressed as figures.

In 30 days the accounts of seven customers will be past due.

Within two months, all 24 students will have celebrated their seventh birthday.

The sign is 3 feet high.

The First Word of a Sentence

When a number is the first word of a sentence, the number is spelled.

Forty years ago this organization was founded.

Six children participated in a theatrical production.

The Same Kind of Data

If one number in a list of a particular category of data is larger than ten, all numbers relating to that category of data within the sentence may be represented in figures.

The class consisted of 9 girls and 12 boys.

They purchased 6 suits, 10 shirts, and 14 neckties.

Two Numbers Together

Very often when two numbers occur together, one is part of a compound expression modifying a noun. One of the numbers should be spelled, the other expressed in figures. The first number should be spelled unless its spelling would make an awkwardly long word.

Please send me sixteen 2- by 4-foot sheets of plywood.

The summer camp consisted of seven 2-room cabins.

Spelling Tips

Understanding the following common families of spelling patterns may help to avoid spelling errors.

Double Consonants

Double L

al•lo•cate	dis•al•low	hol•low
al•lot•ment	al•le•vi•ate	fal•la•cy
ex•cel•lent	chal•lenge	gal•lery

Double M

com•merce	com•mu•ni•cate	sum•ma•ry
rec•om•mend	im•me•di•ate	ac•com•mo•date

Double S

as•sis•tance	suc•cess	ac•cess
nec•es•sary	ad•mis•sion	pos•ses•sion
as•sign•ment	per•mis•sion	busi•ness

Adding *-ly* to Words Ending in *e*
Most words ending in *e* retain the *e* when the ending *-ly* is added.

bare·ly	ac·tive·ly	nice·ly
com·plete·ly	name·ly	sure·ly
mere·ly	for·tu·nate·ly	unique·ly
like·ly	sin·cere·ly	late·ly

In the following words, however, the *e* is dropped when *-ly* is added.

| tru·ly | du·ly | whol·ly |

Dropping Silent e Before *-ing*

chal·leng·ing	mak·ing	sav·ing
hav·ing	man·u·fac·tur·ing	stim·u·lat·ing
hous·ing	pre·par·ing	su·per·vis·ing
in·creas·ing	re·ceiv·ing	typ·ing

Past Tenses in Which *r* Is Doubled

oc·curred	de·ferred	trans·ferred
pre·ferred	in·ferred	con·ferred
con·curred	re·ferred	blurred

Past Tenses in Which *r* Is Not Doubled

| of·fered | cov·ered | hon·ored |
| dif·fered | ma·jored | suf·fered |

Adding *-ed* and *-ing* to Words Ending in *t*

When the last syllable of a word ending in *t*, preceded by a single vowel, is accented, the *t* is doubled before *-ed* and *-ing*.

al·lot	al·lot·ted	al·lot·ting
com·mit	com·mit·ted	com·mit·ting
omit	omit·ted	omit·ting
per·mit	per·mit·ted	per·mit·ting

When the last syllable is not accented, the *t* is not doubled.

ben•e•fit	ben•e•fit•ed	ben•e•fit•ing
cred•it	cred•it•ed	cred•it•ing
lim•it	lim•it•ed	lim•it•ing
so•lic•it	so•lic•it•ed	so•lic•it•ing

When the *t* is preceded by more than one vowel or by a consonant, the *t* is not doubled.

coat	coat•ed	coat•ing
seat	seat•ed	seat•ing
greet	greet•ed	greet•ing
alert	alert•ed	alert•ing
at•tract	at•tract•ed	at•tract•ing
grant	grant•ed	grant•ing

Adding *-ed* and *-ing* to Words Ending in *l*

When the last syllable of a word ending in *l*, preceded by a single vowel, is accented, the *l* is doubled in forming derivatives ending in *-ed* and *-ing*.

com•pel	com•pelled	com•pel•ling
con•trol	con•trolled	con•trol•ling
dis•pel	dis•pelled	dis•pel•ling
ex•cel	ex•celled	ex•cel•ling

When the last syllable is not accented, the *l* is not doubled.

can•cel	can•celed	can•cel•ing
mod•el	mod•eled	mod•el•ing
to•tal	to•taled	to•tal•ing
trav•el	trav•eled	trav•el•ing
equal	equaled	equal•ing

Changing *y* to *i*

In the following words *y* is changed to *i* in the past tense and in the *s* form.

ap•ply	ap•plied	ap•plies
im•ply	im•plied	im•plies
com•ply	com•plied	com•plies
re•ply	re•plied	re•plies
re•ly	re•lied	re•lies

Hyphenation of Compound Adjectives

When two or more words form an expression which conveys a single meaning in modifying a noun, that expression, called a compound adjective, is hyphenated.

> Winning the award is considered a once-in-a-lifetime honor.

> We were delayed by a five-car accident.

Abbreviations and Acronyms

Basic Abbreviations

Some latitude exists in the extent to which abbreviations may be used. In reports, statistical data, in-house documents, or communications of an informal nature, abbreviations are appropriate.

The more formal a piece of written communication is, the more abbreviations should be avoided. The very common abbreviations of people's titles, educational degrees, or times of day (a.m. or p.m.) are always acceptable.

Many abbreviations end with a period. If a period occurs within an abbreviation, no space follows it. Examples of some abbreviations follow:

> Dr., Mr., Mrs., a.m., p.m., A.D., B.C., R.S.V.P., govt., blvd., dept., co., e.g., etc., S. Dak., Ph.D., and B.S.

Very Frequent Abbreviations

Some abbreviations, particularly the initials of well-known organizations, are pronounced in their abbreviated form. These very common abbreviations are represented by all-capital letters with no spaces or punctuation.

Some examples of very frequent abbreviations follow:

IRS, IBM, IOOF, BPOE, RCA, CBS, ABC, ICC, FCC, UAW, IQ, FM, FBI, AT&T, YMCA, AFL-CIO, UN, and SEC.

Acronyms

The very frequent abbreviations shown above are pronounced by individual alphabetic letter. Acronyms, on the other hand, are a series of letters which are read as words. They are represented by all-capital letters with no spaces or punctuation.

Some common acronyms are:

COBOL, FORTRAN, BASIC, PERT, GANT, ZIP (code), SALT, UNICEF, AMVETS, ANOVA, CAD, IRA, and MASH.

Troublesome Place Names

The following list of geographic locations includes the most troublesome names which the writer and keyboarder are most likely to encounter.

United States

Alabama	*Alabama (cont.)*	*Alaska*
Anniston	Montgomery	Anchorage
Badsden	Phenix City	Fairbanks
Bessemer	Tuscaloosa	
Mobile		

Arizona
Flagstaff
Mesa
Phoenix
Scottsdale
Tucson
Yuma

Arkansas
Arkadelphia
Fayetteville
Texarkana

California
Alameda
Anaheim
Berkeley
Beverly Hills
Burbank
Eureka
Guadalupe
La Mesa
Long Beach
Los Angeles
Modesto
Montecito
Monterey
Novato
Pasadena
Pittsburg
Sacramento
San Bernardino
San Diego
San Francisco

California (cont.)
San Luis Obispo
Santa Barbara
Santa Cruz

Colorado
Alamosa
Durango
Greeley
Pueblo
Trinidad

Connecticut
Bridgeport
Danbury
Greenwich
Hartford
Norwich
Stamford
Waterbury
Willimantic

Delaware
Wilmington

Florida
Fort Lauderdale
Gainesville
Hialeah
Miami
Orlando
St. Petersburg
Sarasota
Tallahasee

Georgia
Athens
Macon
Marietta
Savannah
Valdosta

Hawaii
Hilo
Honolulu
Kauai
Lahaina
Maui
Molokai
Oahu

Idaho
Boise
Coeur d'Alene
Lewiston
Nampa
Pocatello

Illinois
Aurora
Belvidere
Bloomington
Champaign
Decatur
Elgin
Glencoe
Joliet
Kankakee
Moline

Illinois (cont.)
Peoria
Skokie
Urbana
Waukegan
Winnetka

Indiana
Elkhart
Evansville
Fort Wayne
Huntington
Indianapolis
Kokomo
Terre Haute
Vincennes
Warsaw

Iowa
Cedar Rapids
Des Moines
Ottumwa
Sioux City
Waterloo

Kansas
Emporia
Pittsburg
Topeka
Wichita

Kentucky
Bowling Green
Covington

Kentucky (cont.)
Lexington
Louisville
Paducah

Louisiana
Baton Rouge
Natchitoches
New Orleans
Shreveport

Maine
Bangor
Biddeford
Gardiner
Lewiston
Presque Isle

Maryland
Bethesda
Cumberland
Hagerstown
Towson

Massachusetts
Brockton
Brookline
Charlestown
Chicopee
Fitchburg
Framingham
Gardner
Gloucester
Haverhill

Massachusetts (cont.)
Holyoke
Leominster
Methuen
Natick
Pittsfield
Springfield
Waltham
Wellesley
Worcester

Michigan
Ann Arbor
Berkley
Dearborn
Escanaba
Hamtramck
Ishpeming
Kalamazoo
Marquette
Menominee
Muskegon
Saginaw

Minnesota
Bemidji
Brainerd
Duluth
Faribault
Minneapolis
Moorhead
St. Paul

Mississippi
Biloxi
Hattiesburg
Meridian
Natchez

Missouri
Chillicothe
Joplin

Montana
Anaconda
Bozeman
Havre
Kalispell
Lewistown
Missoula

Nebraska
Chadron
Kearney
North Platte
Omaha

Nevada
Las Vegas
Reno
Winnemucca

New Hampshire
Laconia
Nashua
Portsmouth

New Jersey
Asbury Park
Bayonne
Camden
Guttenberg
Irvington
Kearny
New Brunswick
Newark
Paramus
Passaic
Paterson
Pennsauken

New Mexico
Alamogordo
Albuquerque
Artesia
Clovis
Gallup
Las Cruces
Los Alamos
Santa Fe
Tucumcari

New York
Binghamton
Brooklyn
Elmira
Huntington
Jericho
Johnstown
Merrick
Newark

New York (cont.)
Newburgh
Ossining
Patterson
Peekskill
Plattsburgh
Poughkeepsie
Schenectady
Syracuse
Tarrytown
Utica
Westchester

North Carolina
Asheville
Durham
Fayetteville
Gastonia
Goldsboro
Greensboro
Kannapolis
Morganton
Raleigh
Winston-Salem

North Dakota
Bismarck
Devils Lake
Fargo
Minot

Ohio
Ashtabula
Berea

Ohio (cont.)
Bucyrus
Chillicothe
Cincinnati
Conneaut
Cuyahoga Falls
Dayton
Elyria
Euclid
Findlay
Lorain
Massillon
Newark
Sandusky
Wooster

Oklahoma
Bartlesville
El Reno
Enid
McAlester
Muskogee
Sapulpa
Tulsa

Oregon
Corvallis
Eugene
Klamath Falls
Medford

Pennsylvania
Altoona
Harrisburg

Pennsylvania (cont.)
Hazleton
Huntingdon
Johnstown
Lancaster
Lebanon
Lewistown
Phoenixville
Pittsburgh
Reading
Scranton
West Chester
Wilkes-Barre
Wilkinsburg

Puerto Rico
Arecibo
Mayagüez
Ponce
San Juan

Rhode Island
Johnston
Narragansett
Providence

South Carolina
Charleston
Greenville
Spartanburg

South Dakota
Aberdeen
Belle Fourche

South Dakota (cont.)
Pierre
Sioux Falls

Tennessee
Chattanooga
Knoxville
Memphis
Nashville

Texas
Beaumont
Cleburne
Corpus Christi
Corsicana
Edinburg
El Paso
Galveston
Lubbock
Odessa
San Angelo
San Antonio
Tyler
Waco
Waxahachie
Wichita Falls

Utah
Kearns
Orem
Provo
Salt Lake City

Vermont
Barre
Brattleboro
Montpelier
Rutland
St. Albans
St. Johnsbury

Virginia
Alexandria
Charlottesville
Lynchburg
Newport News
Petersburg
Roanoke

Washington
Bremerton
Hoquiam
Kennewick
Olympia
Puyallup
Seattle
Spokane
Tacoma
Walla Walla
Yakima

West Virginia
Charleston
Clarksburg
Huntington
Morgantown
Parkersburg
Wheeling

Wisconsin
Beloit
Brodhead
Eau Claire
Fond du Lac
Green Bay
Janesville
Kenosha
La Crosse
Manitowoc
Milwaukee
Sheboygan
Waukesha
Wausau

Wyoming
Casper
Cheyenne
Laramie

Canada

Alberta
Calgary
Edmonton
Grande Prairie
Lethbridge
Medicine Hat
Red Deer

British Columbia
Nanaimo
New Westminster
Penticton

British Columbia (cont.)
Prince George
Prince Rupert
Trail
Vancouver

Manitoba
Brandon
Portage la Prairie
St. Boniface
Winnipeg

New Brunswick
Bathurst
Chatham
Fredericton
Saint John

Newfoundland
Corner Brook
St. John's

Nova Scotia
Dartmouth
Glace Bay
Halifax
New Glasgow
New Waterford
Sydney
Truro

Ontario
Brantford
Hamilton

Ontario *(cont.)*
Kenora
Kitchener
London
Ottawa
Peterborough
Sault Ste. Marie
Sudbury
Toronto
Windsor

Prince Edward Island
Charlottetown
Summerside

Quebec
Drummondville
Granby

Quebec *(cont.)*
Montreal
Quebec
Sherbrooke
Trois-Rivières

Saskatchewan
Moose Jaw
Prince Albert
Regina
Saskatoon
Swift Current

Mexico
Aguascalientes
Chihuahua
Ciudad Juarez
Ciudad Madero

Mexico *(cont.)*
Cuernavaca
Culiacán
Durango
Guadalajara
Hermosillo
León
Mazatlán
Mérida
Monterrey
Morelia
Orizaba
Puebla
Saltillo
Toluca
Torreón
Veracruz Llave

Abbreviations of States, Territories, and Possessions of the United States

AL	Alabama	Ala.		MO	Missouri	Mo.
AK	Alaska	. . .		MT	Montana	Mont.
AZ	Arizona	Ariz.		NE	Nebraska	Nebr.
AR	Arkansas	Ark.		NV	Nevada	Nev.
CA	California	Calif.		NH	New Hampshire	N.H.
CZ	Canal Zone	C.Z.		NJ	New Jersey	N.J.
CO	Colorado	Colo.		NM	New Mexico	N. Mex.
CT	Connecticut	Conn.		NY	New York	N.Y.
DE	Delaware	Del.		NC	North Carolina	N.C.
DC	District of Columbia	D.C.		ND	North Dakota	N. Dak.
				OH	Ohio	. . .
FL	Florida	Fla.		OK	Oklahoma	Okla.
GA	Georgia	Ga.		OR	Oregon	Oreg.
GU	Guam	. . .		PA	Pennsylvania	Pa.
HI	Hawaii	. . .		PR	Puerto Rico	P.R.
ID	Idaho	. . .		RI	Rhode Island	R.I.
IL	Illinois	Ill.		SC	South Carolina	S.C.
IN	Indiana	Ind.		SD	South Dakota	S. Dak.
IA	Iowa	. . .		TN	Tennessee	Tenn.
KS	Kansas	Kans.		TX	Texas	Tex.
KY	Kentucky	Ky.		UT	Utah	. . .
LA	Louisiana	La.		VT	Vermont	Vt.
ME	Maine	. . .		VI	Virgin Islands	V.I.
MD	Maryland	Md.		VA	Virginia	Va.
MA	Massachusetts	Mass.		WA	Washington	Wash.
MI	Michigan	Mich.		WV	West Virginia	W. Va.
MN	Minnesota	Minn.		WI	Wisconsin	Wis.
MS	Mississippi	Miss.		WY	Wyoming	Wyo.

Use the two-letter abbreviations on the left when abbreviating state names in addresses. In any other situation that calls for abbreviations of state names, use the abbreviations on the right.

≡ ELECTRONIC OFFICE ≡ GLOSSARY

acoustic coupler A data communications device that converts electrical signals to tones which are transmitted over a telephone line using a conventional telephone. An acoustic coupler is a type of modem.

administrative secretary A support person who handles word processing, mail, answering phones, filing, making travel arrangements, and other administrative tasks.

archive To save data on a storage medium such as a floppy diskette.

author The person who creates a document. Also called a word originator or a principal.

backup A duplicate copy of a storage medium such as a floppy diskette.

bit The smallest unit of information recognized by a computer.

blind word processor A word processor that does not have a video display.

boilerplate Stored paragraphs that can be combined with each other or with new material to create individualized documents.

cassette A magnetic recording tape permanently housed in a plastic case which plugs into a recording device.

cathode-ray tube (CRT) An electronic vacuum tube used to display text and graphics. Also referred to as a video display terminal.

central processing unit (CPU) The component of a data or word processing system that controls the interpretation and execution of instructions and performs arithmetical and logical functions. Also called the internal processor.

character printer An impact printer that prints a single letter, number, or symbol at one time.

communicating word processor A word processor that can transmit text to and receive text from another word processor.

computer output microfilm (COM) A process by which computer output is produced directly as microfilm.

configuration The components and peripherals which make up a word processing system and the manner in which they are arranged.

cursor A lighted indicator on a display screen that marks the working position of the operator. Equivalent to the printing point indicator on a typewriter.

daisy wheel A kind of printer-type element on which the characters are engraved at the end of spokes or bars which resembles a daisy.

data file Related information that is stored under one file name.

data processing The manipulation of numbers or symbols, usually done by a computer.

disk drive The unit of a computer or word processor into which a disk is inserted, thereby programming the machine.

display word processor A word processor equipped with a video display terminal.

document Any business communication such as a letter, memo, table, or report.

dot matrix A printing pattern in which closely spaced dots form alphanumeric characters.

downtime The period of time that a word processor is not in working order.

editing Changing or rearranging the text by deleting, substituting, inserting, and moving. Also includes reformatting.

electronic mail The transmission and display of business communications via satellites, cables, or telephone wires at very high speeds with no physical movement of paper.

electronic typewriter A low-level blind word processor that houses all components (keyboard, internal processor, storage unit, and printer) in one unit. Automates many typing tasks.

electrostatic printer A type of printer in which images are burned into paper electrically.

facsimile A copy of a document that is transmitted electronically from one location to another, usually by telephone lines.

feasibility study A detailed study to determine a company's information processing needs in an effort to increase productivity.

floppy diskette A magnetic storage medium for word processors that looks like a small phonograph record in its protective jacket.

format The visual arrangement of elements of a document on a page.

function keys Special keys that communicate commands to the internal processor of a word processor.

hard copy Paper output from an information processing system.

hardware Equipment such as a word processor or computer.

impact printer Any type of printer that generates characters by striking type through a ribbon onto paper.

information processing The coordination of people, equipment, and procedures in order to handle information in both word and data processing.

ink-jet printer   A nonimpact printer that sprays tiny droplets of ink to form alphanumeric characters.

input   The facts or data which are entered into the processing system.

intelligent copier/printer   A copier or printer that can manipulate data.

internal processor   The component of a data or word processing system that controls the interpretation and execution of instructions and performs arithmetical and logical functions. (See *central processing unit*.)

internal storage   The storage of data or text within the word processor. Also called memory.

justified text   Copy in which line endings line up evenly at both the right and left margins.

keyboard   The part of an information processing system that looks like a typewriter keyboard but which has additional keys for different functions.

keyboarding   The entering of data into the memory of a word processor by depressing keys on a keyboard.

laser printer   A type of printer in which the characters and symbols are burned into the paper with a laser beam.

line printer   A high-speed printer which prints an entire line at a time instead of a single character.

logic   The basic operating instructions for a computer.

magnetic media   Media that record by means of magnetism. Magnetic media include magnetic cards, cassettes, cartridges, and disks.

mainframe computer   The largest, fastest, most costly type of computer.

memory   The storage of data or text within the word processor.

menu   A screen display offering choices for various processing functions or tasks.

microcomputer   A small computer, about the same size as a display word processor, that can perform many functions including word processing.

microform   A miniature image of a document. Types include microfilm and microfiche.

minicomputer   A middle-size computer having less storage capacity than a mainframe.

modem (modulator/demodulator)   A device used with computers or word processing equipment that transmits signals over telephone lines.

network   A series of points connected by communications channels.

nonimpact printer   A printer that has no printing element that strikes the paper or ribbon.

off-line   An operation done on a computer that is not connected with other computers for the exchange of information. (See *stand-alone*.)

on-line   An operation performed by a computer that is connected with other computers for the exchange of information.

optical character reader (OCR)   A device or scanner that reads printed or typed characters and converts them into digital signals for input into a word or data processor.

output   The product (usually hard copy) of an information processing operation.

password   An authorized code known only to legitimate users of an electronic information system.

peripheral   A device that is not essential to the operation of a word processor but which extends its capabilities.

playback The process of printing or displaying material that has been input into a word processor.

principal The person who creates a document. Also called an author or a word originator.

printer A device used for the creation of printed output.

printout Hard copy output.

program A set of instructions to a computer for the performance of a task.

random-access memory (RAM) Temporary memory.

read-only memory (ROM) Permanent memory that cannot be altered.

retrieve To gain access to stored information.

scrolling Moving text vertically or horizontally across a display screen.

shared logic system A system comprised of several terminals sharing one CPU.

shared resource system A system comprised of several word processors, each having its own internal memory, but sharing other peripherals such as a printer or central storage system.

soft copy Text displayed on a video screen. Compare *hard copy*.

software The programs used to control the operation of a computer.

stand-alone A single station word processor that is not linked to any other piece of equipment.

telecommunications An electronic method of transmitting information from one location to another over telephone lines.

telecommuting A computer at home connected with an information system in the office.

teleconference A meeting of geographically separated people who may have two-way audio, video, and text communications often via telephone and/or closed-circuit television.

terminal A device equipped with a keyboard which is capable of sending text to and receiving text from a computer.

text editing A general phrase referring to a wide variety of word processing systems and procedures.

turnaround time The time it takes for information to be processed and returned to the word originator.

upgrade To add to the features or capabilities of a word processor.

vendor A supplier of office equipment.

video display terminal (VDT) A device consisting of an electronic screen that displays text and graphics.

voice recognition The ability of a computer to receive commands spoken with the human voice.

word originator A person who creates a document. Also called an author or a principal.

word processing A system designed to improve the efficiency and effectiveness of business communications through the integration of people, procedures, and equipment.

word processing operator An employee whose chief function is to produce communications on word processing equipment.

word processing specialist An experienced word processing operator who is skilled at producing complicated documents such as statistical reports.

workstation The place where an employee performs the majority of his or her work. Encompasses the desk and any equipment necessary to perform the job, such as a word processor or typewriter.

wraparound The ability of a word processor to begin a new line of display when the previous line is filled, without the operator initiating a return.